On Nuclear Terrorism

On Nuclear Terrorism

Michael Levi

Viva Books

New Delhi | Mumbai | Chennai | Kolkata | Bangalore | Hyderabad | Kochi | Guwahati

Founded in 1921, the Council on Foreign Relations is an idependent, national membership organization and a nonpartisan center for scholars dedicated to producing and disseminating ideas so that individual and corporate members, as well as policymakers, journalists students, and interested citizens in the United States and other countries, can better understand the world and the foreign policy choices facing the United States and other governments. The Council does this by convening meetings; conducting a wide-ranging Studies program; publishing *Foreign Affairs*, the preeminent journal covering international affairs and U.S. foreign policy; maintaining a diverse membership; sponsoring Independent Task Forces; and providing up-to-date information about the world and U.S. foreign policy on the Council's website, www.cfr.org.

THE COUNCIL TAKES NO INSTITUTIONAL POSITION ON POLICY ISSUES AND HAS NO AFFILIATION WITH THE U.S. GOVERNMENT. ALL STATEMENTS OF FACT AND EXPRESSIONS OF OPINION CONTAINED IN ITS PUBLICATIONS ARE THE SOLE RESPONSIBILITY OF THE AUTHOR OR AUTHORS.

First Indian Edition 2010

VIVA BOOKS PRIVATE LIMITED

- 4737/23 Ansari Road, Daryaganj, New Delhi 110 002
  E-mail: vivadelhi@vivagroupindia.net, Tel. 42242200
- Plot No. 76, Service Industries, Shirvane, Sector 1, Nerul, Navi Mumbai 400 706
  E-mail: vivamumbai@vivagroupindia.net, Tel. 27721273, 27721274
- Jamals Fazal Chambers, 26 Greams Road, Chennai 600 006
  E-mail: vivachennai@vivagroupindia.net, Tel. 28290304, 28294241
- B-103, Jindal Towers, 21/1A/3 Darga Road, Kolkata 700 017
  E-mail: vivakolkata@vivagroupindia.net, Tel. 22836381, 22816713
- 7, Sovereign Park Apartments, 56-58, K. R. Road, Basavanagudi, Bangalore 560 004
  E-mail: vivabangalore@vivagroupindia.net, Tel. 26607409, 26607410
- 101-102 Mughal Marc Aptt., 3-4-637 to 641, Narayanguda, Hyderabad 500 029
  E-mail: vivahyderabad@vivagroupindia.net, Tel. 27564481, 27564482
- First Floor, Beevi Towers, SRM Road, Kaloor, Kochi 682 018, Kerala
  E-mail: vivakochi@vivagroupindia.net, Tel: 0484-2403055, 2403056
- 232, GNB Road, Beside UCO Bank, Silpukhuri, Guwahati 781 003
  E-mail: vivaguwahati@vivagroupindia.net, Tel: 0361-2666386

Published by arrangement with

Harvard University Press
79, Garden Street, Cambridge
Massachussetts 02138-1499
USA

ISBN 978-81-309-0999-8

Published by Vinod Vasishtha for Viva Books Private Limited, 4737/23, Ansari Road, New Delhi - 110 002. Printed and bound by Anand Sons, Delhi - 110 092.

To my parents

Contents

Preface

Nuclear terrorism is an immediate challenge for the entire world. Experts are studying it, policymakers are responding to it, and the public also needs to understand it.

Yet open discussion of nuclear terrorism can present problems. Those of us who write about terrorism face a perpetual dilemma. When should we point out that a security system in widespread use is imperfect, as I do in this book? If the vulnerability is obvious, identifying it publicly can, without introducing any new dangers, prompt authorities to address it. If the problem is more obscure or easier to exploit, things become more difficult: is it best to stay silent and hope that the gap is and will remain unknown, or is it more prudent to expose it and possibly provoke governments to fix it?

Almost all experts who work in this field self-censor, because they fear helping terrorist groups. I talked to people with long experience in these matters, and settled on a few simple rules. This book does not contain calculations that could give meaningful help in designing nuclear weapons; this omission may come at the expense of slightly weakening my arguments for technically inclined readers, but that is unavoidable. (I suspect that most readers will be quite happy to be spared as many calculations as possible.) I have relied on simple, obvious examples to make the same points. Other situations are less clear, and in each case, I asked three questions. Does identifying a way terrorists might fail help point them in a better direction, or does it describe an inevitable problem? Does the analysis have important policy implications? Is there another way to make the same point? With these questions in mind I have sought a balance between two responsibilities: to avoid helping potential nuclear terrorists, and to promote more effective strategies for defense against them.

Nuclear terrorism is not, fundamentally, a technical topic. Defenses are as much about intercepting airplanes as they are about improving radiation detection, as much about human intelligence as they are about the technical demands of bomb-building. But nuclear terrorism is not a nontechnical subject, either. A full understanding of the defenses we need is impossible without knowing something about the underlying science and technology of nuclear weapons. I have written this book so that both technophiles and technophobes can understand it. Early in Chapter 3 the reader will find brief tutorials on the basics of nuclear weapons technology and radiation detection. The book avoids mathematical calculations, though it often explains their basic contours. For the more technically inclined reader, mathematical details that support assertions in the text are explained in the endnotes. A handful are also included in the appendix.

While writing, I found myself noticing parallels to *On Thermonuclear War,* an infamous book published by Herman Kahn nearly half a century ago—hence the title of this book. Addressing specialists and the public alike, Kahn drew both on his imagination and on the long history of warfare to challenge basic assumptions about nuclear war. Many rightly questioned his principles, but he provoked everyone to think anew about a grave danger. I hope that in writing *On Nuclear Terrorism,* I have succeeded in doing the same.

Abbreviations

C/S	Containment/Surveillance
CBRN	Chemical, biological, radiological, nuclear
DBT	Design Basis Threat
DNDO	Domestic Nuclear Detection Office
DOE	U.S. Department of Energy
FMSF	Mayak Fissile Material Storage Facility
HEU	Highly enriched uranium
IAEA	International Atomic Energy Agency
IND	Improvised nuclear device
INS	U.S. Immigration and Naturalization Service
ISG	Iraq Survey Group
keV	Kilo-electron-volt
LASCAR	Large Scale Reprocessing
MCC	Russian Mining and Chemical Combine
MeV	Mega-electron-volt
MOX	Mixed oxide
MPC&A	Materials Protection, Control, and Accounting
NATO	North Atlantic Treaty Organization
NORAD	North American Aerospace Defense Command
NRTA	Near-real-time-accounting
NSG	Nuclear Suppliers Group
Pu	Plutonium
SAFF	Safing, Arming, Fusing, and Firing
SNM	Special nuclear material
U	Uranium
WMD	Weapons of mass destruction

On Nuclear Terrorism

Prologue

In the early hours of July 29th, 2002, a ship carrying fifteen pounds of uranium encased in a lead-lined steel pipe slipped into the New York harbor.[1] Twenty-five days earlier, it had begun its journey in Austria, from whence it had traveled by train through Hungary, Romania, and Bulgaria, to Turkey. There the uranium had been loaded into a shipping container, and on July 10th, it had departed by sea for America. It did not enter the United States entirely unnoticed—it was selected upon arrival for scanning by X-ray and radiation monitoring equipment. It passed their tests with flying colors.

This was not a terrorist plot but a scheme cooked up by *ABC News* and a handful of outside experts, designed to expose holes in American defenses against nuclear terrorism. The uranium was "depleted," making it unusable in a nuclear bomb, but had it been suitable for use in weapons—"weapons-usable" or "highly enriched"—a few shipments would have been enough for the simplest type of nuclear bomb.

Most politicians and many homeland security experts drew at least one of two lessons from the episode. Some called for more investment in port security, so that nuclear material could never again slip through unseen. For others, the scheme showed the futility of such efforts, and thus emphasized the need to focus attention on preventing terrorists from ever acquiring nuclear materials in the first place.

Yet understanding defense against nuclear terrorism is impossible if we only look at isolated tests and at each part of a terrorist plot by itself. Small odds of defeat at different stages of a plot can add up, and a single incident cannot tell us what those odds are. More important, it is impossible to separate any one stage from the rest of the plot, since in evading one part of a defense, a terrorist group may make itself vulnerable elsewhere.

Consider a fictional analogy. At New York police headquarters, a debate rages over how to deal with bank robbers. Some propose erecting roadblocks in the aftermath of any theft, in order to stop robbers who might leap into their getaway cars. But critics argue that those barriers are largely useless, since any thief can evade them by escaping on foot. Some conclude that the only possible solution is to design more effective barriers. Others insist that the only answer is to prevent all bank robberies in the first place.

A third group argues that while better barriers and more secure banks would help, their colleagues are missing much of the bigger picture. A thief might escape on foot, but only at the expense of slowing his flight, giving the police more time to find and catch him. He might flee in a car, but he would have a much harder time avoiding the roadblocks. Or he might attempt a much smaller theft with the hopes that he could pull it off unnoticed, making the details of a hypothetical police chase unimportant. The police group proposes that to reduce the chances that a thief will evade roadblocks with a large hoard of cash, the department should not only improve those barriers and better secure banks, but also improve both its ability to chase down robbers on foot and the ability of banks to alert authorities quickly to even the smallest thefts.

Nuclear terrorism is not all that different. Go back to the *ABC* plot, and imagine that the uranium had been of the sort that one could use in a weapon. Surely the brain behind the plot would have had to think through more than just how to cross the U.S. border. Would he have been confident that every stage of his plot would succeed? He had shaped his plot to make crossing the border as easy as possible, but would that have made other parts of his plot harder? How willing would he have been to accept possible failure? How worried would he have been that, however well thought out his plans, one small stroke of bad luck might separate victory from humiliating defeat?

The terrorist leader would have had to ponder many questions before attempting an attack. What were the odds that his group would be able to execute its theft of weapons-usable uranium undetected, so that rather than having authorities hot on its trail, it would be able to move quietly from Austria to Istanbul? Where would it hide while it shaped its material into the form needed for a weapon? How would it recruit the scientists and engineers it needed for that task? And how would it move the other, bulkier, and perhaps more noticeable parts of the bomb into the United States?

And, unlike the *ABC* reporters, his people would have been terrorists. The group would need operatives who would buy or steal the uranium, procure the other weapon parts, move the materials across borders, and build the bomb. Others would have to recruit the right people and raise the money needed for the plot. Did the group have natural connections to engineering talent and to crackerjack thieves? The list of conspirators might have been large. How would the terrorist leader ensure that no one snitched while he also avoided using terrorists so experienced (and thus trusted) that governments the world over would be on their tails? What if no one had noticed the uranium on the train to Turkey, but someone had spotted the terrorist carrying it?

The group might also need to make sacrifices to minimize the chances that its uranium would be spotted crossing the U.S. border. The group had decided to look only for weapons-grade uranium, since plutonium might have been too hard to sneak past detectors, but as a result, the terrorist leader might judge, the group would have to wait longer for the right theft or purchase opportunity to come along. Would the delay give law enforcement and intelligence more time to uncover the plot? Perhaps the group could use a large team of thieves to attack the nuclear facility of its choice, ensuring that it would acquire the uranium it wanted. But if it tried to keep its plot small, and thus secure from intelligence agents, that decision might limit the number of skilled engineers, fund-raisers, and other specialists it would feel comfortable involving.

The bad news for us is that all these questions, and the many more the leader would have had to ask himself, could have had answers that led to a successful nuclear attack. But the good news is that any single, seemingly simple element of a nuclear plot—in this case, smuggling uranium through an American port—becomes far more complicated when it is embedded in the bigger picture, just as the police roadblocks make more sense when combined with a broader plan. Nuclear terrorism is a genuine possibility, but its complexity expands the universe of ways for preventing it. This book is about understanding how to see the big picture of nuclear terrorism, and how to use that understanding to defeat it.

— 1 —

Principles for Defense

On learning of the bombing of Hiroshima, Bernard Brodie, a leading strategist of his generation, declared, "Everything that I have written is obsolete."[1] Since the first atomic bomb exploded over sixty years ago, the awesome power of nuclear weapons—a Cold War nuclear exchange might have killed hundreds of millions within hours—has often driven even the most careful thinkers to similar conclusions. One scholar recounts the prevailing attitude in the 1950s: "In order to approach nuclear war properly, one had to become a perfect amnesiac, stripped of the intuitions, judgments, and habits cultivated over a lifetime."[2] Strategists once had viewed war as a complex interplay between enemies. By the 1950s, nuclear wizards were viewing war as mutually assured destruction: states could prevent nuclear war only by threatening to annihilate an adversary in response to any nuclear attack. These experts' intellectual predecessors would not have recognized this strategy.

Yet as the Cold War evolved, many of the most influential strategists, Brodie among them, began to turn away from mutually assured destruction as it became clear that the strategy was far from guaranteed to work. The new approaches still differed from traditional military strategy, but they borrowed far more from its basic principles than mutually assured destruction had.

Similarly, though we must always remain mindful that nuclear weapons are in a class of their own, we can find the most effective strategies against nuclear terrorism only by drawing from our wealth of knowledge about traditional counterterrorism.[3]

Three principles intuitively obvious to most counterterrorism experts (and to military strategists too) should drive our approach to nuclear terrorism. First, no single tool can defeat nuclear terrorism: instead, we must combine all the means we have available—controls over nuclear materials and weapons, military power, diplomacy, intelligence, covert action, law enforcement, border security, and consequence management, among others—into a comprehensive system that is aimed at thwarting nuclear terrorists.[4] Second, knowing the worst-case scenarios for nuclear terrorism is important, but these scenarios should not dominate our strategic thinking: instead, we should prepare to fight against a range of possible terrorist groups and terrorist plots. Finally, we should be realistic about our goals, recognizing that we will never build ironclad defenses: instead, we should seek to make nuclear terrorism as unlikely as possible, and we should also aim to minimize the consequences of any attack that might, despite our best efforts, occur.

Policymakers and experts have long recognized that the most powerful tools for preventing nuclear terrorism are those that directly deny nuclear materials and weapons to terrorists: locking up those weapons and materials as best we can in states like Russia and Pakistan, and keeping them from states like North Korea and Iran that are either unable or perhaps unwilling to keep their weapons away from terrorists. This view is reflected in a steady stream of books written over more than three decades; its dominance was recently confirmed in a major survey of leading experts on weapons of mass destruction.[5] There is a growing realization, though, that a much broader defense can contribute to our security. But while careful and sophisticated discussions of locking up materials and preventing proliferation are commonplace, the quality of our debate over broader defenses is far poorer. Exceptions, of course, exist, most notably a partially unclassified 2004 Defense Department study aimed at promoting the integration of defenses against nuclear terrorism; some careful writing on shipping container security; and several other studies that advocate layered defenses but still devote most of their attention to the security of nuclear weapons and materials.[6] Others have promoted a layered approach to defense against terrorism more generally, but without delving into the details of the nuclear threat.[7] We still largely lack an understanding of how effective broader defenses can be against nuclear terrorism, and, most important, of how best to go about designing them. It will take hundreds of individuals with diverse experience and knowledge to design a comprehensive system. Before anyone does that, however, we must understand something more basic: how to *think* about nuclear terrorism.

Defense as a System

Defenses against nuclear terrorism make the most sense as integrated systems, with each part of the defense not only complementing other defensive elements but also reinforcing them. How can we make sense of such a vast system, with its thousands of distinct parts? Consider a simple analogy.

The New York Yankees, displaying remarkably bad judgment, hire a new manager who has no baseball experience. Lacking intuitive understanding of the game, he adopts a systematic approach to assessing his team. He begins by studying each player alone, examining his range of skills. But the manager cannot stop there—after all, he is looking at a team. To be sure, he could, for example, analyze each outfielder only in isolation, but he would come to the nonsensical conclusion that outfielders are useless—after all, with only a right-fielder, opposing batters would simply hit the ball to left field.

Should he then jump to studying the team as a whole? Perhaps, but he would quickly run into big problems. Still unguided by intuition, his obvious next step would be to analyze each pair of players, but with thirty-six possible pairs, doing so would be a tall order. If he went further and studied every possible combination of players—pairs, groups of three, and so on—he would have to look at over five hundred combinations. Almost certainly he would conclude that there must be a better way.

Instead, he divides the players into groups. He studies how the pitcher and catcher work together, how the infield operates as a team, and how the outfielders complement one another, all of which simplifies things a great deal. Only then does he look at the team as a whole, exploring how the groups interact. By studying the pitcher and the infielders together, for example, he discovers that with a bad pitcher, even good infielding might be useless, but with a pitcher who forces batters to hit easy balls, even relatively bad infielding may be effective. Indeed real baseball teams have sometimes used variations on this way of thinking in order to isolate the contributions of individual players.[8]

The manager then examines his limitations. How does his limited budget constrain the combinations of players he can field? How does his need for strong batting limit his flexibility in building the most effective possible defense?

A similar approach makes sense for studying defense against nuclear terrorism. It is impossible to look at every interaction—every "synergy"—between a policeman and a radiation detector, for example, each of which are deployed in the many thousands, but it is useful to study law enforcement as a whole and radiation detection as a whole, and then to look at how law enforcement and radiation detection work together. To understand nuclear terrorism, we must study the defense from its fine details to its broader structure.

A few numbers suggest the potential power of a broad defense. Imagine a scenario in which, at each step of its plot, a terrorist group has a 90 percent chance of success. Then a plot requiring ten steps will have less than a 40 percent chance of succeeding, since its overall odds of success are reduced with each step.[9] This compounding effect also means that improvements in each layer of the defense are magnified. (A defense of this sort is called a "layered defense.") Imagine that the defense doubles its odds of defeating the terrorist group at each layer, so that the chances of terrorist success are now 80 percent at each stage of its plot. Then the overall odds that a terrorist plot will succeed drops to 10 percent.

This perspective turns a cliché about terrorism on its head. It has often been said that defense against terrorism must succeed every time, but that terrorists must succeed only once. This is true from plot to plot, but within each plot, the logic is reversed. Terrorists must succeed at every stage, but the defense needs to succeed only once.

Even if this way of thinking makes perfect sense, we often ignore it. An intuitive explanation is suggested by what philosophers call the "lottery paradox."[10] In a large, simple lottery drawing, the chance that any given ticket will win is essentially zero, so, intuitively, the chances of winning, even with a large number of tickets, seems to be zero as well. But it is obvious that if you buy half of the available tickets, you have a 50 percent chance of winning. Still, many follow the first, patently wrong, way of thinking. (In moral philosophy, the result is that people are willing to accept many small wrongs even if they would never countenance a large evil.) Analysis of nuclear terrorism is often no different—each element of a defense might be intuitively dismissed because, alone, each may only have a small chance of working, leading to the possibly incorrect conclusion that the defense as a whole is ineffective. In evaluating defenses against nuclear terrorism, it is essential not only to avoid quickly dismissing relatively weak defensive tools, but indeed to deliberately look for small odds of terrorist failure. Among other things, this approach means searching for unusual ways that terrorists might fail, rather than just for unusual ways that they might succeed.

Perhaps the most fruitful source of potential terrorist failure is simple bad luck. Call it Murphy's Law of Nuclear Terrorism: What can go wrong might go wrong. (In the traditional version of Murphy's Law, of course, what can go wrong not only might go wrong—it will go wrong.) A 1995 plot to explode airliners over the Pacific Ocean was thwarted when plotters started a fire while preparing explosives.[11] A plot to bomb the Los Angeles airport at the millennium was stopped by an officer who noticed a nervous terrorist at the Canada–U.S. border, leading to a "chance discovery" of explosives in the trunk of his car.[12] The September 11, 2001, al Qaeda attacks on the United States, in contrast, might have been stopped had terrorist errors, such as conspicuous behavior at flight schools, been better exploited.[13] A defense must be prepared to take advantage of such terrorist error or bad luck, lest a terrorist plot succeed despite such misfortune because the defense fails to exploit it.

Even the picture painted above tells only half the story. In thinking about nuclear terrorism, it is not enough simply to assess the odds that any piece of the defense will defeat a terrorist plot. In a true system, the ways defensive elements *fail* to stop terrorist plots are equally important. Just like our fictional policemen, we must think about the costs a terrorist group incurs in defeating a particular defensive component. A group may, for example, avoid recruiting skilled engineers to build its bomb in order to avoid detection by intelligence agents or law enforcement officers—but that decision will come at the expense of increased odds that the group will be unable to build a bomb.

Another numerical example makes this point more concrete. Imagine, just as in the last example, that against each of ten defensive measures, a terrorist group has a 10 percent chance of failure. The group dreams up ways to cut each chance of failure in half, letting it apparently improve its overall odds of success by 40 percent. But there is a catch: each change the terrorist group makes to evade one element of the defense doubles its odds of failure in another part of its plot. (Perhaps the terrorist group hires additional scientists to make bomb-building easier, but is now more vulnerable to law enforcement.) The net result is that none of the terrorist group's clever ideas increase its overall chance of success. For any given terrorist group, plot, and defense, this system effect will differ in its precise details. It will, however, almost always exist, making a true defensive system more effective than a simple layered defense.

All these ideas have been the subjects of careful study outside the context of nuclear terrorism. Some systems analysis takes a top-down and heavily mathematical approach, describing the entire system in detail and then simulating it, just as many companies simulate and analyze their supply chains. But nuclear terrorism is so complex and so poorly understood that such an approach normally becomes intractable or meaningless.[14] The better alternative is what is called a qualitative approach, through which one studies the basic properties of the system without making (often meaningless) numerical assessments of its effectiveness.[15] Qualitative systems analysis focuses on identifying patterns. These patterns typically involve synergies, where the combined effect of several elements of the system is greater than the sum of the individual effects of each element alone. This approach, essentially the one our fictional baseball manager used, allows us to better understand the system without formal simulation or intensive computation.

Another technique developed by students of defense planning can help us too. Arthur Brooks and his colleagues at the RAND Corporation have studied the use of scenarios to understand complex systems. They distinguish two varieties of scenario analysis, traditional and exploratory.[16] Traditional scenario analysis attempts to find the most likely scenario the defense will face and then studies slight variations on it. Exploratory analysis is far less restrictive in choosing scenarios; it looks, instead, at a wide range of possibilities. Since this book seeks to understand a broad universe of terrorist plots and defenses, such explanatory analysis will be enlightening.

Understanding the Enemies

Before we can design or judge a defense, we must know something about the enemies it might face and the plots that those enemies might construct. There may seem to be an obvious way to acquire this knowledge: figure out what the worst possible threat is, and design a defense that can defeat it. Intuitively, we might think that if a defense can do that, it can also stop any other, apparently lesser, group or plot.

History has shown, however, that this way of thinking often makes little sense. Take the Cold War as an example: the United States spent an enormous amount of money on defense, but it never came close to perfect security against the worst-case threat, an all-out Soviet attack. And yet the United States not only survived the Cold War but won it. Defenses that fall short against worst-case threats can still be very valuable.

Meanwhile, after the Cold War ended, the United States quickly learned that the military it had built to confront the Soviets—a more powerful opponent than those who confront the United States now—is ill suited to combat today's supposedly lesser threats.[17] A defense optimized against the worst case may not be the most effective defense against more likely threats.

Military planners often employ the so-called threat-based approach to deal with this problem. They measure their defensive options against a handful of likely threats rather than against a single worst-case scenario. During much of the 1990s, for example, the United States developed its military primarily with two scenarios in mind: "aggression by a remilitarized Iraq against Kuwait and Saudi Arabia, and by North Korea against the Republic of Korea."[18] (Special capabilities were added for other requirements, such as nation building and counterterrorism, but were not at the core of planning efforts.)

This approach is better than focusing on the worst case, but the two schemes still share important potential flaws. The small number of scenarios used may not be representative of a wide enough range of potential enemies, but an accurate representation may demand so many scenarios as to be unwieldy. If we are good at predicting the future, such limits may not pose a problem. But if the future is murky, and we have trouble identifying the tactics and enemies we might face, finding the right set of scenarios may be impossible.

The alternative is to focus on a potential enemy's range of capabilities rather than on narrowly described future threats. Defense experts call this approach to confronting an uncertain future "capabilities-based planning."[19] Nuclear plots and nuclear terrorists may take many different forms that, at best, can be loosely predicted. This diversity makes capabilities-based planning the best approach to thinking about broad defenses against nuclear terrorism.

To understand this approach better, imagine a simple traditional military example where the enemy is described by the number of troops in its army, the type of warning you expect to get before it attacks, and by its ultimate objectives.[20] In traditional planning, strategists would study a handful of opponents and determine the sizes of their armies, the different warnings the defense expects before each enemy attacks, and the objectives of each potential enemy. They would then design forces and strategies for each case. But what if future enemies and attacks are unpredictable? Faced with a wide range of possible sizes for an enemy army, strategists might explore ways to quickly increase or decrease the size of their deployed defensive forces; confronted by uncertainty about early warning of an attack, they might recommend improving intelligence. This way of thinking is not always correct—if, for example, the sizes of enemy armies are well known, it makes little sense to plan against a wide range of potential enemy armies. But it does make sense in many cases, such as when dealing with an enemy whose goals are difficult to know.

Potential nuclear terrorists are notoriously hard to understand or predict. What capabilities and features characterize different terrorist groups? Financial, technical, recruiting, and operational capabilities are a few of the most important, and we will learn about them throughout this book. All these affect the odds of terrorist success. Groups can often trade among these capabilities—for example, the ability to fund-raise might be converted to technical skill if money raised is used to hire scientists and engineers. There are limits, though, to how flexible groups can be.

Terrorist attitudes toward outcomes, risks, and innovation also play central roles. Nuclear terrorism is not a reward in itself for any but perhaps the most pathological terrorist leaders, such as the nuclear analogues of Japanese cult leader Shoko Asahara, who was so obsessed with poisons that he wrote a paean to Sarin gas.[21] Most terrorist groups, though, assess nuclear terrorism through the lens of their political goals and may judge that it does not advance their interests. Others may believe that nuclear terrorism would advance their goals under certain circumstances. A group may, for example, decide under some circumstances that it must escalate its attacks in order to maintain popular support while, at other times, it might conclude that it must limit its level of violence for precisely the same reason. For others, most notably some motivated by religion, killing the enemy may be an end in itself.

Terrorist groups also vary widely in their attitudes toward risk and failure. Analysts differ in their assessments of terrorist groups, in part because understanding terrorist groups is difficult, but also because this dimension of terrorism is understudied.[22] Most analysts who have looked carefully at terrorist decision making, however, reject the popular image of all terrorist groups as being willing to risk everything in pursuit of spectacular results. Paul Davis and Brian Jenkins, citing several leading authorities on terrorism, have written that the "empirical record of terrorism" shows that "terrorist actors are often concerned about operational risk—they may be willing to risk or give their lives, but not in futile attacks."[23] Gavin Cameron, in a book on nuclear terrorism, writes that "many terrorist organizations also appear to be risk-averse: the emphasis is often on the group's survival."[24] More recently Jenkins, one of the foremost American experts on terrorism, has written that for al Qaeda in particular, operations "must be successful."[25] He draws an explicit religious connection: "Jihadists believe that God's will is expressed in success and failure. To succeed is to have God's support."

Ultimately it may be unnecessary for a defense to directly defeat a terrorist plot. If a terrorist leader is unwilling or unable to have his group or cell marshal and expend the resources necessary to achieve what, in his mind, are acceptable odds of success, he may never approve an attempt at nuclear terrorism.[26] Even if the odds of success are high enough, he may decide that the impact of an attack does not justify the risk or expense. As a plot progresses, he will reevaluate these factors: what may appear worthwhile initially may become less attractive.

Most terrorist groups are also quite tactically conservative. Bruce Hoffman writes that "the organizational imperative to succeed . . . imposes on some terrorist groups an operational conservatism that makes an ironic contrast with their political radicalism."[27] Thus the degree to which a given terrorist group is conservative will affect its approach to nuclear plots. There is, for example, nothing tactically conservative about building a nuclear bomb, a task far different from those that terrorist groups commonly face. That does not preclude conservative groups from tackling such challenges, but when those groups cannot avoid innovating in one part of their plot, they face increased pressure to use their bread-and-butter tactics as much as possible in its remainder. Such basic tactics could be identified in the 9/11 attacks: while the culmination of that plot was innovative, the underlying operations—in particular, the movement of money and operatives—were similar to those in past al Qaeda efforts, despite the potential risks associated with continuing to use them.[28] The tactics did, however, allow al Qaeda to minimize the chance of making mistakes while attempting to innovate.

Setting Realistic Goals

The choice of goals for any defense has important consequences for how strategy is designed and for its ability to succeed. Much of the Western debate over arms control during the Cold War was fundamentally a debate over whether the main goal was avoiding nuclear war or confronting communism. For those in the majority who were unwilling to dismiss either objective, a strategy that ranked the two but still pursued both was essential.[29]

Nuclear terrorism presents a similar challenge. The main goal of defense against nuclear terrorism should be to prevent nuclear attacks, but if perfect defense is impossible, it is essential to also reduce the damage inflicted by any attack that succeeds. A nuclear terrorist attack might kill anywhere between hundreds and hundreds of thousands of people, depending on the power of the terrorist weapon, where it explodes, and the effectiveness of any emergency response. Smaller weapons kill fewer people, as do larger weapons that explode farther away from major population centers, while smaller weapons that explode far away from densely populated places kill fewer still.

To predict with any precision how many fatalities a weapon will cause in an urban area is quite difficult, since buildings may shield the blast as well as the radiation in different ways; the radiation emitted by a nuclear weapon is also hard to predict in the first place. It is still useful, though, to have a basic understanding of some numbers.[30] Reducing the explosive power of a weapon detonated in a uniformly populated area from ten kilotons to one kiloton might reduce the number of fatalities by anywhere between a factor of three and five; reducing that power from ten kilotons to one hundred tons (a factor of one hundred) might reduce the number of fatalities by anywhere between a factor of five and twenty. (A kiloton is an explosive force equal to that of 1,000 tons of TNT explosive). Moving a detonation away from a city center will also reduce immediate fatalities. Imagine a ten-kiloton weapon detonated in a city whose population is concentrated primarily within two kilometers of the city center. Displacing that detonation by one, two, three, or five kilometers from the city center will reduce the number of fatalities by 20, 40, 60, or 95 percent, respectively.

Although there is no question that any nuclear attack would be terrible, the difference between hundreds, thousands, and hundreds of thousands dead matters deeply. And these differences may not matter only to defensive planners—terrorist groups might find the distinctions important in deciding whether to proceed with any nuclear attack. Still, regardless of how many people are killed in an attack, the mere fact that the attack is nuclear will have far-reaching social, political, and strategic implications, which is why prevention must remain our most important goal.

The Alternative

It is easy to imagine alternative principles that might guide our thinking about nuclear terrorism. Systems analysis might be replaced with any of several other, less holistic, approaches: defense could be approached as a series of independent layers, as a set of completely separate components, or even as a single layer. Capabilities-based planning could be replaced by a focus on worst-case scenarios or on a small set of possible threats. And the set of goals just proposed could be replaced by a singular focus on preventing attacks. To conclude that systems analysis, capabilities-based planning, and setting multiple goals should guide our thinking not only requires that their principles help us to understand nuclear terrorism—it demands that they do a better job than the alternatives. It now remains for us to understand exactly how to apply these principles in practice and to show that they are solid foundations for thinking about nuclear terrorism.

— 2 —

Security at the Source

No material occurring in nature can be used to make a nuclear bomb, which requires either enriched uranium or plutonium. Uranium mined from the ground must be processed extensively—enriched—before it can be used in a bomb. Plutonium does not occur naturally aside from minuscule quantities and must be produced in a nuclear reactor. Both capabilities are widely agreed to be beyond the reach of even the most sophisticated terrorists.[1] Thus state stockpiles of these nuclear materials and weapons are the gateways to nuclear terrorism. If nuclear weapons and materials can be locked up by capable, well-behaved states, and if those unable or unwilling to lock up materials or weapons can be denied them, nuclear terrorism can be made impossible.

This sort of strategy is so compelling that it should form the foundation of any sensible approach to preventing nuclear terrorism. Only nine countries have nuclear weapons. Policymakers are confident that in seven of them—the United States, Britain, France, Russia, China, India, and Israel—no government imaginable would ever want to allow terrorists access to a bomb or to the materials needed to make one. A more contentious debate exists over what the other two states, Pakistan and North Korea, might do with their arsenals, but many believe that they would not part with them either. Many more countries retain civilian stocks of highly enriched uranium (HEU) or plutonium, the indispensable ingredients of nuclear bombs. Fourteen states without nuclear weapons are estimated to have at least twenty-five kilograms (about fifty pounds) of HEU each, the minimum amount required for a bomb according to the International Atomic Energy Agency.[2] Another twenty-six have at least one kilogram (about two pounds) of the material. Three countries without nuclear weapons also have sufficient plutonium with low enough radioactivity to be used in a bomb.[3] Although these numbers may appear to indicate a widespread problem, they actually describe a limited challenge. In contrast with, for example, conventional explosives, nuclear weapons and materials are available only at a relatively small, known, group of facilities that in theory can either lock their materials down or end their operations if adequate security proves impossible. Meanwhile only one state, Iran, explicitly threatens to acquire highly enriched uranium or nuclear weapons in the near future, in theory a problem that can be managed using a mix of international diplomacy, inducements, economic pressure, or military action.

It was against a similar backdrop that cooperative efforts to keep weapons and materials under responsible control originated in the immediate aftermath of the Cold War. Following the fall of the Soviet Union, Western analysts and politicians worried that lax security exposed ex-Soviet nuclear weapons and materials to theft or illicit sale, and scientists and engineers to recruitment by rogue states or by terrorists pursuing nuclear arms.[4] The Soviet Union had relied primarily on the loyalty of its employees, backstopped by its internal security services, to control its nuclear assets—yet as the Soviet Union dissolved, that loyalty became questionable, while security services became weaker (though by no means sidelined) as successor states began to reform. Economic malaise produced new incentives for employees to sell nuclear weapons or materials, or their own services, to rogue states and terrorists.

The United States, widely agreed to have good security over its own nuclear weapons and materials, pioneered efforts to address the situation. Defense Department programs, which began in 1991, originally engaged several states of the former Soviet Union, applying American funding and expertise to dismantle or destroy nuclear arms, focusing on those missiles slated for elimination under arms control treaties. At the same time, the U.S. Department of Energy pursued its own initiative, focused on securing materials and human capital rather than weapons themselves. Efforts to work with others to secure nuclear weapons, materials, and expertise are known collectively as Cooperative Threat Reduction.

Beginning in 2002, American efforts were substantially supplemented by contributions made through the G-8 Partnership against the Spread of Weapons of Mass Destruction, often referred to simply as the Global Partnership. Under that initiative, the United States committed $10 billion over the next ten years to extend its decade-old efforts, while its G-8 partners committed to match that $10 billion over the same period. Since the Global Partnership was announced, it has become an umbrella for efforts extending beyond the G-8.[5] (Non-U.S. contributions to cooperative materials control existed before 2002, but were not comparable to the level of American contributions.) Also in this period, following the 9/11 terrorist attacks, the United States and others began to expand their cooperative threat reduction programs beyond the former Soviet Union to other states, like Pakistan, that appeared to need assistance.

Efforts to bring existing materials under control have been two-pronged. Materials Protection, Control, and Accounting (MPC&A) and Weapons Protection, Control, and Accounting (WPC&A) have aimed to secure nuclear explosive materials. Parallel efforts have aimed to reduce stockpiles of materials and weapons, both to lower the overall burden on MPC&A and WPC&A and to eliminate nuclear explosive materials and weapons in cases where establishing effective security appears to be impossible.

To get a deeper understanding of these tools, focus for now on nuclear materials rather than on weapons.

These initiatives have produced important results. Over 49 percent of former Soviet nuclear explosive material outside weapons has received so-called rapid security upgrades, which "include items such as installing nuclear material detectors at the doors [of nuclear facilities], putting material in steel cases that would take a considerable time to cut through, bricking over windows, and counting how many items of nuclear material are present."[6] These upgrades contribute substantially to preventing simple thefts. Items such as steel cases and bricked-over windows will prevent some thefts by nonemployees (referred to as outsiders) and slow others down so that guard forces can respond. Material detectors will promptly detect some theft attempts by facility employees (referred to as insiders) as well, reinforcing physical security upgrades.

In addition to the rapid upgrades, so-called comprehensive upgrades have been undertaken at 29 percent of former Soviet facilities. These upgrades focus in particular on systems to defend against insider threats, including both materials control upgrades to directly defeat theft attempts, and materials accounting upgrades to better deter thefts.[7]

Many have argued that these upgrades can be perfected, making materials and weapons theft impossible. Perhaps the most intuitively persuasive case for that proposition is a recently popular argument: since it has been possible to provide absolute security for gold at Fort Knox, it should be possible to provide similar absolute security for nuclear facilities against thefts of nuclear weapons and explosive materials. This analogy has been made most notably by Graham Allison in his book *Nuclear Terrorism*, and has since been publicly endorsed by a host of others, such as Thomas Kean, co-chairman of the 9/11 Commission.[8] Indeed the Fort Knox analogy is not new. After describing standards for materials security, Bernard Feld wrote in 1985 that "I refer to this as the 'Fort Knox solution', in view of its similarity to the procedures used in our country [the United States] for the transport and storage of gold. Plutonium is more valuable than gold, and much, much more lethal. Surely, it deserves at least as much care in its handling."[9]

Many advocates of cooperative materials and weapons security have noted, however, that those efforts will be undercut if new and irresponsible states acquire nuclear materials or weapons. These observers support a strategy for preventing nuclear terrorism that mixes cooperative efforts to control existing nuclear weapons and materials with vigorous efforts to prevent more states from acquiring nuclear materials or bombs.[10]

Efforts to prevent the spread of nuclear weapons and materials have evolved over the last sixty-plus years and incorporate a wide range of tools. They rest on a mixture of incentives for states to forgo sensitive technologies and nuclear bombs, punishments for states that acquire nuclear weapons or dangerous technologies, systems that provide warning that states might be moving toward nuclear weapons or technologies, and tools that slow the progress of states that embark on that path.[11]

As a result of these efforts, the spread of nuclear weapons has been far more limited than many predicted when John F. Kennedy warned in 1960 of a world with "ten, fifteen, or twenty nations [with] a nuclear capacity . . . by the end of the presidential office in 1964."[12] Instead, only one new state has acquired nuclear explosives in each of the last three decades. (India acquired nuclear explosives in the 1970s; Pakistan in the 1980s; and North Korea most likely in the 1990s.) Only one state, Iran, threatens to acquire nuclear weapons in the first decade of the twenty-first century, itself a testament to the effectiveness of efforts to prevent nuclear proliferation. Although the world could take a sharp turn for the worse, it is not unreasonable to be largely optimistic about the future potential of nonproliferation.

Limits to Controls

While controls over nuclear weapons and material should always form the core of our efforts to prevent nuclear terrorism, they will never be perfected.[13] To understand why, we can first dissect the Fort Knox analogy. The analogy is intuitively appealing, and sometimes close to reality. Yet nuclear facilities often differ from Fort Knox in important, unavoidable, and revealing ways. According to the United States Mint, "The only gold removed [from Fort Knox] has been very small quantities used to test the purity of gold during regularly scheduled audits. Except for these samples, no gold has been transferred to or from the [Fort Knox] Depository for many years."[14] Given this history, any attempt to remove significant quantities of gold from Fort Knox would be identified immediately as unauthorized, and authorities could quickly attempt to stop the thieves. But distinguishing between allowed and illegal withdrawals of nuclear materials requires fundamentally different tools from those used at Fort Knox: as long as nuclear facilities generate products that will be used elsewhere, many legitimate movements of significant quantities of nuclear material will occur. Preventing thefts is not as simple as replicating Fort Knox.

Fort Knox's setting also makes massive response to any attempted theft relatively straightforward: the facility is next to the U.S. Army Armor Center.[15] Many nuclear materials facilities, however, are not located next to similar military installations.

The contrast between Fort Knox and many nuclear facilities is suggestive, but it is no substitute for careful analysis of the finer details of weapons and materials security. Focus for now on the protection of nuclear explosive materials: the most persuasive argument explaining why it is impossible to lock all these materials up permanently can be found by looking at what MPC&A systems—the systems that "lock up" nuclear materials—actually do. MPC&A has three components: protection ("P"), control ("C"), and accounting ("A"). An authoritative report from the National Research Council defines the three MPC&A elements:

1. *Materials protection* "should allow for the detection of any unauthorized penetration of barriers and portals, thereby triggering the use of force if necessary."
2. *Materials control* "should prevent unauthorized movement of mate-

rials and allow for the prompt detection of the theft or diversion of material."

3. *Materials accounting* "should ensure that all material is accounted for, enable the measurement of losses, and provide information for follow-up investigations of irregularities."[16]

Materials protection is directed at keeping thieves out of a facility; it is aimed primarily at facility outsiders. (It might also be used against facility insiders attempting to break into a part of the facility that they are not authorized to enter.) Materials control is, in contrast, fundamentally directed at keeping material inside a facility; its job is primarily to prevent theft by facility insiders. To be sure, no bright line divides physical protection and materials control—for example, the same guards might keep thieves out of a facility (physical protection) and keep insiders trying to smuggle nuclear material from leaving the facility (materials control).

In contrast to these prongs, materials accounting does not involve actively and directly controlling nuclear materials. Instead, it is used to observe the state of materials stocks in order to determine if materials have been removed without authorization. To be useful, it must be used to trigger further actions—"follow-up investigations of irregularities" and, if those confirm that materials have been stolen, pursuit of thieves. Those follow-up actions fall outside the scope of MPC&A.

Only two conclusions are possible. The most obvious is that MPC&A is not a self-contained system—it cannot provide complete security alone. It requires other defensive tools, such as the ability to pursue and apprehend thieves, to be fully effective. The second possible conclusion is that perfect protection and control can indeed be achieved, so that the accounting dimension of MPC&A is superfluous. But perfect protection and control are not in fact attainable.

The limits to physical materials protection ("P") come mainly from culture and budgets. They are cultural, because some settings—for example, universities or many urban locations—do not naturally or readily admit strongly fortified facilities defended by large numbers of armed forces.[17] The limits are budgetary in that increasing physical protection costs money, and governments or corporations will at some point decide to limit investment. Theoretically, these barriers can be universally surmounted. Graham Allison makes the point most clearly, but not dissimilarly to others, arguing that looking "through the lens of 9/11," governments should be able to muster "steadfast determination" that will "run over . . . objections about difficulty and expense."[18] With regard to nuclear reactors used for academic research that are fueled with highly enriched uranium, he, like many others, argues that "reactors that cannot be converted to LEU [material that is effectively impossible to use in nuclear weapons] must be closed"—presumably because cultural and budgetary factors would prevent those facilities from being adequately secured.[19]

Whether this case is persuasive depends on what it is supposed to prove. It shows that technically steps do exist that can be taken to create robust physical security for all nuclear facilities. But that truth does not mean that such steps *will* be taken, even though they should be. The political will needed to spend funds or to force facility closures may not be attainable; it certainly has not been thus far. We must prepare for the possibility that this vulnerability will persist.

Perfect materials control ("C") is even harder to implement than perfect materials protection, even when the desire for such programs, along with the necessary funds, exists. In contrast with materials protection, where problem individuals simply need to be kept away from sensitive material, materials control must deal with insiders who legitimately handle nuclear material as a part of their normal work. Possible misuse of this access poses a more difficult challenge.

Control efforts generally focus on three areas: monitoring stored materials for any unauthorized changes; monitoring facility exits for any unauthorized removal of materials by insiders; and personnel security, including personnel screening and special procedures for handiing materials.[20] Although such systems can be highly effective in most cases, several situations bring them under stress.

The same cultural problems that can hamstring physical protection can also deeply undermine the effectiveness of materials control. Because most control efforts must ultimately rely on the ability to physically restrain any insider who attempts to steal nuclear materials, they must include a ready ability to use significant force. (The exceptions involve cases where material almost never needs to be moved; there, access controls inside the facility that do not depend on human elements, such as extremely heavy blocks sealing storage containers, can essentially preclude theft.) Research reactors are again an example of where this problem occurs—if thieves cannot be physically stopped, no amount of monitoring will prevent an inside team from removing materials. This problem also exists, though to a lesser extent, in industrial facilities, where armed forces are still not as acceptable as in military facilities.

In cases where enough force is available to stop thefts in progress, the central challenge is timely detection of thefts, since no amount of force is useful if a theft is detected only after all the stolen material has already been removed from the site. Again the feasibility of this step depends on specific circumstances. Facilities used primarily for storing materials are the most easily protected, because any movement of materials by facility employees, other than planned and highly restricted movement, can be immediately identified as inappropriate.[21] (This is the Fort Knox case.) In cases where materials must be handled regularly by facility staff, the other two prongs of materials control—portal monitoring and personnel reliability—become more important. Personnel screening, though valuable, is still limited—a broad insider conspiracy can never be ruled out, especially one that might be provoked or aided by outside bribery. Portal monitoring, meanwhile, is fallible too, particularly in cases where facility workers might force their way through exit points that are not monitored.

Accounting is thus not a superfluous part of MPC&A. Physical protection and materials control may be effective most of the time, but we cannot expect them to always work.

Terrorist acquisition of nuclear materials, furthermore, may not even involve the failure of good-faith MPC&A efforts. Most obviously, state leaders might be complicit in the transfer of nuclear materials to terrorists. The deliberate transfer of nuclear weapons or materials from leaders of a state to a terrorist group is, in a sense, the extreme instance of insider assistance, particularly when those leaders involved are subverting state policy. What distinguishes this case is that any MPC&A systems in place are not designed specifically to prevent or detect movement of nuclear materials by state leaders—rather, those individuals are in positions accorded such great trust that these systems are considered unnecessary. The group of state leaders who might participate includes those implementing state policy and those subverting state policy. Perhaps the poster child for both of these possibilities is the Pakistani scientist A. Q. Khan. Over the course of nearly two decades, Khan helped spread nuclear technologies (though not nuclear materials or weapons) to a host of states, including Iran, Libya, and North Korea.[22] Some of those activities were likely sanctioned by the Pakistani leadership; others were probably not.

Scholars and other observers have worried most about three scenarios.

Subversion of state control over Pakistani nuclear weapons or materials could let terrorists acquire nuclear materials or weapons. As David Albright has written, "Pakistan must also increasingly worry that experts from the nuclear complex could steal sensitive information or assist nuclear weapons programs of other countries or terrorist groups."[23] North Korea might sell materials or weapons to wealthy terrorist groups. Richard Clarke, for example, contends that given "North Korea's well-known reputation for sponsoring organized crime and selling missile technology to anyone with hard currency, and Kim Jung-Il's hatred for the United States, the possibility that the country would provide terrorists with a nuclear capability is not unrealistic."[24] Iran might also work with Hezbollah to deliver nuclear weapons, were Iran to acquire those weapons.[25]

These specific possibilities are matched by three potential motivations for leaders to be complicit in transferring nuclear weapons or materials, though each possibility and motivation can be challenged. Leaders might transfer weapons or materials in order to further what they see as their states' strategic interests. Their willingness to do so could be bolstered if they worked with terrorist groups that shared their ideology—transfers from Iran to Hezbollah would be a natural example.[26] Others might part with weapons for purely financial reasons, as North Korea has done with conventional weapons.[27] State leaders might also transfer weapons or materials to terrorists as a means for revenge in the face of imminent hostile regime change; this scenario was cited by many, prior to the 2003 invasion of Iraq, as the most likely under which Iraq would have transferred nuclear, chemical, or biological weapons to terrorists.[28]

At the same time, a large community of scholars contend that no state would transfer materials to terrorist groups. They too cite three reasons. (The description below follows one by Matthew Bunn and his colleagues, but the same themes appear in other places.)[29] They argue that a state will be deterred by even a remote prospect of retaliation; this contention responds to the claim that a state might transfer weapons or materials in the pursuit of strategic aims. They also argue that problem states are normally dictatorships whose leaders are loath to relinquish control, so such leaders would not give control over their nuclear weapons or materials to terrorists; moreover, according to this line of argument, those just below the top leadership would not have the authority to transfer weapons or materials. This argument counters claims that individuals not acting in the state's best interest might transfer materials. Some make yet another argument, saying that since nuclear weapons are difficult and expensive to acquire, a state would not want to part with them; this objection serves as a response to arguments about financial, ideological, and strategic motivations. Few people argue against the possibility that a state facing regime change might transfer weapons; instead these observers use this point to counsel against forced regime change.[30]

Determining which of these positions is correct is a theoretical, and futile, exercise. In the final analysis, scholars and policymakers will have to make judgments about the weight to place on each possibility. To guide them, the most useful approach is to briefly explore and illuminate each pair of competing claims just introduced.

Most of the arguments that states would not transfer weapons or materials to terrorists depend on the assumption that any transfer will be made by someone attempting to promote the best interests of his or her state. If that is not the case—as one might argue was the situation with A. Q. Khan when he engaged in sales of Pakistani nuclear technology that were not sanctioned (likely a subset of his broader work)—then arguments relying on deterrence normally fail, since the individuals in question will not worry about the dangers their activities bring upon their countries. In addition, arguments centered on a need to conserve scarce nuclear material resources fall apart, since the problem individual may not care much about the size or shape of his state's nuclear stockpile. In such a situation, only the likelihood that dictatorial leaders would not allow others sufficient control to divert weapons or nuclear materials remains a major barrier to the spread of nuclear arms. One might argue that A. Q. Khan's freelance work eviscerates this argument, since Khan, despite being entrusted to trade nuclear technologies as part of state policy, was not adequately controlled. But the Khan case may be fundamentally different, in that it did not involve nuclear weapons or explosive materials, the most sensitive parts of the Pakistani nuclear program.

What about states that might transfer weapons or materials to further their strategic aims? If nuclear explosive materials are scarce, leaders may not be willing to part with any, unless they are using a terrorist group to deliver a weapon to a specific intended target. But with more weapons, there is no fundamental reason why a state would not sell one; North Korea, for example, could live with seven rather than eight bombs.

The argument that state leaders would be deterred from transfers is more vexing. Skeptics are right to suggest that the possibility of retaliation creates a high bar to nuclear transfers, even if the chances of retaliation are low. At the same time, states like North Korea *do* risk small chances of regime change in pursuit of national objectives. For example, North Korea probably saw at least a small chance of war—and hence of regime change—when it extracted plutonium from its used nuclear fuel in 2003, given past American assertions that such a move would cross a red line and invite attack (though no red line was articulated during the 2003 crisis).[31] Yet North Korea proceeded with the action anyway.[32] Again, it is impossible to rule out risky behavior.

Yet another possibility should make us suspicious of claims that materials and weapons security can be perfected: state collapse. If a state collapses, nuclear weapons or materials might be transferred to terrorist groups as centralized control evaporates. The most commonly cited scenario here is the collapse of the Pakistani government, though North Korea is sometimes mentioned as well.[33] This scenario's plausibility depends on both the likelihood of state collapse and the likelihood of theft or transfer of nuclear weapons or materials following collapse. The chance that weapons or materials will be transferred to terrorists rather than recovered by responsible governments depends not only on the particular circumstances of collapse but on the responses of other governments.

Even if all states manage to control their nuclear materials and weapons in the future, horror stories of past nuclear security raise concerns that meaningful amounts of nuclear materials may have already been diverted and may already be in circulation. There are several known instances of nuclear theft as well as many instances of foiled theft attempts.[34] Because nuclear material is often difficult to recapture, the thefts indicate that there may be stolen nuclear material floating around the world.[35] The most obvious counterargument to these claims is that, since no terrorist nuclear attack has taken place, there must not be meaningful amounts of nuclear explosive material in circulation. All this shows, though, is that no buyer has been able to gather sufficient material for a nuclear weapon in a single place, or that no terrorist group has been able to execute an attack even with sufficient stolen material.[36]

Although attempts to control nuclear weapons and materials will and should always be at the heart of any strategy to defend against nuclear terrorism, the world must contend with the possibility that those efforts will occasionally fail. And even if all new proliferation can be prevented, substantial gaps will inevitably remain.

To understand defense against nuclear terrorism, then, we need to learn about other defensive tools. To best understand them, it is useful to at least temporarily narrow and sharpen our focus. The next three chapters will look only at bombs terrorists build themselves, so-called Improvised Nuclear Devices (INDs), which a majority of leading experts have recently identified as the most likely route to nuclear terrorism.[37] These chapters will also look only at plots that involve stolen materials, which the same group of experts identified as the most likely source of materials for terrorist plots, rather than materials provided deliberately by states.[38] We'll return to the other cases toward the end of the book.

— 3 —

Building Blocks

Acquiring nuclear materials is only one necessary step for nuclear terrorists. Any nuclear plot, even at its most basic, has at least two other major components.[1] First, a terrorist group that obtains nuclear materials will still need to build a bomb. Second, to build a bomb, the group will need to transport those materials, other weapons components, and the tools they need to build their bomb; they will also have to move the actual terrorists who will be involved. These demands can in principle be countered by matching sets of defensive tools, those aimed at disrupting bomb-building and those designed to stop the movement of materials and personnel. If a terrorist group succeeds in detonating a nuclear bomb, another group of defensive tools, those used to manage the consequences of an attack, comes into play. And even the most difficult step, acquiring nuclear materials, may involve more than stealing them—if the terrorist group does not steal the materials on its own, it will need to find another way to acquire them.

This set of terrorist requirements and defensive measures needs to be broken down into many small pieces. That makes analysis complicated: as a result, the only way for us to understand the big picture is to work in stages. The first stage is to study the acquisition of nuclear materials, bomb-building, transporting nuclear and non-nuclear materials, and consequence management each in isolation. To keep things as simple as possible, when we explore any one segment of the defense, we will pretend that it is the *entire* defense. For example, when we look at barriers to terrorist bomb-building, we will imagine that, facing no defense, acquiring and transporting materials is a trivial task. (This method is the same one taken by our fictional baseball manager when he studied his outfield all alone, as if there were no infield.) Only after we start to understand each piece of the defense alone will we begin looking at how the different pieces work together. This approach will, eventually, make clear the advantage of looking at the defense as a system rather than as a collection of isolated parts.

Acquiring Nuclear Explosive Material

Acquiring nuclear explosive materials may involve more than the execution of a theft. Acquisition may, for instance, happen in two stages: one group might steal the materials, and a terrorist group might then buy them.[2] Understanding the barriers to this second stage—understanding the so-called black market—is as important as understanding the barriers to the initial theft.

Why might a terrorist group choose to acquire materials from others rather than stealing them itself? Some groups may not be particularly good at penetrating defenses at nuclear facilities or at subverting their security systems, but may be more able to arrange and execute transactions. This capability may derive from a group's stronger skills in the latter arena. Geography may also play a role: Russia or Pakistan may be places where nuclear materials might be stolen, but some groups may have more difficulty operating in those countries than in states where those materials might be bought. Groups may also decide that acquiring materials indirectly will help them hide their tracks more effectively, by making it unnecessary for them to ever come close to a nuclear facility. But if a group decides to look to buying materials, its abilities to raise money and to hide large transactions—which may vary drastically from group to group—will determine its odds of success.

If nuclear explosive material is expensive, price will present a big barrier to all but the richest terrorist groups. One immediate implication for defense is thus that broad efforts to restrict terrorist funding could make a major contribution to preventing nuclear terrorism. Beyond that, even wealthy groups would run into problems if they could not effectively hide large transactions. Similarly, if a defense could increase the risk of exposure for groups that attempt to buy materials from strangers, it would raise barriers for groups with relatively weak connections to established smuggling networks. In pursuing this line of thought we are already seeing capabilities-based thinking at work—some defensive measures may not be universally effective, but they might make meaningful contributions nonetheless.

Indeed nuclear material may be very expensive. Publicly available data indicating the price terrorists would have to pay for nuclear materials are sparse. Simple and suggestive estimates, however, are possible.

Why is it so difficult to predict the price of illicit market nuclear explosive material? No attempted underground sale of enough nuclear explosive material for a bomb has been publicly recorded.[3] (A terrorist-built uranium-based nuclear bomb requires approximately twenty kilograms of nuclear explosive material, and could easily need at least one hundred kilograms or more. The corresponding numbers for plutonium are smaller but similar.) On the one hand, a terrorist group might attempt to accumulate enough material for a bomb through a series of small purchases, making past records of small sales more relevant. But such repeated attempts would leave the group highly vulnerable to stings, in which government agents pose as sellers. Repeated transactions would also extend the group's plot over longer timelines, increasing its chances of being detected by law enforcement or intelligence.

On the other hand, buying enough material for a bomb in a single transaction could be expensive. Past records are of little use for inferring price, since there is a fundamental difference between buying enough nuclear material for a bomb and buying an amount of material insufficient for a bomb. (Barely enough material for a simple bomb is certainly worth much more than slightly less than enough material for a bomb, which in a simple design cannot produce an explosion. In this way, nuclear materials are like art—half a painting has far less than half the value of a whole painting.) At best, the price negotiated for small quantities of nuclear material puts a floor on the possible price for enough material for a bomb. Al Qaeda seems to have negotiated a price of $1.5 million for a cylinder (of unknown mass) of highly enriched uranium (HEU) in 1993, which suggests a possible minimum price. The group found out the material was fake after acquiring it.[4]

Al Qaeda's experience points to a second problem: most recorded transactions for nuclear material involve frauds (sometimes sting operations) planned by either the seller or the buyer. Yet if a seller is fraudulent, the price he agrees to says nothing about what a genuine seller might accept. Still, episodes involving fraudulent sellers might give some insight into what terrorists would be willing to spend, and active intelligence operations, in which government agents pose as potential sellers, could help gather such information, helping to improve defenses.

How else might one predict price? Think about the role of states in the marketplace for nuclear weapons, and imagine a hypothetical example in which a perfectly efficient market attempts to match a buyer to a seller of enough nuclear explosive material for a single bomb. (In a perfectly efficient market, the buyer pays the lowest possible price, and the seller receives the highest possible payment.) A terrorist group can only buy the material if it can outbid every state in the market. The price a state is willing to pay for a nuclear weapon therefore suggests a minimum price a terrorist group will have to pay. Libya is reported to have spent between $40 million and $100 million over roughly five years purchasing nuclear weapons assistance from Pakistan.[5] A. Q. Khan, who ran the Pakistani smuggling ring, is reported to have amassed a fortune of approximately $400 million through his activities; assuming his major clients are those that have already been made public (Iran, North Korea, and Libya), at least one state other than Libya must have spent more than $100 million as well. To be certain, those states were buying the *means* to make weapons, not just weapons or materials themselves. But presumably, the exact path to the bomb was less important to these countries than their ultimate goal of getting nuclear weapons. Imagine that a state like Libya had $100 million to spend and required ten weapons. It would have been willing to spend roughly $10 million for each; if it needed fifty weapons, that price would drop to $2 million. The first weapon would likely be much more valuable to the buyer than any subsequent weapons, pushing the cost of a single weapon toward the upper end of this range, if not higher. In this way one can make a crude estimate of what terrorists might need to pay for enough nuclear material for a bomb.

In a hostile environment, sellers may not be able to connect with all potential buyers, and those that can connect may not be able to enter into careful negotiations. Such circumstances might prevent a seller from getting the highest payment for his materials, or a buyer from getting the best deal possible. But the sale price of any material would only be substantially smaller than in the scenario just described if no state seeking nuclear materials were able to connect with the seller and drive the price up. Because state intelligence networks, through which states would attempt to buy nuclear materials, tend to be better developed than terrorist ones, the absence of a state buyer is unlikely (though certainly not impossible).

To assess how widely-varying terrorist capabilities clash with the requirements for a successful purchase, it is essential to understand more about terrorist financing and about illicit transactions. The amount of money available to a terrorist group is the most obvious constraint on its ability to buy materials. (We will see later that money will also constrain the rest of the group's plot, by making it more difficult, for example, to sustain operatives, bribe security officials, or hire scientists.) Total assets, though, do not give the full picture. For those assets to be useful, a terrorist group needs to be able to transfer them to its intended recipient. This task can be complicated if, for example, a group's resources are distributed throughout its membership, rather than held in central accounts. Even when money can be moved, the potential for a defense to detect transactions adds other barriers that vary from group to group.

Assume that enough material for a bomb is likely to cost a terrorist group at least several million dollars. The magnitude of this sum already suggests that measures targeted at combating terrorist financing, many of which are already being pursued by the United States and others, may have a major effect on the ability of terrorist groups to execute nuclear plots.[6] For example, before its attacks on the World Trade Center and the Pentagon, al Qaeda operated on roughly $30 million per year, enough to allow a several-million-dollar purchase of nuclear explosive materials.[7] Yet according to a report by the 9/11 Commission staff, "intelligence analysts estimate that al Qaeda's operating budget may [now] be only a few million dollars per year."[8] This lower figure may mean that, as a result of measures taken to combat terrorist financing, al Qaeda is simply unable to spend more than a few million dollars a year, indicating that it may not be able to purchase enough nuclear explosive material for a bomb. Or the lower figure may indicate only a lack of opportunities for new spending, which would suggest that al Qaeda could still muster the funds for a nuclear purchase. This second interpretation is supported by the claim that "Al Qaeda probably paid between $10 to 20 million per year to the Taliban": the Taliban's demise would have removed any reason to spend that money, and hence might have reduced al Qaeda's total spending.[9] Yet even if that were the case, the purchase of a large quantity of nuclear explosive materials would require a major change in al Qaeda's spending patterns, which might be observed by law enforcement and intelligence analysts on the lookout. Other groups might face similar problems.

If a terrorist group has the needed funds and holds its money centrally, there is no challenge (beyond evading detection) in transferring money to an intended recipient. But many prominent terrorist groups do not function this way. Al Qaeda, for example, is currently believed to raise and hold money primarily at the level of individual terrorist cells. (Since September 11, 2001, central authority over al Qaeda spending has collapsed.)[10] Although the aggregate financial capacity of a network may be very high, transferring large amounts of money to single recipients may require persuading a large number of cells to send money to a particular part of the network. (A single wealthy donor could, of course, short circuit this demand.) Making such a transfer without severely damaging operational security—without having to widely disclose the reason for needing money or, at a minimum, sparking intense curiosity within the network that could lead to broader knowledge of a nuclear plot—could be challenging. Between these two extremes, the need to consolidate large sums of money before executing a transaction involves both a growing number of terrorists and the growing possibility that intelligence or law enforcement will penetrate the terrorist plot.

A defense's ability to monitor and potentially disrupt transfers may be affected by terrorist capabilities and influence terrorist decisions, even when such transfers are technically possible. Many scenarios can be imagined. Transactions between trusted partners lie at one extreme. Russian mafia and Chechen terrorists might, for example, have long-standing relationships; if Chechen terrorists bought nuclear materials from well-known mafia, a direct cash transaction, free from government monitoring, might be possible. At the other extreme, high-value transactions for single items between strangers, which might be required for the illicit purchase of nuclear materials, present far greater difficulties. One might expect challenges similar to those involved in other illicit transactions. The drug trade, which may seem a ready source of insight, actually provides little: transactions of drugs for money in amounts over ten thousand dollars normally occur between established partners.[11] In contrast, the black market in arms, particularly in single pieces of major equipment like aircraft, provides more insight into the challenges a terrorist group might face.

The need for large transactions leads to a requirement that they be carefully structured, in order to create some reliability in an interaction between mutually suspicious partners. R. T. Naylor, an expert on covert transactions, notes that "typically, in an arms deal, neither side trusts the other. This is particularly true if the transaction is underground, because there is no dependable way to resolve disputes."[12]

For a terrorist group whose large transactions through legitimate financial institutions are monitored and often blocked, choosing not to go underground presents its own risks. Naylor expands on how mistrust is normally managed: "Most private-sector arms deals seem to involve the [buyer's] bank advancing commercial credit. It might be an open line to be drawn upon at will. This arrangement likely is offered only to customers with a long-standing relationship with the bank or to those who have pledged assets to back the full amount. In such a case, the bank can disclaim direct involvement in the actual deal. More commonly, though, arms sales involve dedicated letters of credit issued by the buyer's bank and tied to a specific transaction."[13]

How would payments be made under such an arrangement? Most commonly, "payments to the seller are made in tranches as the contract proceeds, with agreed-upon neutral parties (perhaps bank officials) determining when sufficient progress has been made."[14] It is unclear, however, how such a procedure would work with nuclear-specific purchases. At a minimum, it would require involving a third party with a level of intimacy that might expose the transaction—and while corrupt officials might turn a blind eye to the sale of AK-47s or even military aircraft, dealing in nuclear materials would pose a much greater risk to those individuals if they were caught.

Since big-ticket nuclear transactions between mutually suspicious partners present special problems, those involved might depart from the normal approach and forgo using a broker. If a terrorist group worked directly with a seller, it could benefit by avoiding the banking system or the need for a third party. But a significant risk of cheating by either side would then be introduced, as the reliable third party would be eliminated. Direct interaction between buyer and seller would also eliminate anonymity, increasing the risk to both sides of being exposed. For terrorist groups without trusted relationships with suppliers for nuclear materials, financial transactions involved in nuclear terrorism will present special dilemmas, and potentially force terrorist groups either to cut down on the options they are willing to consider or to accept greater risk.

Many possibilities exist between the two extremes. Levels of trust between partners may vary. In some cases, mutually trusted third parties may exist, but involving them could still compromise operational security. In other cases, it may be possible to divide transactions into smaller units, in order to build trust progressively or to work through legitimate financial systems without triggering typical government requirements that transactions over certain amounts (typically tens of thousands of dollars) be declared.

States aiming to complicate illicit transactions related to nuclear terrorism might improve their defenses in at least two ways. Intelligence and law enforcement agents might attempt to purchase nuclear materials themselves, driving terrorists out of the market. Such purchases would also allow the development of good information about what is available so that its sale might be defended against. But at the same time these inquiries might establish incentives for nuclear thefts where none would otherwise exist. For this reason, the purchase approach should be viewed with caution (though not dismissed outright). In contrast, sting operations aimed at terrorist buyers rather than at sellers appear more promising. In addition to the possibility of uncovering terrorist plots, stings, by increasing uncertainty for terrorists in the market for nuclear materials, could raise their perceived chances of failing and hence the odds that a risk-averse terrorist group would be deterred. These two possible outcomes would have to be balanced—more publicity about sting operations would improve deterrence but decrease the odds of catching terrorists in the act, and vice versa. This tactic would also be more effective against groups with relatively weak established connections to those who might have nuclear materials to sell.

The challenges involved in acquiring nuclear materials also point to the importance of the nature of terrorists' relationships with states. States and terrorists can cooperate actively, as al Qaeda did with the Taliban and as Hezbollah does with Iran.[15] States can take a mixed approach toward terrorist activity, often balancing leadership opposition to terrorist groups with popular support for them.[16] Some failed or weak states such as (at times) Somalia or the Sudan are incapable of controlling terrorists within their borders.[17] Each situation provides a terrorist group with a stronger platform from which to launch a nuclear attack. When it comes to acquiring nuclear materials, states willing to actively cooperate might provide necessary funds or help terrorist groups make connections that would otherwise be more difficult to establish. Indifferent or collapsed states would be of no help to terrorists here, though we shall later look at other cases in which they are.

The need to maintain strong relations with a state whose political goals may conflict with abetting nuclear terrorism may, however, strongly constrain terrorist groups. Such constraints may be present even if states are far more willing to assist with lower-level terrorism. The relationship between Hezbollah, Syria, and Iran provides an interesting example of how terrorist–state relations can be a double-edged sword. Kim Cragin asks: "Why would Hizballah, with the support it receives from Syria and Iran, risk establishing an international logistics network?" The answer is illuminating: "Part of the explanation might be its desire to retain some independence from its state sponsors."[18]

If states can play important roles in facilitating nuclear terrorism beyond directly transferring nuclear materials to terrorists, targeting such relationships could undermine attempts at nuclear terrorism in a variety of ways. In the face of potential cooperation between states and terrorists, diplomacy might be used to break state–terrorist relationships, or at least to convince states that supporting *nuclear* plots would be unwise. At the other extreme, military action might be used to the same end.

Developing a Nuclear Weapon

A terrorist group plotting an attack using an improvised nuclear device must build a nuclear weapon. To isolate this stage and the options for defending against it, imagine for now that acquiring and transporting nuclear materials are trivial tasks for the terrorist group. Assuming this means, among other things, that the terrorist group will have its pick of nuclear materials. Observers have consistently identified roughly one hundred kilograms of pure weapons-grade uranium metal as the easiest material to build a weapon from, so for now assume that this is what terrorists will have.[19]

How Nuclear Weapons Work

To carefully examine the barriers to building a weapon, it is useful to first know some facts about how nuclear weapons work. This section provides a basic introduction to the science.

Every atom contains a mix of protons, neutrons, and electrons. The protons and neutrons are contained in the nucleus of the atom, and for our present purposes, that nucleus is all that matters. The number of protons determines the element—hydrogen, for example, has 1 proton, oxygen has 8 protons, uranium has 92 protons, and plutonium has 94 protons. Each nucleus also comes in a variety of isotopes, variations that contain different numbers of neutrons. Uranium, for example, can exist as the isotope U^{235}, which has 92 protons and 143 neutrons for a total of 235 protons and neutrons; as U^{238}, which also has 92 protons but 146 neutrons for a total of 238 protons and neutrons; and in several other isotopic variations. The material in a uranium-based nuclear weapon is a mix of U^{235}, U^{238}, and other elements and isotopes.

Nuclear weapons exploit a process known as the chain reaction. When a single neutron strikes a uranium nucleus, it can be absorbed, it can change direction (be "scattered"), or it can induce fission, in which the uranium nucleus is split into smaller pieces and energy, along with several more neutrons, is released. Imagine that each fission produces two neutrons. (That number is fairly close to the actual total.) One fission will produce two neutrons; each of these can induce another fission, making a total of four neutrons; these can in turn produce eight neutrons, which can make sixteen neutrons, and so on. This process runs away quickly—after forty-five stages, over ten trillion neutrons have been produced and massive amounts of energy have been released. The energy release can manifest itself as an explosion.

Neutrons that hit U^{238}, however, are much less likely to cause fissions than those that hit U^{235}. They are also more likely to be captured by U^{238}—to essentially disappear and be unable to cause additional fissions. It is, therefore, easier to sustain a chain reaction in uranium with a higher fraction of U^{235} than in uranium with a lower fraction, which makes it easier to create an explosion—that is why uranium with a particularly large fraction of U^{235} (usually 90 percent or higher) is considered weapons-grade.

Aside from being captured by uranium atoms, neutrons can disappear, and thus fail to cause additional fissions, by escaping through the surface of the uranium. Imagine that you have an infinite amount of uranium: it is impossible for neutrons to escape. In contrast, assume that you have a tiny speck of uranium. Now all neutrons that are produced escape, and it is impossible to sustain a chain reaction. At some size and shape in between, the material is barely able to sustain a chain reaction—just enough neutrons leak to balance their production through fission. That configuration is referred to as critical, and the amount of material in it is referred to as a critical mass. A configuration with less material is subcritical, and one with more material is supercritical.

Criticality can also be affected by using a neutron reflector. Reflectors, when placed around nuclear explosive material, are good at sending escaping neutrons back into the mass. The return of those neutrons reduces the fraction that ultimately escape the core of nuclear explosive material, and hence reduces the amount needed to create the critical mass. Different types and amounts of reflector material change the critical mass in different ways. The critical mass without a reflector is called the bare critical mass; a critical mass in the presence of a reflector is called a reflected critical mass.

In the nuclear weapon design most commonly associated with enriched uranium, two subcritical pieces of uranium are brought together to form a supercritical piece. Initially, a chain reaction is impossible, but once the pieces are assembled, a chain reaction quickly produces neutrons and releases energy. Because one piece (called the bullet) is typically fired at the other (the target), this combination is known as a gun-type design.

As a chain reaction proceeds, it releases energy, causing the uranium to expand. That expansion increases the space between uranium atoms, making it easier for neutrons to escape. At some point, the uranium expands so much that too many neutrons escape. The material again becomes subcritical, and the chain reaction stops. If enough fissions have occurred at this point, one has an explosion; if too few have occurred, one does not.

What determines how many fissions can happen before the chain reaction stops? The number of fissions that occur depends on when the chain reaction starts. If the reaction starts soon after the material becomes supercritical, it takes only a small amount of expansion—and a small amount of time—for the material to become subcritical again, keeping the number of neutrons released relatively low. If the reaction starts well after the material becomes supercritical, once the two pieces of uranium have come closer together, it takes a larger amount of expansion, and a longer time, to make the system subcritical again. As a result, more neutrons are produced and a large explosion is more likely.

A chain reaction can start each time a neutron enters the uranium (though not every neutron will start a chain reaction). The more neutrons are emitted, the higher the odds that a chain reaction will start earlier, when the system is less critical, resulting in a lower explosive power, or yield. At the same time, the faster the bullet is fired, the higher the chances are that the system will reach a greater degree of supercriticality before the chain reaction begins, which increases the yield. Low neutron emissions and high bullet speed thus maximize weapon yield. Pure weapons-grade uranium emits so few neutrons that a maximum yield is very likely even for relatively low bullet speeds.

Adding a tamper increases a weapon's explosive power. A tamper is a mass of heavy material that surrounds the uranium core. When the uranium expands, it must now push more material outward. The weight of the surrounding tamper slows down the expansion, allowing more fissions to occur before the material becomes subcritical again, in turn increasing its yield. The tamper and the reflector are often the same piece of material.

Yield, in turn, determines the destructive effects of a nuclear weapon. Yield is measured in thousands of tons (kilotons, or kT) or tons (T) of TNT. The bomb dropped on Hiroshima had a yield of approximately ten kilotons; a weapon built by terrorists would have at most a similar yield. A bomb that large, detonated at ground level, would destroy an area roughly one kilometer in radius. (In central Manhattan, that could kill a hundred thousand or more people.) Every time the yield is reduced by a factor of ten, the area destroyed is reduced by approximately a factor of between three and five. A bomb with a yield of ten tons, then, would destroy an area roughly fifty times smaller than a bomb with a yield of ten kilotons would.

Barriers to Building a Bomb

Building a weapon with one hundred kilograms of pure weapons-grade uranium metal is not a trivial task, but it is still far from impossible. A gun-type weapon, which analysts assess as the easiest to build, has two necessary and two optional major components. An appropriate gun and two or more properly shaped pieces of uranium metal are essential, while a tamper/reflector and initiator are optional. The gun fires one piece of uranium metal at another to form a critical mass; a tamper/reflector surrounds the two pieces of uranium when they have been brought together, reducing the amount of material required and possibly increasing the yield of the weapon; the initiator makes sure the explosive chain reaction starts at the right time, maximizing the weapon's yield.

A gun of the appropriate size could probably be adapted from a small commercially available conventional artillery piece.[20] (An artillery piece is essentially anything that can launch a projectile.) Taking that route would introduce the possibility of being caught purchasing the artillery piece, but would eliminate most of the technical demands involved in building a gun.

Still, the group would need to test the gun at least once using natural or depleted uranium, introducing at least a small probability of detection if the group did not have an appropriate sanctuary. The sound of a single shot might not raise many suspicions, but the impact of the test projectile—it would cause a great deal of damage if fired openly—or the construction of a facility needed to contain a test shot, could attract attention. This scenario assumes that someone in the group has a strong understanding of the type of artillery used; if no such person could be recruited, additional, similar tests would probably be needed to be sure the gun had been successfully adapted. In contrast with a single test shot, multiple shots would be more likely to raise suspicions. Still, building the right gun for a weapon based on weapons-grade uranium metal would probably be one of the smaller hurdles in a terrorist plot.

Some have gone so far, though, as to claim that terrorists might even be able to build and detonate a bomb without an actual gun while still inside the facility where they had stolen their nuclear material. These claims are variations on a theme made famous by Nobel laureate Louis Alvarez, who wrote that "with modern weapons-grade uranium, the background neutron rate is so low that terrorists, if they have such material, would have a good chance of setting off a high-yield explosion simply by dropping one half of the material onto the other half."[21] One scholar gave this added detail when he asserted that "a 100-pound mass of [weapons-grade] uranium dropped on a second 100-pound mass, from a height of about 6 feet, could produce a blast of 5 to 10 kilotons."[22] These assertions are correct, but they can easily be misinterpreted. Making a nuclear weapon is harder than they suggest.

How can they be misinterpreted? The experts making these claims assume the two pieces of uranium are in ideal shapes for creating an explosion. Take the last example, where the final mass of uranium is about one hundred kilograms (or about two hundred pounds). This weight would provide about two critical masses for a spherical piece of uranium, which leads to a blast of five to ten kilotons, as claimed. Yet for other shapes, one hundred kilograms of material may not even form a critical mass, in which case no explosion will occur; alternatively, the two shapes may form more than a critical mass, but not the two critical masses that would lead to a five- to ten-kiloton explosion. Depending on the shapes and sizes of nuclear material a terrorist group acquires, then, the group may have to reshape the material, or, in some cases, decide between reshaping the material and accepting a reduced yield. In the second case, the lower expected payoff may drive some groups to reconsider their plot.

If a terrorist group must (or chooses to) reshape the material it acquires, it will encounter more challenges and create new vulnerabilities. Casting and working uranium metal into the best shapes for a nuclear bomb is feasible but not necessarily straightforward. Twenty years ago, a group of experienced nuclear weapons designers and engineers made the critical distinction between description and implementation of the tasks, asserting that "the methods of casting and machining the nuclear materials, can be (and have been) described in a straightforward manner, but their conduct is most unlikely to proceed smoothly unless in the hands of someone with experience in the particular techniques involved, and even then substantial problems could arise."[23] Groups with lower technical capacity or ability to recruit technically skilled individuals may face particularly important challenges here. The problem also introduces a more general one: there is a big difference in difficulty between describing something and actually doing it.

Many have asserted that standard machine shop tools are adequate for manipulating uranium. As early as 1978, John Daugherty of Los Alamos Scientific Laboratory (later renamed Los Alamos National Laboratory) wrote that "casting and machining uranium can be done in any modern foundry and machine shop. No part of these operations is beyond the capabilities of equipment and tools normally used in such a facility."[24] More recently, Andrew Bird and Simon Anthony of the UK Atomic Weapons Establishment wrote similarly that "uranium can be cast and heat treated in conventional vacuum melting furnaces and machined using conventional machine tools," though it is important to note that they were not writing about building weapons and hence may have assumed different demands from those a terrorist group would face.[25] In any case, one must parse such statements carefully. Simply because casting and machining *can* be done doesn't mean either is certain or even likely to succeed. Moreover, having equipment and tools with sufficient capabilities is different from having individuals skilled enough to use them successfully. Many terrorist groups may still get past this stage. Yet as we add up the chances of failing at each stage of a terrorist plot, this barrier, even if relatively small, cannot be neglected—anything that raises that bar may be of interest to a defense.

What particular problems might a terrorist group encounter? Accidents might expose a terrorist plot or damage its nuclear material; two potential types of accidents that have been widely discussed stand out. Uranium metal is vulnerable to spontaneous ignition when finely divided, creating the risk of fire during processing, and of ensuing detection.[26] Such an event could expose a terrorist group, just as the 1995 plot to explode eleven U.S. airliners over the Pacific was thwarted when its leader started a small fire in his Manila apartment.[27] Even uranium processing in advanced states has seen no shortage of fires—for example, a 1954 study reported that "one [government] contractor (National Lead at Fernald) has experienced upward of 300 [uranium] fires in a single month."[28] This statement falls well short of showing that fires are inevitable—uranium handling has improved since then—but the possibility of an accident in a primitive terrorist operation cannot be ruled out. A group, seeking to perfect its approach, might practice with natural or depleted uranium. Yet preparatory work involves the same potential for fires as work with weapons-grade uranium, and it still does not guarantee the development of a successful process.

The report of the Iraq Survey Group (ISG), chartered in 2003 to investigate Iraq's former weapons of mass destruction (WMD) program, provides additional insight into the potential for accidents. The ISG, summarizing its findings on casting and machining uranium, noted that "working with molten highly enriched uranium requires special consideration for criticality during the melting and solidification process." Criticality accidents, which occur when so much nuclear material is collected together that a chain reaction takes place, may kill or disable scientists who would be difficult to replace in a group with few technical experts. Such accidents would also change the chemical composition of the uranium, which might then require additional processing before it could be used in a bomb.

The potential for accidents reinforces the importance of relationships between terrorists and states or their publics, since the right relationship can provide a group with sanctuary—a place to hide—that would make accidents, if they occurred, far less likely to expose a plot. Active state cooperation may not be necessary here: an indifferent or a failed state may provide equally effective sanctuary. Indeed a failed state may provide ideal sanctuary, since it would have no leadership that could reject a terrorist group. From a defensive perspective, preventing failed states may also contribute to preventing nuclear terrorism.

Support from local populations can also be an important asset—if people are unwilling to report suspicious people, packages, or activities, terrorists will be more able to hide what they are doing. But reliance on support from local populations can place constraints on terrorist activities that are similar to those a group faces in its relations with states—societies that support low-level terrorism may feel differently about supporting murder on a massive scale. Many analysts have studied ways to address this challenge: tools range from public diplomacy aimed explicitly at winning over potential partners, to crafting broader foreign policy in ways that do not lead societies to be so hostile that they support or turn a blind eye to terrorist groups.[29]

The difficulties involved in shaping uranium, though, go beyond the potential for accidents. The ISG reported that it "found no evidence that Iraq had acquired or developed the technology of dealing with casting and machining issues of highly enriched uranium."[30] This finding suggests that a terrorist group, with fewer resources than a state like Iraq, might well meet the same fate. It is important, however, to be careful not to infer too much, since a terrorist group might have requirements that are different from those of a state. The ISG noted that "Iraqi scientists encountered difficulties in use of vacuum casting furnaces to melt uranium metals prior to pouring into molds and with the molds. According to inspections, several small spherical and cylindrical pieces were produced, but of relatively poor quality as pertaining to void and impurity inclusions."[31] These problems would have a different impact on terrorists building a gun-type weapon than they would have had on Iraq, which aimed to build an implosion weapon (another type of nuclear weapon, discussed in the next chapter), but the "impurity" problem the ISG refers to could still be significant.[32] If a terrorist group encountered the same technical problems as Iraq did, it might only obtain a yield of roughly ten tons, still devastating but a thousand times smaller than a typical crude nuclear weapon.

The impurities the ISG is referring to are most likely traces of light elements like oxygen and nitrogen. When radiation (alpha particles) emitted by the uranium strike these impurities, neutrons are occasionally released. Large numbers of stray neutrons cause greater problems for gun-type weapons than for implosion weapons, so impurities would cause problems for terrorist gun weapons well before they would cause problems for the sorts of bombs Iraq was trying to build. Indeed, after asserting that HEU metal can be used in a gun-type design, Carson Mark and his colleagues note that for their claim "to be true, it is necessary to have rather pure uranium metal, since even small amounts of some chemical impurities can add appreciably to the neutron source."[33] To be certain, many states have succeeded in casting uranium for a nuclear weapon, including the United States as early as 1945. Still, no amount of discussion about the theoretical ease of manipulating uranium, or evidence of cases where states have succeeded, can change the fact that major problems have arisen in practice, and that terrorists might fail.

Any terrorist group also faces a choice of whether to develop an initiator, which generates neutrons to start the chain reaction at a time that maximizes a weapon's yield. If the group forgoes an initiator, it will face additional design challenges in producing the uranium bullet and target, or it will have to accept the possibility of reduced or zero yield. The technical implications of forgoing an initiator are best understood by looking at South Africa's nuclear weapons program, which produced a successful weapon without using an initiator.[34] Instead, writes David Albright, "South African devices were designed to use background, or stray, neutrons to initiate the chain reaction." This approach is only possible if the weapons are designed to hold the bullet in place after it has been fired, for tens of milliseconds.[35] Such a design would parallel that of the first uranium-based U.S. weapon, Little Boy, which was intended to hold the bullet in the target (though that weapon also used an initiator as backup).[36] Designing and testing such a weapon would require special skill, a strong understanding of the materials involved, and presumably careful testing. Such requirements would, in turn, place a time burden on a terrorist group, putting pressure on its ability to maintain operational security, and would demand special technical skills as well. More crudely, a source that emitted neutrons continuously could be added, reducing the odds of an explosion that might be measured in the tens of tons. Yet emitting neutrons continuously would also increase the probability of predetonation, making an explosion as large as ten kilotons extremely unlikely.[37]

The final option would be to design and build an initiator. This still presents challenges to any terrorist group (particularly for one with weaker abilities to acquire special materials) and thus opportunities for the defense. Design and manufacture do not appear to be particularly difficult. Richard Rhodes notes that "in the case of the [Little Boy/Hiroshima] uranium gun [the] requirement [for an initiator was] relatively easy to meet."[38] The main barrier is acquiring a substantial source of alpha particles, which are used to produce neutrons in an initiator. A calculation of the quantity needed requires either sophisticated modeling of initiator physics or experimental study. Rhodes, however, has reported that the first

American implosion bomb used approximately fifty curies (a measure of radioactivity) of polonium-210 (Po^{210}) as its alpha emitter.[39] Although the initiator for that bomb could conceivably have used more polonium than necessary, and while less material may be required for a gun-type weapon, this figure roughly suggests how much Po^{210} a terrorist group might decide it needed, especially if it lacked the technical ability to carefully calculate how little material was actually necessary for an effective initiator.[40] More material would be needed for testing, since the conditions under which an initiator is activated are violent, making it hard to recover any material used in tests.

Although Po^{210} is most commonly cited, other alpha emitters might be used—R. R. Paternoster lists plutonium-238 (Pu^{238}), polonium-208 (Po^{208}), actinium-227 (Ac^{227}), and radium-226 (Ra^{226}).[41] Including Po^{210}, these are all currently controlled, in a variety of ways. For example, the United States regulates exports of these materials to states that are outside the Nuclear Suppliers Group (NSG), the cartel of industrial countries that controls trafficking in nuclear-related materials. For each export of Po^{210}, Pu^{238}, and Ac^{227}, the United States requires that the material "be contained in a device" where it is already mixed with another material that converts alpha particles to neutrons; if a terrorist group is not able to separate the two materials, a task demanding some technical skill, the initiator will emit neutrons prematurely, risking predetonation.[42] American law also prohibits export of individual sources larger than 1/10 of a curie. In the case of radium, exports outside the NSG of amounts exceeding 1/100 of a curie are controlled, with the exception of material in "medical applicators."[43] Less information is available about Po^{208}, though it appears to have no commercial uses, and it has been noted that, compared with Po^{210}, it is "very expensive."[44] In each case, attempts to control these materials suggest that at least some decision makers believe exports can be monitored at low levels. A defensive option may be to extend these controls, in some form, to all purchases. If that were done, terrorist groups with relatively weak abilities to steal materials or subvert controls would be particularly stressed.

The final possible weapon component is the tamper. With sufficient nuclear explosive material—and one hundred kilograms of weapons-grade uranium metal would be enough—the terrorist group could forgo a tamper, though with some loss in yield.[45] If the terrorist group wanted to maximize its yield, a heavy tamper would be necessary. If the tamper was also good at reflecting neutrons, the terrorist group would be able to build two or perhaps three gun-type weapons with its uranium, rather than just one, because less uranium would be needed for each weapon.

For clarity, focus on two pairs of materials often associated with tampers for gun-type designs—tungsten and tungsten carbide, and beryllium and beryllium oxide—as well as on iron. Tungsten carbide was used in the first U.S. nuclear weapon, and beryllium has been used in many others, while iron has been identified as a likely candidate for a terrorist tamper in at least one famous analysis of nuclear terrorism.[46] Natural and depleted uranium have also been used as tamper materials, most notably in the Fat Man bomb dropped on Nagasaki, but they emit too many spontaneous neutrons to be a reliable option as a tamper for a gun-type design.[47] For an implosion design, discussed in greater detail later, uranium would be a natural candidate for a tamper material; the difficulty of forming a uranium tamper would be similar to the difficulty of forming uranium components for a gun-type bomb (without the risk of a criticality accident).

Tungsten, a very dense material, was reportedly used in the first U.S. nuclear weapon (as tungsten carbide, a compound of tungsten and carbon).[48] As of 1980, an authoritative guide to metallurgy reported that "present knowledge and techniques are such that very great difficulty exists in working the [pure] metal."[49] Public information on the difficulty of producing appropriate shapes in tungsten carbide is sparser, possibly because such shapes are not commonly produced. Nonetheless, it is suggestive that the Nuclear Suppliers Group includes on its list of controlled items appropriately shaped hollow cylinders made of either tungsten or tungsten carbide, indicating the group's judgment that acquiring those materials can be a challenge to those seeking to build nuclear weapons.[50] As a material with roughly the same density as uranium, a tungsten tamper would also increase the yield of a weapon (by a publicly unknown amount).

Beryllium and beryllium oxide are less dense than tungsten and tungsten carbide, resulting in a lower yield, but are more effective neutron reflectors, allowing a terrorist group to make multiple weapons with one hundred kilograms of weapons-grade uranium metal.[51] Like tungsten and tungsten carbide, beryllium is difficult to form. One specialist notes that for producing hollow cylinders, "the material is difficult to form compared with other metals and rather sophisticated methods must be employed."[52] The journalist John McPhee, on the basis of former weapons designer Theodore Taylor's comments, claims that fabricating a beryllium reflector is "an accomplishment in itself, since beryllium is both toxic and brittle."[53]

This statement contrasts with the overall attitude of the rest of McPhee's interviews with Taylor, which largely downplay difficulties a terrorist group might face. Less information is publicly available for beryllium oxide, although it appears that the material can be formed through relatively simple techniques.[54] As with beryllium, however, beryllium oxide can present significant health hazards.[55] Such risks may not affect the decision making of suicidal terrorists, but may deter outside experts who might otherwise be recruited by a terrorist group.

Iron may be a more likely candidate. Blacksmiths have been forging iron for millennia, which suggests that an iron tamper would be relatively easy to build. An iron tamper can potentially reduce the critical mass of weapons-grade uranium twofold from the bare critical mass, making it less effective than tungsten or beryllium as a reflector but still potentially valuable to a terrorist group. A weapon using an iron tamper may have a different yield than one using a tungsten tamper; it will certainly have a greater yield than one using a beryllium tamper (which is less dense and is also a lighter element).[56]

Although many terrorist groups may be able to construct a nuclear weapon with a yield of roughly ten kilotons given one hundred kilograms of weapons-grade uranium metal, significant hurdles remain. Chief among these are transforming the uranium to an appropriate shape and procuring material for an initiator (or designing and building an initiator-free system). Depending on the skills of a group and its requirements for a bomb (or several bombs), machining or purchasing a tamper may add another hurdle. Each of these might be surmounted, but together they stress both the operational and the technical capacities of any terrorist group and introduce multiple opportunities for failure or reduced impact.

Groups that have or are able to acquire strong technical expertise will, of course, have less trouble managing the barriers just discussed. But how hard is it to acquire those capabilities, and what might affect terrorist decisions about the risks involved?

No one has ever claimed that terrorist groups normally contain members experienced in building or transporting nuclear weapons. The more important unknown is how effective a given group can be at gaining the knowledge and skills necessary to execute a plot. Understanding this problem requires knowing both about the particular knowledge and skills necessary to execute a plot—something this chapter has started to explore—

and about the ways particular terrorist groups go about acquiring that knowledge and skill.

The process by which groups acquire particular capabilities—in this case, primarily the ability to make nuclear weapons—is called organizational learning. Organizational learning, in the context of terrorism, is "a process through which members of a group acquire new knowledge that can be applied in strategic decision-making, tactical planning or design, and operational activities." Some observers further narrow this to include only knowledge that "is integrated into routines and is institutionalized."[57] This second restriction is too narrow for our purposes. Learning that is truly institutionalized certainly provides value well beyond learning by a handful of terrorist operatives; in particular, it makes the group far more resilient to member turnover, to the capture of skilled members, and to accidents. That said, so long as terrorist knowledge exists for long enough to execute a nuclear attack, it will be useful to a group and need not be genuinely institutionalized.

No study explains correctly and universally how terrorist groups learn (and no serious study aspires to), because each group follows a different approach, driven at least in part by the nature of its membership, by its attitude toward risk, and by its demands for operational security. These constraints yield different balances between "learning by doing," "learning through training," "learning through research," and "learning from others."[58] Coincidentally, these types of learning divide themselves into learning that happens within the group and learning that involves more extensive interaction outside the group. Learning by doing lies at the first extreme; learning through training involves passing on knowledge and skills internally, but to new recruits (or to more veteran members moving to new tasks); learning through research involves attempting to assimilate knowledge from the outside, but in a way in which outsiders do not play an active role; and learning from others, either by receiving training from them or by recruiting them, involves the greatest degree of external interaction. As a group moves along this spectrum, it increases its chances of executing a successful plot, but it also increases the risk of compromising its operations by involving less trusted people. This tradeoff, as well as the different starting points of different groups, can help explain the wide range of approaches to learning.

A 2005 RAND study provides insight into the spectrum of potential approaches through in-depth assessments of organizational learning in five terrorist groups.[59] The authors deliberately excluded al Qaeda because the group was rapidly changing when the study was written, but other scholarship, as well as the narrative of the September 11 plots contained in the 9/11 Commission Report, provide insight into how that group too has approached learning.[60]

John Parachini studies how the Japanese cult Aum Shinrikyo went about learning how to develop and disseminate Sarin gas in advance of its 1995 chemical weapons attack on a Tokyo subway. He concludes that the group had a strong preference for internal learning. Even then, the group's internal learning was itself circumscribed; Aum Shinrikyo involved only the most committed individuals in its most sensitive plans to develop and use the weapons.[61] Aum Shinrikyo's approach had both positive and negative consequences, leading Parachini to observe that "while the small size of this group greatly facilitated its operational security, it . . . probably impeded the development of its capabilities, which may in part explain the crudeness of some of its efforts as well as its failures."[62]

Parachini reviews several illuminating cases. For example, he writes that "Aum's activities in Australia [to test chemical weapons and acquire uranium] are another example of its attempts to develop knowledge even though the funds it used for those attempts could have been used to more efficiently acquire the knowledge from external sources." He also notes that "given its resources and contacts in Russia, it is surprising that Aum was unable to lure a former Soviet scientist to work in its program or train some of its personnel." Parachini attributes this inability to the fact that "Aum was basically uncomfortable with people from outside the organization."[63]

Al Qaeda has been different, and somewhat more aggressive, balancing incentives to adapt with the desire to maintain operational security. In the initial phases of the 9/11 attacks, Osama Bin Laden selected would-be pilots from the ranks of the most experienced, and hence most trusted, members of the group, implicitly valuing loyalty over skill.[64] When it became clear that two of those operatives would not learn to fly airplanes, he was willing to turn to relatively (but not entirely) new recruits, who had first traveled to Afghanistan in 1999, and train them at American flight schools. Although using less veteran operatives may have increased the danger of betrayal, they "added the enormous advantages of fluency in English and familiarity with life in the West."[65] Later, still facing a shortage of pilots, al Qaeda got lucky: a new recruit, already trained as a pilot, showed up in Afghanistan in early 2000, and was added to the plot. He had, however, previously traveled to Afghanistan for jihad in the late 1980s, perhaps allaying some potential concerns about operational security by demonstrating his long-standing commitment to the cause.[66] A clear pattern emerges: while some in al Qaeda were, like those in Aum Shinrikyo, skeptical of using relatively new members, al Qaeda was considerably more flexible in adapting to difficulties at the expense of some operational security. But it still had its limits—al Qaeda never went so far as actively recruiting pilots for its plot.

As in financing nuclear terrorism, building necessary skills and capabilities for nuclear terrorism involves tradeoffs. A group that can steal nuclear materials will not necessarily be able to acquire the skill needed to turn those materials into a weapon, and some that may be able to build a weapon may not be willing to take the necessary risks. Conversely, some groups may have technical skill readily available, but may not have immediate access to the skills necessary to acquire nuclear (or associated non-nuclear) materials. This problem might occur were a group of disgruntled scientists to consider attempting a nuclear plot, a scenario analysts occasionally conjure up.[67] Rather than assuming a single model of skill and capability building, an intelligent defensive strategy will prepare to take advantage of a wide range of terrorist approaches presented to it, juxtaposed with the particular demands of nuclear terrorism.

Transportation

Scholars generally hold that transporting a gun-type weapon based on weapons-grade uranium to a target within a major Western state would present little challenge to a terrorist group. Many analysts at least implicitly equate transporting a weapon with transporting nuclear material. This equivalence is ultimately wrong, but it is the right way to approach the analysis here, since we want to isolate transportation from the other demands of nuclear terrorism. Because we are assuming that the other parts of the plot, most notably building a weapon, are easy, we should also assume that a terrorist group can build and assemble its weapon near its target. If it can do that, it has little incentive to transport its weapon whole.

Shipments of pure metallic weapons-grade uranium are, indeed, difficult to detect. Although it might be possible to detect materials in a wide range of places, I will look at international borders to focus our analysis; much of that analysis can usefully be adapted to other situations. Even with significant advances in technology, moving weapons-grade uranium metal through official points of entry, such as airports, without triggering detectors may remain relatively straightforward, obviating most reasons for terrorists to cross at unmonitored border points. In contrast, for many other nuclear explosive materials, detection at official points of entry is far more feasible. When that is the case, the ability of terrorists to move nuclear materials across unmonitored border crossings becomes more important. Since this chapter focuses on weapons-grade uranium metal, it will assess detection at official points of entry; nonofficial points of entry will be explored in the next chapter.

Transporting weapons-grade uranium metal is not entirely trivial, and defensive measures can make it more difficult. Advances in radiation detection can improve the probability of detecting material at close range. And to the extent that using official border crossings forces not only materials but also terrorists to pass through checkpoints, the probability of detection and failure will be increased as well.

Indeed, perhaps the most straightforward way to detect terrorist smuggling of nuclear materials through official crossing points is to detect the terrorists first. In that case, neither the terrorist nor the nuclear material accompanying him will be allowed into the target country. This possibility, of course, does not exist if the material is unaccompanied by a terrorist, as would be the case, most prominently, for nuclear materials shipped as cargo.

How Radiation Detection Works

How hard is it to detect weapons-grade uranium metal directly? Answering this question requires understanding some facts about radiation detection. This section provides an introduction to the science; we will focus on specific details throughout the rest of the book.

Nuclear materials emit particles—nuclear radiation—that can in principle be detected. The primary targets of the radiation detectors normally associated with defense against nuclear terrorism are gamma rays and neutrons. I have already provided a simple description of neutrons. Gamma rays (which I will sometimes refer to as photons), are packets of energy much like light. Both are characterized by how much energy they have, which can be measured in electron-volts, or eV. Most gamma rays of interest in nuclear detection have energies on the order of MeV, or millions of electron-volts. Most neutrons of interest also are emitted with energies on the order of MeV.

Neutrons are produced primarily in two ways. As already discussed, they are emitted as the result of fission. This includes spontaneous fission, which occurs naturally, and so-called (α,n) reactions, in which an alpha particle—the nucleus of a helium atom—is emitted by nuclear material and strikes the nucleus of a lighter atom, such as oxygen, producing a neutron. (The second process does not involve fission.) Other sources of neutrons exist, but these two are the largest. Like neutrons, gamma rays are emitted naturally by radioactive elements. They can also be emitted when a neutron is captured by a nucleus—most notably, when a hydrogen nucleus captures a neutron, it emits a gamma ray with energy 2.2 MeV.

The main challenge nuclear detectors face is distinguishing the radiation emitted by nuclear materials from so-called background radiation that is present in any environment. If the amount of background radiation were well known, this task would be straightforward, but instead, it is known only with some uncertainty. To put it somewhat roughly, if the amount of radiation from a source of nuclear material is substantially greater than the uncertainty in the background, one can be confident that the material will be detected and that few false alarms will occur. Larger detectors, detectors placed closer to nuclear material sources, and longer observation times all make detection easier. In the case of gamma rays, the ability to distinguish effectively between different energies, described by what is called the energy resolution, can also be useful. The basic gamma detectors I examine are based on impure ("doped") sodium iodide, referred to as NaI(Tl), and high-purity germanium, referred to as HPGe. High-purity germanium has a higher energy resolution but is also much more expensive than NaI(Tl). Several other attributes of radiation detectors influence their effectiveness, but these are the most important.

The other critical factor affecting radiation detection is shielding, material placed between a radiation source and a detector to hide radiation. Effective gamma shielding is normally very heavy—lead is a frequent candidate—while effective neutron shielding normally contains a large amount of hydrogen and is thus, for the most part, relatively light. Such hydrogenous materials include water and polyethylene. Neutron and gamma ray energy is important in the hunt for illegal nuclear weapons material—higher-energy gamma rays and neutrons are more effective at penetrating shielding, making them easier to detect.

Detecting Weapons-Grade Uranium Metal

With the basics of radiation detection under our belts, we can return to our original question: how hard is it to detect weapons-grade uranium metal directly?

If the material is unshielded—if the terrorist group makes no attempt to hide its radiation—detection at a reasonable range is possible. A sphere of weapons-grade uranium metal twelve centimeters in diameter (weighing roughly seventeen kilograms, slightly less than a well-reflected critical mass), enriched to weapons grade can be detected within one second at a distance of roughly ten meters, with a false alarm rate of less than one in a million, using even a basic handheld germanium-based detector.[68] (Like the other estimates for detection ability given later, this estimate is only an approximation.) These circumstances are depicted in Figure 3.1a, in which the radiation from the nuclear material is stronger than the background radiation. This scenario provides a large enough range, short enough observation time, and low enough false alarm rate for detection at essentially any border-crossing portal. However, a small amount of lead shielding, as introduced in Figure 3.1b, dramatically lowers the chances of detection. Imagine that the same sphere is surrounded by a mere one centimeter of lead, weighing six kilograms (roughly thirteen pounds). Even at a distance of two meters, though the radiation from the uranium would substantially exceed the background, the same handheld detector would now be expected to detect only one telltale gamma ray every forty seconds.[69] A set of forty detectors, shown in Figure 3.1c, would be expected to detect one gamma ray each second, suggesting that in some cases improving radiation detection is as at least as much about developing larger detectors—or developing cheaper small detectors—as it is about developing more advanced detection technology.

(In assessing detector performance, I will always assume that nuclear explosive material is in a spherical form, maximizing self-shielding and thus representing a worst case from the perspective of the defense. Other analysis would profit from studying cases that are less challenging from a defensive perspective, but, as the introduction to one government standards document notes, using worst-case analysis here allows open assessments of detector capabilities without providing useful information to potential adversaries.)[70]

Of course, a group could easily use more than six kilograms of lead shielding. Imagine that, instead, the group used a three-centimeter-thick,

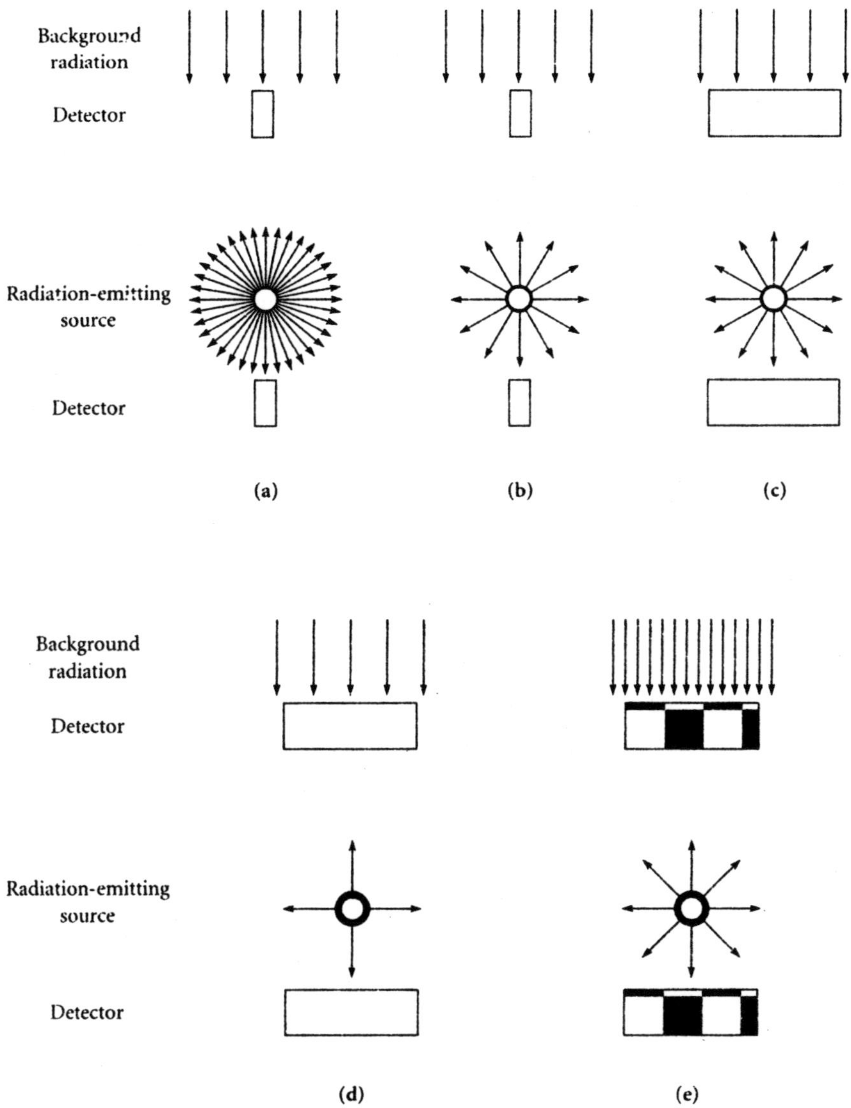

Figure 3.1. Detecting weapons-grade uranium metal. If radiation from the uranium exceeds the background radiation, the uranium may be detected.

twenty-five-kilogram mass of lead shielding, as in Figure 3.1d. A single handheld germanium-based detector at a distance of two meters would see one telltale gamma ray only every four minutes.[71] The array of forty detectors just suggested would still require several seconds of observation. A larger sodium iodide detector, shown in Figure 3.1e, would be cheaper, as well as large, efficient, and sensitive enough to see one telltale gamma ray roughly every second. That signal, however, would be over two hundred times smaller than the detected background radiation, which would also be increased, requiring unreasonable observation times of at least several hours to have any meaningful chance of successful detection. Passive gamma ray detection, even with large, cheap, high-resolution detectors is fundamentally limited.

Neutron detection would be even less effective. The same seventeen kilograms of unshielded weapons-grade uranium metal just explored emit roughly thirty neutrons each second. A typical handheld detector at a distance of two meters would detect one neutron roughly every thirty minutes; an array of forty, similar to that studied above, would still require observation times on the order of a minute or more. A typical transportable (but not handheld) detector at that distance would detect one neutron every forty-five seconds, but the background would now be at least ninety neutrons in that same time period.[72]

Beyond passive detection, at least five technological possibilities remain: direct detection of dense materials (whether shielding or uranium itself), detecting neutrons during transit, active interrogation of nuclear materials, neutron radiography, and other more exotic detection technologies. Each has some potential, though all have fundamental limits. Studying them is important for three reasons. It confirms past claims that detecting radiation from weapons-grade uranium metal is very difficult, but it does that while looking at a far wider range of potential technologies than most normally study. It shows how the effectiveness of new detection schemes will depend on the contexts in which they are employed. And it provides insight into the demands driving much development, deployment, and assessment of radiation detection technology.

Detection of dense uranium and shielding material using gamma radiography, combined with gamma ray detection, is promising for small targets such as backpacks and perhaps vehicles, but it may be of less value against large targets such as shipping containers. (X-ray scanning, similar in principle, might also be used.) In this approach, gamma rays are fired at an object and detected on the other side. Knowing what fraction of them make it through provides information about how much material is in between—empty space will remove none (Figure 3.2a), light material will remove few (Figure 3.2b), somewhat heavier material will remove more (Fig-

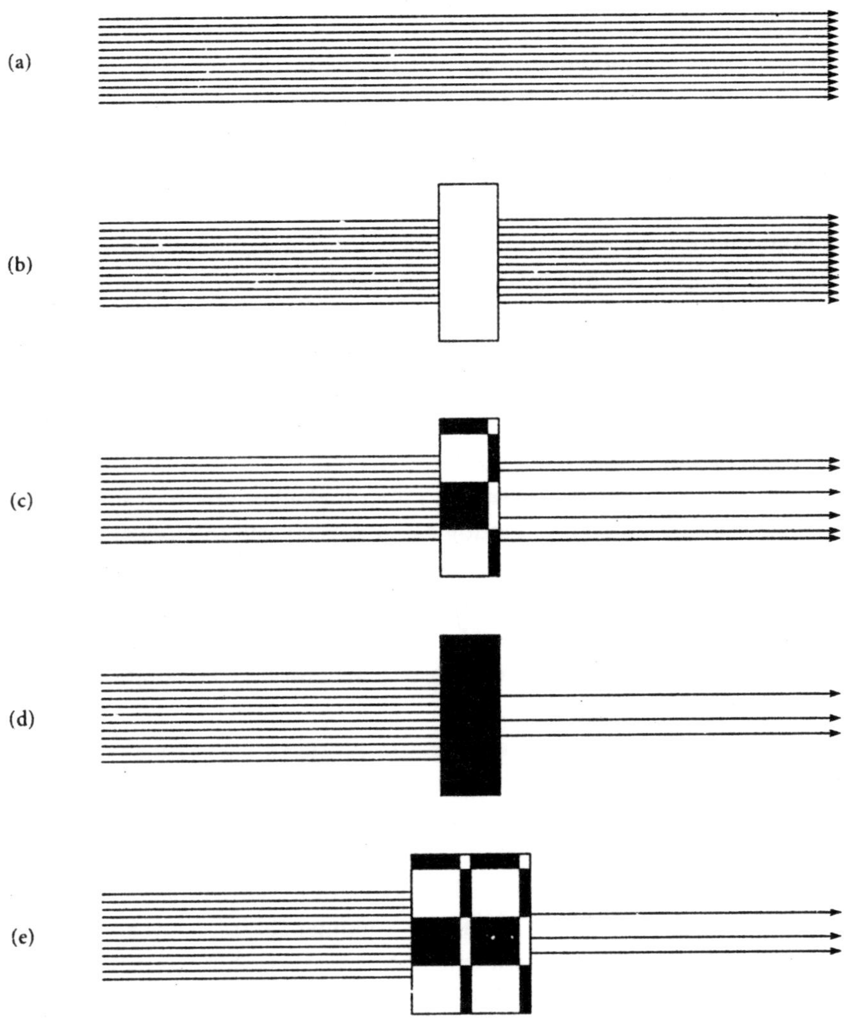

Figure 3.2. Gamma radiography. A photon beam is emitted at the left of each figure, passes through intervening material, and is detected at the right of the figure.

ure 3.2c), and very heavy material will remove more still (Figure 3.2d). The observations can be used to create a two-dimensional image of the intervening object that approximately describes the density of the materials in it. If portions of the target have a density exceeding some preset threshold, suggesting the possible presence of uranium or dense shielding, an alarm is triggered and the target is searched more thoroughly.

This approach, however, potentially involves a high rate of false alarms. If many common targets contain materials whose densities are similar to or greater than that of minimally shielded nuclear material, a system that looks for materials with similar density to uranium may produce false alarms in unmanageable numbers. Thick amounts of lower-density material may look just like thinner amounts of high-density material, since thicker amounts of material will remove more gamma rays, as shown in Figure 3.2e. Even if shielded nuclear material is much denser than most cargo, radiography may not be sensitive enough to tell the difference. Alternatively, to keep the number of false alarms down, governments may use higher detection thresholds (looking only for thicker or denser material) and miss situations where shielding is thick enough to prevent passive detection of gamma rays but too thin to trigger a radiography alarm.

At its thickest point, the seventeen-kilogram ball of uranium shielded by three centimeters of lead just studied contains six centimeters of lead and twelve centimeters of uranium. This amount of material would measure one and a half feet across, making it unlikely that it could be disguised as something more common in a relatively small package such as a suitcase. (A suitcase would need to contain more than a foot of steel to produce the same radiography image.)

Shipping containers present a larger technical problem for the defense. Indeed most detailed analysis of border security against nuclear smuggling has focused on defense against the use of shipping containers as smuggling vehicles. These standardized containers, either twenty or forty feet in length, eight feet wide and normally eight-and-a-half feet tall, are carried by the tens of thousands on specialized container ships.[73] They account for 37 percent of all port calls worldwide.[74] Many observers have criticized the focus on these containers, but there are legitimate reasons to pay special attention to them (though not to the exclusion of other possibilities).[75] They allow terrorists to separate themselves from nuclear materials as they cross borders, removing one possible detection opportunity. And they accommodate so much bulk and mass that they provide a special opportunity for terrorist groups to use large amounts of shielding. (They have also attracted attention because many believe that the container and port system might be chosen as a target for terrorists attempting to disrupt the economy.)[76]

Unfortunately, a container filled with (for example) steel pipes might produce an image with regions that look just like shielded uranium. So might one filled with water. Indeed, one of the more commonly discussed gamma radiography machines—the VACIS—is advertised as being able to penetrate approximately 15.9 cm of steel, meaning that any containers with large sections that contained more than that thickness of steel or similarly dense material would have to be subjected to further inspection. (A container completely filled with fruit, which is mostly water, might well cause the same problem.) More data are needed before the utility of this approach can be fully assessed, since the false alarm rate for various thresholds will, most likely, have to be determined experimentally by deploying radiography systems and analyzing the data they produce. (A recent deployment of detectors at the port of Hong Kong has produced a large amount of data that could be usefully exploited.)[77] It would also be valuable to extensively field-test radiography systems that use higher-energy gamma rays, which could penetrate several times deeper into cargoes. Cost will also be a limiting issue, affecting the proportion of containers that can realistically be scanned.

Several scientists have argued that both low emission rates and low signal-to-background ratios that plague passive detection can in principle be addressed by another approach: dramatically increasing the amount of time a detector can observe a suspect object.[78] Most of these researchers have focused on the container shipping case, arguing that detectors attached to shipping containers could observe nuclear explosive materials for entire container journeys, usually lasting millions of seconds, rather than for a brief period of time (a small number of seconds and at most about one minute) at a port. Unfortunately, in-container sensors do not appear to provide substantial gains compared with fixed detectors. In order for in-container sensors to provide much more precise detection than fixed detectors, the background radiation must be well known. Within a shipping container, though, that background will depend on the nonradioactive contents of the container; in addition, it will vary over the container's voyage. Although sophisticated schemes might be developed to offset these problems, no approach proposed so far (at least publicly) even addresses the challenge. At a minimum, no one should expect in-container detectors to be a panacea.[79]

So-called active interrogation of suspect cargo may provide important opportunities.[80] In active detection, particles are fired at a suspect target with the expectation that they will induce the emission of some other particles that can then be detected, as shown in Figure 3.3a. Dennis Slaughter and his colleagues write that "there are at least four potentially viable approaches to detection of SNM [special nuclear material or nuclear explosive material] and they are distinguished by the interrogation source (neutrons or γ-rays [gamma rays]), and the induced radiation signature (neutrons or γ-rays)."[81] The number of emitted particles reaching the detector is proportional to the number of particles fired at the material, as shown in Figure 3.3b; thus there is no fundamental limit on the strength of the signature. This approach contrasts with passive detection, where the amount of radiation emitted is limited by the amount of uranium being observed.[82] Using a very strong neutron beam for active interrogation may, however, create a radiation hazard for individuals in its path and possibly make the target material radioactive, creating limits that do not exist for passive detection. Researchers have for a long time sought technology that is effective at detection yet avoids these problems.

Otherwise excellent studies of active interrogation are plagued by an exclusive focus on shielding arrangements that are not entirely determined by real-world conditions. For example, promoting one candidate technology, James Jones and his colleagues study the detection of delayed neutrons produced when high-energy photons are fired at weapons-grade uranium.[83] They explore several shielding options, the most effective being four inches of borated polyethylene (a material found in many nuclear applications) and two inches of lead between the target and both the source and the detector. This combination is potentially effective, because the lead blocks the original beam of photons while the borated polyethylene can capture neutrons that are produced before they are detected. This scenario is illustrated in Figures 3.3c–e: Figure 3.3c shows an arrangement with only neutron shielding, Figure 3.3d shows an arrangement with only gamma shielding, while Figure 3.3e shows an arrangement with both. Yet the authors do not explain why the shielding thickness in their discussion is limited to thirty centimeters (assuming the nuclear material must be shielded on all sides). Their analysis thus says little about whether the technology might be effective under realistic conditions.

Such an approach is typical of active interrogation analyses. Slaughter and his colleagues study an alternative approach, detection of photons produced (through fission) by firing high-energy neutrons at uranium.[84] The authors do not consider shielding explicitly, including it only indirectly by requiring that their system operate in the presence of "cargos ranging from 0–60 g/cm^2."[85] The maximum cargo density is based on the assumption that uranium is hidden in a container of agricultural products,

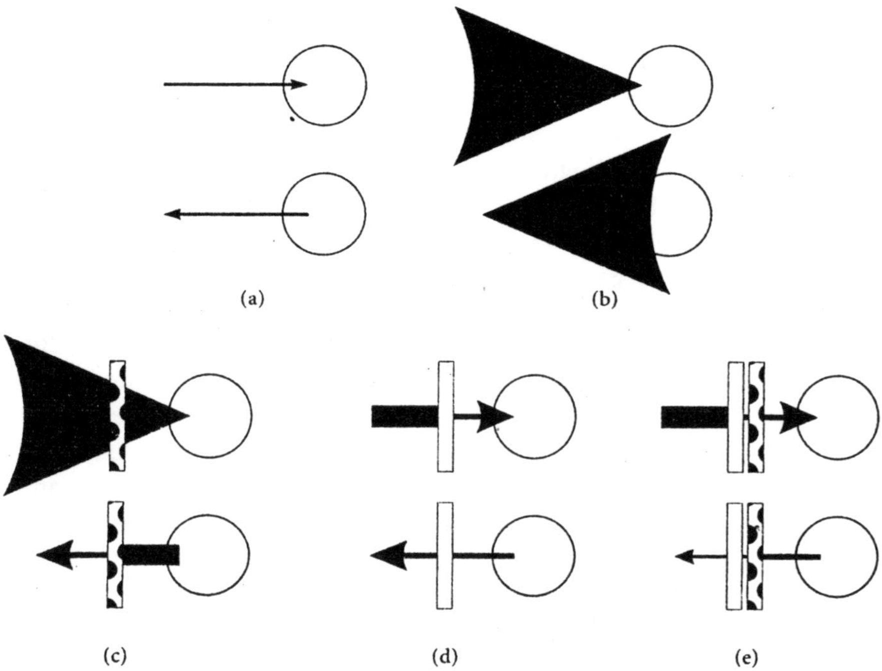

Figure 3.3. Active interrogation. In each example, a photon beam reaches on a mass of weapons-grade uranium, and, below, induces the emission of neutrons. In (c)–(e), shielding is also present.

but no argument is offered for why terrorists would hide nuclear material in that sort of cargo rather than in a more effective mix of shielding materials.[86]

Nonetheless, no study has shown that active interrogation technologies cannot work, particularly in concert with radiography, which could detect shielding. An intensive experimental research program would likely be required to understand the true potential of active interrogation. Researchers would have to identify both the limits to terrorist arrangements due to mass and bulk constraints and the potential for radiography to detect shielding without generating false alarms. Such a study would also need to distinguish between different detection scenarios—the amount of shielding that might be feasible in a shipping container would be different from that which a terrorist could use in a backpack. Given these constraints on shielding, experimenters could properly determine the potential of various active detection schemes.

Scientists would also need to explore different technologies under a range of constraints that might be placed by public concern over radiation. Different limits would likely be acceptable in different circumstances, such as peacetime; when a strong warning of a terrorist attack is present; and after a terrorist group has already exploded one bomb.

Although gamma radiography has been widely discussed, another possibility presents itself in the context of active interrogation (and will reappear later): it may be possible to detect neutron shielding using neutron radiography. Just as gamma rays can be fired at materials to determine whether there is gamma shielding inside, neutrons can be fired at materials to determine if there is neutron shielding inside. Gamma radiography for practical detection applications is far more developed than neutron radiography for the same challenges, and is thus discussed far more frequently. Neutron radiography might, however, be useful, providing an independent measurement of the density of neutron-absorbing materials in a container.[87] If a neutron radiography system detected a sufficiently large mass of neutron-absorbing material, it could raise an alarm. If, at the same time, gamma radiography or visual inspection indicated an extremely dense mass (uranium) amid the neutron-absorbing material, the container could be further inspected. Since few conceivable innocent cargoes enclose high-density material such as uranium within large amounts of (typically low-density) neutron-absorbing material, this approach would produce few false alarms.[88]

Other more exotic detection technologies are also being explored. Some use novel particles (particles other than photons or neutrons) for radiography. The most discussed system uses muons. Muon radiography would use the deflection of naturally occurring muons, subatomic particles that are generated in the atmosphere (though they originate in outer space), to indicate the presence of high atomic number material, the most notable of which is nuclear explosive material.[89] At a theoretical level, the approach appears promising, but the technology is only at the research stage, and many practical challenges remain. This technology suggests, though, that so-called fundamental limits imposed by the gamma and neutron emissions of weapons-grade uranium metal may not be as fundamental as many think.

Other technologies promise to improve the signal-to-background ratio for passive detection. For example, so-called Compton imaging of gamma rays would produce two-dimensional images of gamma emitters, allowing much more sensitive separation of signal from background.[90] This approach is still fundamentally limited by the need to detect *some* gamma rays, regardless of the signal-to-noise ratio. As long as shielding can reduce high-energy gamma emissions from weapons-grade uranium metal to only one every several seconds, these technologies will have limited utility.

In many cases, cost and practical implementation are also fundamental constraints. Gamma radiography and Compton imaging, for example, are currently too expensive for universal deployment at official entry points, although the cost of radiography equipment could probably be substantially reduced for much larger deployments.[91] Muon radiography and Compton imaging, among others, are similarly far from mature enough for deployment.[92]

As long as the defense is restricted to combating transportation in isolation, and to dealing with an enemy equipped with pure weapons-grade uranium metal, interdiction options are limited, if still incompletely understood. Where very close-in inspection is possible, a combination of direct detection and gamma radiography can be effective. Against larger targets such as shipping containers, it remains to be seen whether radiography, active inspection, or more exotic technologies will be able to deliver reliable detection at an acceptable cost. Theory is not enough to tell us where to go—experimental research is necessary to answer many unresolved questions.

Emergency Response

Careful study of postattack response is almost entirely neglected in public discussions of nuclear terrorism. A recent trend has given more credit to this dimension of defense, but few have assessed options in any detail.[93]

This lack may perhaps be surprising, given the enormous range of effects that might follow a nuclear attack (physical, economic, social, political, and strategic) and thus the opportunity to explore a wide spectrum of possible ways to mitigate them. The economic impact of an attack that destroyed a seaport might be mitigated by measures that allowed other ports to continue functioning (most likely while incurring greater costs) without compromising security.[94] The political fallout from an attack that decapitated a government might be lessened by advance preparations to ensure continuity of government.[95] An enormous set of other scenarios, and accompanying responses, deserves at least careful study before those responses are dismissed as not worthy of further attention. This section will focus narrowly, however, on the most immediate consequence of a nuclear attack—fatalities—and on how the right emergency response measures can substantially reduce them. This single example demonstrates the potential value of preparing carefully to respond to a nuclear attack, and should motivate more thinking about other dimensions of response.

Even immediate response to nuclear attack has received little attention, at least in public. Two studies stand out from this pattern. Far and away the most careful quantitative public treatment of the problem is Lynn Davis and colleagues' *Individual Preparedness and Response to Chemical, Radiological, Nuclear, and Biological Terrorist Attacks.*[96] In examining the nuclear case, the authors simulate and describe in detail the events following detonation of a one-kiloton nuclear device, and then develop measures that individuals, with little or no government support, can take to reduce their chances of death or injury. The study is limited by its restriction to individual response and by its choice not to compare its proposed response strategy with other options. Nonetheless, in developing and executing a careful approach to the problem, it elevates the public study of emergency response to a new level.

Charles Ferguson and William Potter adopt a more comprehensive but less numerical approach. They note that "in the new security environment, in which the explosion of a nuclear weapon by a terrorist group appears more likely than thermonuclear war, consequence management preparation plays a greater role in readying first responders and American citizens to weather the ravages of a nuclear detonation"—and they write that "just outside [the zone of near-universal immediate death], first responders can work to rescue trapped and injured people, fight fires, decontaminate individuals and property, and seal off highly radioactive and very heavily damaged areas." They discuss at some length the impact of radioactive fallout, but focus far more on its potential to impede first responders than on its immediate hazard to civilians. Much of their remaining discussion is focused on coordination, prioritization, and the general value of good planning.[97]

Others find that this level of attention to emergency response is excessive. Some appear to address the problem, studying responses to CBRN (chemical, biological, radiological, nuclear [weapons]) or WMD, but while broad strokes about coordination and planning often apply across those categories, treatment of specifics inevitably focuses on chemical and biological (and occasionally radiological) threats, thus saying little about the nuclear problem. A series of five reports by the Gilmore Commission (1999–2003), researched and endorsed by many of the academic and governmental leaders in the emergency response field and cumulatively representing the state of the art as of 2003, does precisely this. Its extensive survey of first responders involves in-depth analysis of chemical, biological, and radiological scenarios, completely excluding nuclear ones without any explanation; it then presents its conclusions as applying to CBRN generally.[98]

Neglect and extreme pessimism are misplaced. Although even the best consequence-mitigation would fail to prevent a bomb's immediate and potentially enormous impact, the analysis in the appendix, reviewed here, shows that mitigation could at least halve the number of deaths expected in even the worst attacks. It also shows that the wrong response measures might lead to far more fatalities than the right ones would.

Assume the worst: a terrorist group detonates a ten-kiloton nuclear weapon in the center of a densely populated area, causing a hundred thousand or more immediate deaths. Many effects of the weapon are near-instant, but one—radioactive fallout—is delayed. Mitigating the effects of that fallout is thus an obvious candidate for emergency response. In their study of individual preparedness, Davis and his colleagues propose that those able to evacuate a zone of intense radioactive fallout do so, while they recommend others stay where they are (normally referred to as "sheltering in place"). But individuals will not be equipped to decide what zone they are in, resulting in confusion and, potentially, even in people "evacuating" into more dangerous areas. There are two simpler alternatives: all people shelter in place, or all attempt to evacuate.

Because we are focused on a worst-case scenario where terrorists detonate their weapon in a densely populated area, we can assume that most people in the area are in large buildings. New York City's Grand Central Station, for example, is frequently cited as a target that would maximize casualties; it would do that because it is in an area dominated by big buildings, and hence one with a high population density. If people move to the center of a large building and away from the top few floors and stay there for twenty-four hours, they can reduce their radiation exposure by a factor of twenty or more. The appendix estimates that this sheltering strategy can reduce deaths twofold or better, relative to one where people are simply exposed to radioactive fallout. This estimate assumes that the population density decreases quickly as one moves away from the detonation point; if it does not, more lives are threatened by fallout, and more people can potentially be saved by sheltering in place.

An evacuation strategy is more complicated, since a potentially significant proportion of people may not be able to evacuate successfully, and will instead be exposed to radioactive fallout as they attempt to flee. The appendix shows that even an extremely effective evacuation strategy does little to improve on a strategy based on sheltering in place—and as evacuation becomes more complicated, it quickly becomes inferior.

Although more sophisticated study is necessary to design specific response strategies for particular settings, this simple analysis demonstrates an important point. Strategy matters when it comes to emergency response—if it is neglected because of a belief that emergency response is useless against nuclear terrorism, a successful attack may cause many more deaths than it needs to. This reality does not in any way lessen the urgent need to attempt to prevent attacks: a nuclear terrorist attack would cause many deaths, and other wide-ranging consequences, regardless of response. But emergency response can save many lives if prevention fails.

— 4 —

The Beginnings of a True System

So far, we have been exploring defense against nuclear terrorism as a set of unconnected layers, much as our fictional baseball manager studied his outfield, infield, and pitcher each in isolation. Defenses become much more effective and interesting, but also harder to understand, when we put those components together. The most powerful set of defensive tools are those used to keep nuclear materials out of terrorist hands in the first place, and thus as a natural next step in our investigation of integrated systems, we will look at what happens when these tools are combined with others in the defensive arsenal.

These combinations can be thought about in a fairly straightforward way. As materials security becomes stronger, groups are likely to become more opportunistic in their acquisition of nuclear materials. Rather than always being able to use the ideal nuclear material, roughly one hundred kilograms of pure weapons-grade uranium metal, they might buy or steal plutonium, uranium oxide, impure uranium, smaller amounts of pure weapons-grade uranium metal, or any of many other widespread but less than ideal nuclear explosive materials. Terrorists are also less likely to be able to acquire materials unnoticed, because better materials security should not only make it harder for terrorists to steal materials—it should also make it easier to quickly discover any thefts that occur. Thus to understand how materials security combines with other defensive tools, consider, first, how the effectiveness of those other tools changes when terrorists are faced with nuclear materials other than pure weapons-grade uranium metal, and, second, how those other tools' utility changes when the defense has warning that a nuclear plot might be well under way. The first question is the subject of this chapter; the second, the topic of the next. Here I examine the first question by studying several common nuclear explosive materials. This discussion will not attempt to be comprehensive: a thorough study of all the ways groups might pursue nuclear terrorism would occupy volumes and require a large team of experts. My goal is simpler: to collect enough examples that a sharper picture of defense as a system begins to emerge.

Acquiring Less than Ideal Nuclear Materials

Each potential less than ideal nuclear explosive material I will explore is widespread. Each also tends to be secured no better than, and in many cases less carefully than, pure weapons-grade uranium metal. Both these attributes increase the chances that an opportunistic terrorist group will acquire such materials.

The simplest departure from one hundred kilograms of weapons-grade uranium metal is a smaller quantity of the same material. Terrorists, having acquired fewer than two critical masses of weapons-grade uranium material, might proceed with their plot rather than risk being caught attempting to find more. Indeed all nuclear trafficking incidents recorded to date have involved less than two critical masses of nuclear material, suggesting the difficulties involved in acquiring even this quantity. Sites with less material are, all else being equal, also likely to have poorer security than sites with more.

A second alternative material is weapons-grade uranium metal contaminated with the isotope U^{232}. Pure weapons-grade uranium contains U^{234}, U^{235}, and U^{238}, each of which is only weakly radioactive. U^{232} is far more intensely radioactive, which has important implications. U^{232} is produced when nuclear fuel is irradiated in a nuclear reactor; if weapons-grade uranium is made using uranium extracted from used reactor fuel, it will contain U^{232}. Most notably, the Soviet Union made its weapons-grade uranium this way prior to 1989, and other states may have followed similar paths.[1]

Another variation on uranium metal involves material that is weapons usable but not weapons grade. Highly enriched uranium, with enrichments as low as 20 percent, can, at least in theory, be used in nuclear weapons. And while the world is awash with weapons-grade material, much of what analysts describe when they survey the state of nuclear security involves HEU that is not weapons grade. Fuel in nuclear research reactors has been one of the most prominent examples in public discussion of poorly secured HEU. In 2002 Robert Civiak identified twenty-six vulnerable Russian-supplied HEU-fueled reactors, most of which are still problematic today.[2] Among those, however, only half used HEU enriched to 80 percent or more. Of the thirteen reactors using uranium enriched to less than 80 percent, ten used material enriched to 36 percent or less. Uranium enriched to 36 percent is prevalent not only in Russian reactors but in the Russian nuclear complex, since it was produced in an intermediate stage in the production of weapons-grade uranium.[3] (Pakistan is also believed to use similarly enriched uranium as an intermediate step in producing weapons material.)[4] An opportunistic terrorist operation might draw on these sources and find itself with HEU that was not weapons grade.

Such a group might also acquire plutonium, which makes up over half of the nuclear explosive materials in the world.[5] Two national weapons programs, the Indian and the North Korean, are based nearly exclusively on that material; most others have significant plutonium elements too.[6] Moreover, in the civilian nuclear sector, far more plutonium than highly enriched uranium exists, a product of power plant operation and the subsequent separation of plutonium from used nuclear fuel.[7]

Other slightly more exotic possibilities also exist. Weapons-usable materials not only exist as metals but can be found in chemical compounds combined with the elements oxygen, fluorine, nitrogen, and hydrogen as well as in mixtures of materials. In particular, both uranium and plutonium are often found in the forms UO_2 and PuO_2, uranium and plutonium oxide, powders in which each uranium or plutonium atom is attached to two oxygen atoms. Uranium oxide is widespread—HEU is often stored or processed in oxide form. For example, many HEU-based nuclear reactor fuels use uranium oxide, and HEU from dismantled Russian nuclear weapons is converted to oxide as part of a process that converts it to fuel for power plants.[8] Indeed, uranium oxide has been stolen in the past.[9] Plutonium oxide is also common. In particular, the United States and Russia expect to dispose of tens of tons of weapons-grade plutonium in so-called mixed oxide (MOX) fuel, which uses both plutonium and uranium in their oxide forms.[10] Oxide is also widely used as a form for storing plutonium—for example, the Russian government has "mandated that, as of October 1, 1994, all newly produced plutonium cannot be used in weapons and must be stored in oxide form."[11]

Many other varieties of nuclear explosive materials are possible, but those just discussed will be enough to begin painting a picture of how a defense against nuclear terrorism works as a system.

Smaller Quantities of Weapons-Grade Uranium

If a group finds itself with less than two critical masses of weapons-grade uranium metal and does not want to attempt any more acquisitions, it will have two options. If it wants to avoid introducing any new twists, and hence possible vulnerabilities, into its plot, it will have to accept a reduced yield.[12] Figure 4.1 shows approximately how the yield of a simple gun-type weapon decreases when less material is used. If only 1.5 critical masses are available, the yield will be reduced to approximately 10 percent of its full value, or roughly one kiloton, while if only 1.2 critical masses are available, it will be reduced to approximately 1 percent of its full value, roughly one hundred tons. A terrorist group that is unsure of exactly how many critical masses it has (since that depends not only on the mass of the material but on the details of the weapon) will have to expect even less explosive power, especially for relatively small amounts of material. Imagine that instead of having 1.2 critical masses of uranium, the group actually has only 1.1: that difference in mass of less than 10 percent will drop the yield by another factor of ten, to approximately ten tons. The potential upside would not be as great: if the group actually has 1.3 critical masses, its explosive power would increase only by a factor of approximately three, to three hundred tons.

How will all these numbers translate into reduced casualties? Focus on the extreme but still quite plausible case involving 1.2 critical masses of material. The appendix shows that the area affected by the nuclear blast is reduced between five- and tenfold from its value for a weapon involving two critical masses of weapons-grade uranium metal. If one originally expected 100,000 deaths, one would now expect 10,000 to 20,000. (This calculation assumes that population density is uniform over the affected area, a reasonable approximation in a dense downtown region.) This total is still horrific, but it is very different from the original number.

The other parts of the terrorist plot will remain largely unaffected if the group has less material to work with. Building the weapon is unlikely to proceed much differently from the case with two critical masses, since the weapon design will not be very different. Evading radiation detection will

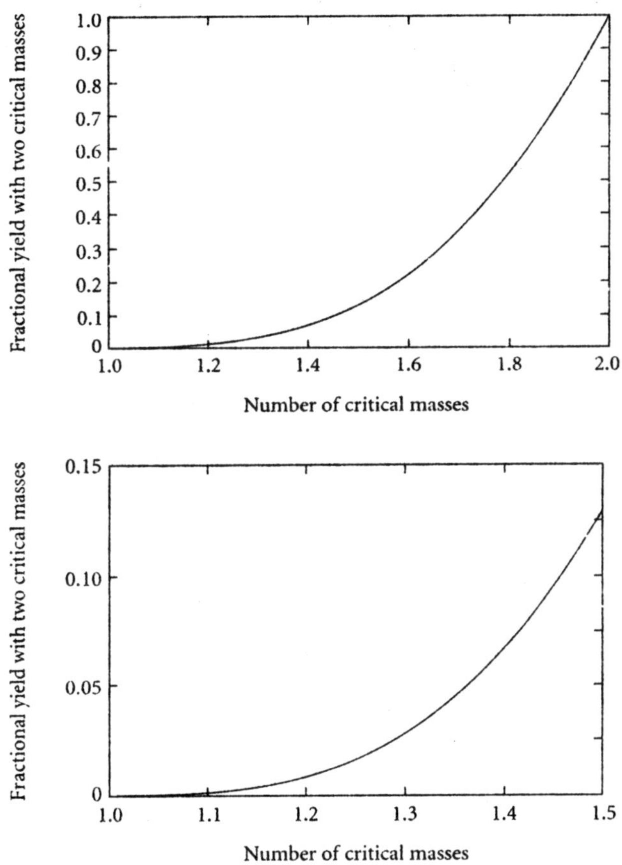

Figure 4.1. Yield reduction due to reduced fissile material.

be slightly easier, because reduced mass implies reduced emissions, but the difference is not significant.

The effectiveness of emergency response might, however, change. Imagine again a case involving a terrorist bomb with a hundred-ton yield. The analysis in the appendix strongly suggests that a strategy of sheltering in place could eliminate essentially all near-term deaths from radioactive fallout. In contrast, an evacuation strategy could cause many deaths from fallout if the evacuation did not proceed smoothly. Thus a smart emergency response strategy has the potential to cut down the number of fallout-induced deaths by a much larger fraction than in the case of a ten-kiloton-yield weapon. At the same time, the absolute reduction in fatalities would be smaller, simply because there would be fewer lives to save since the bomb would affect a smaller area with a proportionately smaller population. Defenses that force terrorist groups into using lower-yield weapons and those that prepare to deal with the consequences of lower-yield bombs thus complement each other.

The terrorist group would have two options if it was unwilling to accept a reduced yield: it could use a neutron reflector like those discussed earlier or it could shift to an implosion design, to be introduced later. In either case, the same amount of nuclear explosive material would achieve a greater degree of supercriticality, increasing the yield for a fixed amount of nuclear material. But new construction challenges and new weapon attributes might make the plot more vulnerable to failure or discovery. In the extreme, if the group had substantially less than a critical mass of material, it might be forced to use a difficult-to-produce beryllium tamper. The implosion option, as we shall see later, would introduce substantial design and engineering challenges.

Uranium with Lower Enrichments

How would the use of medium-enriched (that is, uranium enriched 20–80 percent) rather than weapons-grade uranium metal influence a terrorist plot? A terrorist plot might become more difficult in several ways, but to allow for more in-depth analysis, focus on the possibility that, faced with uranium enriched to less than weapons grade, a terrorist group would need to build a large and massive weapon or to accept a reduced or zero yield. (The most prominent other effect of switching to medium-enriched uranium would be an increase in both neutron and gamma radiation, which would increase the odds of discovery by radiation detection.)

A nuclear weapon built using medium-enriched uranium would be bulkier, heavier, and thus more difficult to transport than a device with a similar yield that used weapons-grade uranium. A gun-type weapon using medium-enriched uranium that does not predetonate will have a yield similar to that of a weapon that uses weapons-grade uranium, assuming that each bomb uses two critical masses of uranium and the same type of tamper. The critical mass of medium-enriched uranium needed would be much greater than that needed for weapons-grade uranium, however, forcing terrorist groups to acquire more nuclear explosive material. At the same time, the increased amount of material would tend to increase the weapon's yield relative to a bomb using weapons-grade uranium. That effect, though, would largely be offset by the weapon's lower efficiency.[13] While two critical masses of unreflected weapons-grade uranium metal weigh 100 kilograms, two critical masses of unreflected HEU with 45 percent U^{235} weigh 370 kilograms, and two critical masses of unreflected HEU with 30 percent U^{235} weigh 740 kilograms. A heavy tamper could be used to reduce the critical mass of uranium required, which might be necessary depending on how much material the terrorist group could acquire, but the total mass of uranium and tamper used would need to be greater than two unreflected critical masses of similarly enriched uranium in order to maintain the same yield.

If the group wanted to reduce the mass of material used in order to make the weapon more transportable, it would need to use a light tamper and hence accept a reduced yield. Consider an extreme example that illustrates the range of possibilities. Replace a weapon that uses two critical masses of unreflected 36 percent enriched uranium with one that uses two critical masses of 36 percent enriched uranium inside a fifteen-centimeter-thick beryllium reflector. The mass of uranium needed is reduced fourfold, but the yield will likely be reduced by between two and three orders of magnitude, to between ten and one hundred tons.[14] Thinner reflectors will result in greater yield but less reduction in the amount of uranium required.

Predetonation is also more likely, primarily because medium-enriched uranium includes a far larger mass of neutron-emitting U^{238} and hence emits more neutrons. To compensate, a terrorist group must either fire the uranium bullet at a higher speed than would be needed for a bomb using weapons-grade uranium metal, or risk a reduced yield. The mass of the gun needed depends on many factors, the most important of which is the willingness of the terrorist group to risk reduced yield due to predetonation and the willingness of the terrorist group to risk outright failure due to physical breakdown of its gun. Predetonation problems can be reduced by firing the bullet at a higher speed, but that requires using a heavier gun. Outright failure is possible if, attempting to make the gun lighter, the terrorist group makes it so light that it cannot withstand the stresses involved in firing the bullet; as a result, guarding against catastrophic failure requires a heavier gun too.

Consider a weapon using two bare critical masses of 36 percent enriched uranium: the range of possibilities is broad. For a group willing to accept a fair chance of catastrophic failure, as well an even chance of a yield at least an order of magnitude smaller than the theoretical maximum if the gun does not fail outright, a gun barrel weighing as little as a hundred kilograms may be theoretically possible, though a group is unlikely to be able to create such a weapon in practice. (This lower limit, as well as those below, is also derived from a worst-case calculation—the real weight requirements for a terrorist group might be much higher, and I will not suggest here what they might be.)[15] A group less willing to accept the possibility of catastrophic failure, or less willing to accept a substantially reduced yield if its gun does not fail, will require a gun barrel weighing at least several hundred kilograms. And a group requiring a greater margin of error against catastrophic failure and also unwilling to accept more than a small chance that its weapon will detonate with a yield of one ton or less will require a gun barrel weighing several tons. In each case, a gun would almost certainly need to be built from scratch, unlike one built for a bomb that used weapons-grade uranium. The testing involved would inevitably require multiple shots of a very heavy bullet, creating noise and also requiring a substantial facility to contain the testing. Such issues might stress a group's ability to acquire sanctuary.

Should the terrorist group choose to use a weapon whose total mass, including uranium, tamper, and gun, is more than about one ton, its transportation options will be significantly affected. Both container and bulk shipping could accommodate this much mass, but loading a whole weapon this heavy would require a crane or large forklift, potentially generating attention, especially if port workers were trained to take note of such activity. Even loading just the uranium or the gun barrel alone might, in many cases, attract attention.[16] (This issue would add a special vulnerability to the bulk shipping case, since loading away from port would be much harder than in the container scenario.)

Transportation by aircraft would also be restricted. Loading a several-ton weapon into an aircraft might, depending on the circumstances, risk attracting attention. In addition, aircraft large enough to travel long distances but still relatively small in size simply cannot transport a gun or uranium weighing tons over long distances. For example, the maximum payload capacity of any Gulfstream aircraft is three tons, including fuel, which is typical of private jets that might be used for long flights.[17]

Plutonium

A much more substantial shift from weapons-grade uranium, and one that has been publicly studied in far more detail, involves weapons-grade plutonium metal. Such a shift would affect every dimension of a terrorist plot.

Building a weapon with plutonium would be more difficult than building one with uranium, as many have noted, assuming terrorists aim for the maximum yield possible. Analysts most often observe that plutonium is ideally used in a so-called implosion device. It is widely agreed that an implosion weapon is more difficult to design and build than a gun-type device, quickly leading to the conclusion that plutonium is harder than uranium to use in a weapon.[18] The difficulty of building a weapon is due primarily to the need for new designs, specialized explosives, and appropriate manufacturing equipment and skills. Development will almost certainly require non-nuclear explosive testing to develop a weapon that terrorists are confident will produce a nuclear explosion.

How do implosion weapons work, and why is plutonium normally associated with them rather than with gun-type weapons? Pu^{240}, contained in all plutonium, emits such large numbers of neutrons that it makes a high-yield gun-type design impossible. Even for extremely high bullet speeds, such a weapon is almost certain to undergo a chain reaction when it is barely supercritical, resulting in at best much lower yield than a gun-type weapon using weapons-grade uranium. Instead, plutonium is normally used in an implosion design, which changes the material from subcritical to supercritical much more quickly than a gun-type design can, largely avoiding the problems caused by the high neutron emissions of plutonium. In this design, the plutonium is surrounded by specially designed explosives ("lenses") which when detonated compress the material. Neutrons are now less likely to escape, since the plutonium atoms are more densely packed, turning a mass of plutonium that was previously unable to sustain a chain reaction—a subcritical mass—into a supercritical mass that is.

Disagreement still exists, however, over how hard it would be for a given terrorist group to develop an implosion weapon. Although no definitive conclusion is possible—and even less precision is possible without classified information—much can be understood about the challenges, shedding light on how the capabilities of a terrorist group would affect its odds of succeeding. Building an implosion weapon may be prohibitively difficult, especially for a group with weaker technical capabilities. It is also likely to attract attention unless the terrorist group has an effective sanctuary.

The most commonly offered piece of evidence used to argue that terrorists could build an implosion device with relative ease is the Nth Country Experiment. Yet the experiment is often misunderstood. Between 1964 and 1966, Lawrence Livermore National Laboratory gave three postdoctoral students the task of designing an atomic bomb without any access to classified information.[19] The students quickly rejected a gun-type uranium-based design as too easy (it would hurt their career prospects) and ultimately produced an implosion design that, when simulated by experts, produced a Hiroshima-type (or perhaps more accurately, a Nagasaki-type) yield. Their achievement has been taken by many as proof that designing an implosion bomb without access to secret information may be relatively straightforward. Charles Ferguson and William Potter, while not offering an explicit judgment, comment, without qualification, that "these physicists, using access to only open source information, were able to design a workable implosion-type weapon in less than three years."[20] Morten Braemer Maerli writes that "the researchers, armed with the advantage of knowing that a bomb could be built and having access to the large quantity of open literature on shock waves, explosives, nuclear physics and reactor technology published since 1945, concluded their task successfully."[21] These comments by some of the most perceptive researchers on nuclear terrorism are representative of the prevailing interpretation of the experiment, but they misread its significance.

Designing a nuclear bomb requires a combination of experimental and theoretical work, but the Nth country scientists pursued a purely theoretical project. Their instructions stated that "it is not expected that the experimenters do all of the routine work involved in the design themselves." Instead, the researchers had technical assistance, sending requests to a responsive support team: "The [support] committee simulated the support groups who would have carried out experiments and some computations in the Nth country."[22] Any suggestion that this was a genuinely three-person effort is inaccurate.

Explicit examples of when the committee was used can be found in the heavily censored report on the experiment that the U.S. government has released. Having chosen to pursue an implosion design in December 1964, the group proposed in May 1965 a test of their explosive lens system, used to focus explosive power into an imploding shock wave; a second test was executed in November 1965, and still further changes (though minor) were required before the final design.[23] These tests suggest that for the explosive lenses in particular, theoretical calculations were not sufficient for completing the design—they had to be combined with experiments. That the three scientists had no capability to manufacture or diagnose explosive lenses was made irrelevant by the support team, which contained experts in those tasks.[24] The Nth Country Experiment does not teach us much about how hard it would be to build an implosion bomb, but it does tell us something important: by isolating the experimental aspects of weapons design and engineering, and showing that the remaining design challenges are relatively straightforward, the experiment suggests that if there are any great barriers to a terrorist implosion weapon, they are practical, not theoretical. They thus require recruiting skilled support and possibly purchasing equipment, or incurring greater risk of failing to clear major technical hurdles.

The practical barriers to building a weapon, neglected in the Nth Country Experiment, are significant. The main challenges in the design stage are likely to be experimental. In particular, developing proper techniques for assessing the performance of implosion lenses is far from straightforward. The ultimate test of an implosion system will involve detonating a mock weapon where nonexplosive material such as natural uranium is substituted for plutonium. Determining whether an implosion system is working properly requires "seeing" through the explosives to determine the behavior of the material they enclose, as shown in Figure 4.2. Figure 4.2a shows material surrounded by high explosives before detonation. In Figure 4.2b, the explosives have detonated and have led to the sort of symmetric implosion needed to maximize the yield of an implosion weapon. In contrast, in Figure 4.2c, the explosives have detonated but the material enclosed has not imploded symmetrically; were that material replaced with plutonium, this asymmetry would lead to a reduced or zero yield. From the outside, it is impossible to distinguish visually between the two cases, making it difficult to diagnose what is happening.

Instead, the behavior of weapon cores has been studied in a wide variety of other, more technically demanding, ways. Early in the Manhattan Project, the only diagnostic available was flash X-ray, which captured freeze-frame images of an imploding sphere normally hidden by a layer of explosives.[25] The fact that flash X-ray has been understood for so long suggests that a technically limited terrorist group might attempt to use—and even

(a) (b) (c)

Figure 4.2. Diagnosing an implosion weapon.

rely upon—this technique. Yet flash X-ray technology suitable for weapons design is controlled by the Nuclear Suppliers Group, which suggests that states may have the ability to monitor and control its spread to terrorist groups as well as to other states.[26] Such restrictions appear to have added difficulty to Iraq's nuclear weapons program—Iraqi scientists noted in a 1990 report that "work is continuing to complete the design and manufacture of the 600 kV supplementary [flash X-ray] system which cannot be obtained commercially."[27] In contrast with this mention of flash X-ray, no inspectors' reports on Iraq mention other, more advanced diagnostic techniques, including those introduced later in the Manhattan Project than flash X-ray. Some diagnostic techniques, to be sure, do not require distinctive equipment, and thus might not have been recorded during inspections; one prominent example is the so-called pin method, which in 1945 "was based entirely on familiar technology."[28] A truly authoritative review of the potential roles of different diagnostic techniques in any terrorist plot can only be conducted in a classified setting.

If a terrorist group could not obtain suitable diagnostic equipment, it would have to rely on theoretical calculations. Such an approach would be aided significantly by recruiting knowledgeable scientists or engineers, creating opportunities for intelligence or law enforcement to penetrate a plot. With or without such help, the chances of achieving a full yield without experimental testing would be reduced. The exact impact of this effect cannot be predicted with any confidence, though at a minimum, it is plausible to suppose that it would reduce a terrorist group's own confidence in its weapon, an important factor for some groups in deciding whether and how to proceed with their plots.

A terrorist group may also encounter difficulties in fabricating an implosion device. The first challenge would be obtaining ingredients for fast explosives, many of which are controlled by the NSG.[29] Such explosives are, however, relatively widely available. (In one notorious incident, nearly 380 tons of two such explosives, HMX and RDX, were stolen from a former Iraqi weapons site after Iraq was invaded in 2003.)[30] Fabricating the explosives into appropriate shapes without significant imperfections that might distort the implosion would be more difficult, though, than simply acquiring them.[31]

An implosion device may not, however, be essential. Analysts commonly assert or imply that plutonium is unusable in a gun-type weapon, but that may not be the case.[32] The Russian scientist Stanislav Rodionov has estimated a yield of a "few tons" for a simple plutonium gun, though this has not been confirmed by any government.[33] A terrorist group, particularly one with limited technical skills, might choose this route if it is interested primarily in maximizing its chances of some success and is not as concerned with its weapon's yield.

Regardless of what design is chosen, plutonium, one of the more exotic metals known, may itself present problems.[34] Although uranium metallurgy can be practiced using natural uranium prior to the acquisition of enriched uranium, the same is not possible for plutonium. No chemical and metallurgical substitute for weapons-usable plutonium would be available.[35] Some have suggested that uranium could be used as a stand-in for plutonium, but experienced metallurgists caution that the substitution would entail important limits.[36] (The limits of uranium here suggest that small thefts of plutonium may present a greater danger, from a defensive perspective, than might be intuitively assumed, since they could facilitate metallurgical studies.)

Even with ample time for practice, plutonium's strange properties could present problems. Solid plutonium exists in six different phases, or forms. Plutonium is best used in nuclear weapons in the so-called delta phase, which is readily workable, rather than the alpha phase, which is brittle.[37] It is the alpha phase, however, that is normally present at room temperature. It is widely understood that in order to preserve plutonium in the delta phase at room temperature, it must be alloyed with a small amount of another element, normally gallium. Materials stolen from weapons programs may already be in alloyed form, but those stolen from civil programs will almost certainly be pure, since there is no reason to add impurities to civil

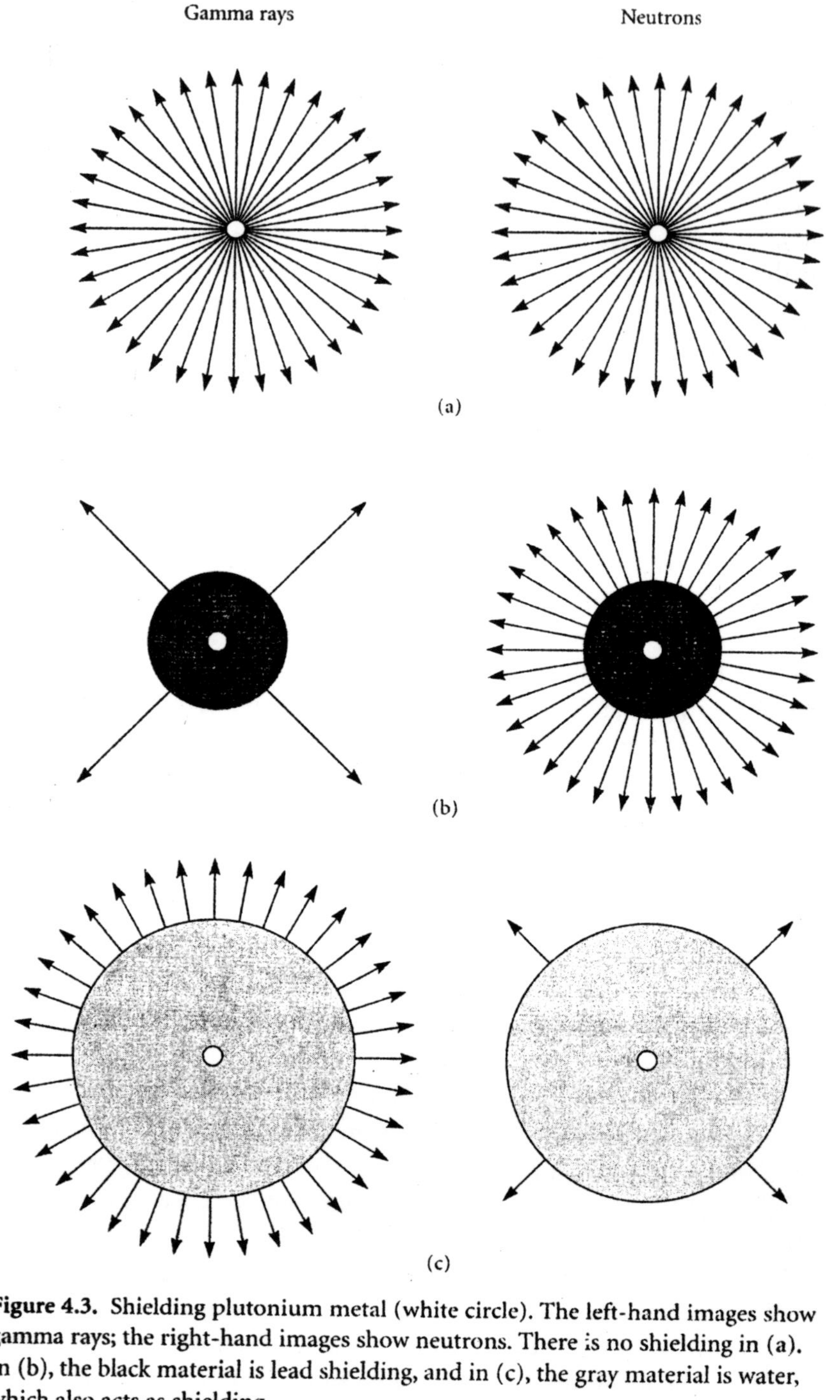

Figure 4.3. Shielding plutonium metal (white circle). The left-hand images show gamma rays; the right-hand images show neutrons. There is no shielding in (a). In (b), the black material is lead shielding, and in (c), the gray material is water, which also acts as shielding.

stocks of plutonium. The need for an alloy adds an extra complication to the terrorist plot. The exact difficulty is impossible to determine from unclassified sources, but at a minimum it will add to the skill and time demands on a terrorist group. Gallium is an extremely common metal in industry, so acquiring it would most likely not add a significant hurdle. Nonetheless, it is probably not on the normal shopping list of any terrorist group, and the chance detection of its acquisition could be immediately flagged as suspicious.

Not only is plutonium metal harder to fashion into a powerful weapon than uranium is, but it is also more difficult to hide from radiation detectors because of its far higher rate of spontaneous fission. Fission generates both neutrons and high-energy photons (gamma rays), and when neutrons scatter off plutonium nuclei, they generate even more high-energy photons. An implosion bomb will also contain large amounts of explosives, potentially presenting another opportunity for detection at official points of entry. This possibility may encourage terrorists to use pathways other than official points of entry, where no detectors would be present.

Imagine that a terrorist group attempts to smuggle four kilograms (roughly nine pounds) of weapons-grade plutonium metal, a fraction of that needed for a nuclear bomb, through an official point of entry.[38] Shaped as a sphere, this material emits half a million neutrons each second, nearly ten thousand times as many as one bare critical mass of weapons-grade uranium (weighing roughly fifty kilograms) emits.[39] The four kilograms of weapons-grade plutonium also emits over 150,000 gamma rays between 100 keV and 10 MeV.[40] This combination of neutron and gamma emissions, if unshielded as in Figure 4.3(a), is fairly easy to detect; thus this situation presents a large challenge to terrorists wishing to shield their weapons from gamma and neutron detectors.

If the group places lead shielding immediately outside the four kilograms of plutonium, large numbers of additional gamma rays will be generated through interactions between neutrons and lead nuclei, partially offsetting the value of the lead shielding. Yet if the group places its *neutron* shielding immediately outside the plutonium, the mass of the lead shielding ultimately required to block gamma rays will increase dramatically, since the lead shielding will need to be placed outside the neutron shielding, and will thus need to cover a much larger area.

Consider a concrete example, shown in Figure 4.3b, in which the terrorist group surrounds its four kilograms of plutonium with twenty centimeters of lead, weighing over six hundred kilograms. Five thousand gamma rays with energies between 1 and 3 MeV will still escape.[41] If a defense uses a basic sodium iodide gamma ray detector to observe a suspicious object for one second at a distance of at most two meters, it will reliably detect the object with less than a one-in-five-hundred chance of a false positive caused by background radiation.[42] This amount of shielding is considerably more than was contemplated in the uranium case, restricting possible methods of smuggling—the material cannot be hand-carried, placed in luggage or light cargo, or even put in a car trunk without potentially arousing suspicion—and making shielding far more vulnerable to detection by gamma radiography in those transport modes that remain possible. Moreover, this analysis completely ignores neutron detection and shielding, which would make the terrorist task even more difficult.

What would happen if, instead, the group sought only to shield neutrons? Assume that the defense uses a typical transportable neutron detector at a distance of two meters for an observation time of one second, wishes to have at most 5 percent false positives, and wants to detect 95 percent of all sources. If the four kilograms of plutonium are unshielded, the detector will detect approximately four hundred neutrons from the source, compared with a detection threshold of, at most, fifteen neutrons.[43] (Depending on the detection scenario, the threshold could be as low as five neutrons.) The terrorist group will thus need to reduce its neutron emissions by a factor of at least thirty to hide them from the detector. Several materials might be used to do that—readily available and well-known studies suggest water, lithium hydride, and borated polyethylene as possibilities.[44] Approximately 40–50 centimeters of water (Figure 4.3c), for example, would provide enough neutron shielding, although additional gamma shielding would still be required if gamma detection was also used.[45] As earlier, this bulk would complicate smuggling options, provide opportunities for detection elsewhere in the plot (lithium hydride cannot normally be obtained in high-density form outside military circles, and borated polyethylene is normally associated with nuclear applications), and introduce the possibility that shielding will be detected using radiography. Gamma radiography might be useful here—one should see a very dense mass of plutonium surrounded by a large, low-density mass of hydrogen-containing material. Alternatively, neutron radiography might be used to spot shielding directly.

Terrorists could also err in the way they shield their material, exposing themselves to detection, and thus even a rudimentary detection capability may be useful. This contrasts with weapons-grade uranium, where neutrons from even carelessly shielded material would be near-invisible to detectors. And in the face of combined gamma and neutron detection, which would be more powerful than either of the two simple detection schemes just considered, more careful shielding schemes would likely need to be evaluated by a terrorist group. Although both of the simple shielding arrangements just noted have been described in well-known writings, more sophisticated ones have not been. The basic analysis of simple detection scenarios already indicates, however, how much more difficult it would be for terrorists to hide plutonium than to hide uranium.

Given that plutonium is considerably easier to detect at official points of entry than uranium is, the possibility that terrorist groups will attempt to move it through illicit border crossings may be much greater.[46] So is the possibility that terrorist groups might do the same with other easier-to-detect materials that we will soon encounter. Unless very long range radiation detection is possible—and most agree it is probably not—terrorists attempting to move nuclear materials through illicit border crossings will need to be intercepted the same way all others attempting to illicitly cross borders might be. Many analysts have strongly emphasized the possibility that terrorists might use illicit crossings, and they often conclude that such tactics would be almost trivially easy to use.[47] Yet as I will show later in this chapter, though it is true that there are many gaps in national borders, within a systems context, border security beyond official points of entry can make a valuable, albeit limited, contribution, not only in the nuclear case but in other cases as well. This is particularly true against groups that may be deterred by a substantial probability of failure, and that may be conservative in their tactics.

Oxide Powder

If a terrorist group acquired uranium or plutonium oxide powder, it could use the powder directly in a nuclear weapon, convert it to metal, or, in the case of plutonium oxide, it could build a radiological weapon.[48] The first of these would yield a less powerful weapon than one using metal, the second option would add technical difficulties, and the third, while simpler, would produce highly uncertain and less devastating results.

A terrorist group is more likely to convert uranium oxide to metal than it is to convert plutonium oxide, since producing a high-yield weapon using uranium metal is much easier than producing one using plutonium metal, making conversion of uranium oxide more worthwhile. Converting either type of oxide to metal is, at least on paper, a fairly straightforward process, though an inexperienced chemist is by no means guaranteed to succeed quickly, if at all. There is disagreement regarding the severity of this barrier. Gunnar Arbman and his colleagues, for example, write that "conversion of the HEU is a fairly simple task."[49] More authoritatively, Carson Mark and several colleagues who were veterans of nuclear weapons design and engineering claimed that conversion would take "a number of days in the event that uranium oxide powder . . . were to be converted to uranium metal" and implied a similar conclusion for plutonium. They noted, however, that "the necessary chemical operations . . . can be (and have been) described in a straightforward manner, but their conduct is most unlikely to proceed smoothly unless in the hands of someone with experience in the particular techniques involved, and even then substantial problems could arise."[50] Such prospects may deter a terrorist group from attempting conversion.

Even if a group did proceed, potential complications could induce it to adopt a slower and more cautious approach than might be expected. For example, the International Atomic Energy Agency reported that Iraq planned to produce uranium metal in fifty- to one hundred–gram batches, even though it was capable of producing it in kilogram quantities, a much quicker and more efficient approach. The stated rationale was that "the choice of the small batch size minimized the losses in the event that a [conversion] went drastically wrong."[51] Such a precaution might be taken by a terrorist group as well, slowing it down. Ultimately the relevance of this barrier will depend on the technical capacity of the group in question, on its goals, and on the amount of material it acquires. The final constraint arises since less material is needed to make a weapon using metal than to make one using oxide, meaning that in some cases, conversion to metal would be the only route to a nuclear explosion.

Several authors have claimed that plutonium oxide can be imploded to produce a nuclear yield on the order of one hundred tons.[52] Those authors do not describe how much nuclear material they assume would be used, the amount of explosives required, and the weight and size of the other weapons components needed, but theirs are probably worst-case judgments from a defensive perspective. Refining their estimates to reflect these parameters requires describing hypothetical weapons. This discussion is thus restricted to a very crude level. More detail can be obtained, and likely has been, in classified settings.

A terrorist group may choose powder implosion because of its relatively low technical demands. Most notably, shaping and compressing a powder is easier than casting and imploding a metal. According to Carson Mark and his colleagues, a simple terrorist weapon might be made with as little as 110 kilograms of UO_2 or 35 kilograms of PuO_2, though depending on the yield sought by a terrorist group, on how much the powder is compressed before it is imploded, and on the sophistication of the weapon, the amount used might be half that or might become as high as several hundred kilograms. Moreover, an actual bomb, which would include not only the explosives needed to compress the powder but also a strong casing to confine the explosion, would be much heavier—the explosives alone would likely weigh considerably more than the uranium or plutonium powder. These are large masses of explosives, posing dangers to any who work with them and possibly presenting difficulties if they are to be acquired in Western countries. At the same time, importing such explosives into target states presents detection opportunities for a defense, if materials are smuggled through official crossing points. Terrorists may find ways to reduce the amounts of explosives used, but that would likely come at the expense of requiring considerably more nuclear material, something that is generally much more difficult to acquire than explosives.[53]

Radiation detection at official points of entry (and in searches of vessels) would become much more effective if used against oxide powder rather than against metal. Focus first on uranium. The radiation emission from uranium oxide is much greater than that of uranium metal. Even if a terrorist group plans to convert oxide powder to metal, the greater radiation signature of uranium oxide would make the group vulnerable before it could convert the material, and would potentially make identification of a contaminated safe house or processing facility easier.

To be conservative (from a defensive perspective), assume that a terrorist group attempts to move one hundred kilograms of UO_2. What would the material's neutron output be? Neutrons are produced in uranium by spontaneous fission and by the interaction of alpha particles with oxygen impurities. In metallic material, spontaneous fission dominates this process, since very little oxygen is present. The situation is different, however, in an oxide powder, where there are two oxygen atoms for every uranium atom. With many more oxygen atoms present, alpha particles have greater odds of hitting an oxygen atom and producing a neutron. That increases the rate of neutron production through alpha particles by a factor of approximately seventy.[54] The net result is that one kilogram of UO_2 emits approximately forty neutrons each second, and one hundred kilograms of UO_2 emit four thousand neutrons each second. This is approximately the same number of neutrons produced by one hundred grams of weapons-grade plutonium metal. (Recall that plutonium metal is much easier to detect than uranium *metal.*) Shielding would make detection considerably harder, but would impose the same difficulties for a terrorist group as it did for plutonium. Shielding would also need to be heavier, since it would surround a bulkier package—while twenty centimeters of lead shielding surrounding four kilograms of plutonium metal weighed about six hundred kilograms, the same thickness of lead surrounding one hundred kilograms of UO_2 compressed to six grams per cubic centimeter would weigh two tons.

Plutonium oxide would present even greater opportunities to detect radiation. Following the same approach as for UO_2 shows that one kilogram of PuO_2 will emit approximately 100,000 neutrons each second. Even a single densely packed thirty-kilogram mass of PuO_2, the absolute minimum needed for a simple powder implosion weapon, would thus emit over three million neutrons each second, more than ten times the number emitted by the four kilograms of plutonium metal studied earlier.

In addition to emitting copious numbers of high-energy neutrons, plutonium oxide emits large numbers of high-energy gamma rays, making shielding extremely difficult. Some of the reactions between alpha particles and oxygen nuclei that increase neutron production also produce high-energy gamma rays. Bruce Geelhood and his colleagues have conducted experiments showing that one kilogram of PuO_2 emits approximately two thousand highly penetrating 2.44 MeV gamma rays each second in this way.[55]

Assume that a terrorist group transports fifty kilograms of PuO_2 with a density of three grams per cubic centimeter, three times the density of water. Then the material will produce five million neutrons each second as well as 100,000 2.44 MeV photons each second. Surrounding the material with ten centimeters of lead shielding (weighing six hundred kilograms) will reduce the number of photons with energies near 2.44 MeV to about five thousand.[56] This emission can still be detected in one second with a one-square-meter sodium iodide detector at a distance of two meters with essentially no false positives.[57] With fifteen centimeters of lead shielding, weighing over one ton, this can be detected in ten seconds with the same detector at a distance of two meters, with one in a thousand false positives.[58] This description actually overstates the ease with which gamma rays can be shielded by terrorists, since neutrons emitted by the plutonium oxide will produce even more high-energy gamma rays that must also be hidden. In addition, a large amount of neutron shielding would be required to hide the neutron emissions. It would thus be all but impossible to move substantial amounts of plutonium oxide undetected through an official point of entry equipped with relatively inexpensive neutron and gamma detectors.

Nuclear Materials Extracted from Fuel

Plutonium or uranium contained in reactor fuel poses additional problems to a terrorist group, since it must be extracted before it can be used in a weapon. Plutonium is found either in fuel that has been irradiated in a reactor, where plutonium has built up over time, or in MOX fuel, where plutonium is incorporated in the design of the fuel. While common—there are hundreds of tons of plutonium in spent fuel around the world—used fuel is an unlikely target for terrorist groups.[59] As argued in a National Academy of Sciences report, "It would be difficult for terrorists to steal a large quantity of spent fuel (e.g., a single spent fuel assembly) . . . Theft and removal of an assembly or individual fuel rods during an assault on the plant might be easier . . . However, the amount of material that could be removed would be small."[60] Since even single spent fuel assemblies (objects containing many pieces of fuel) are likely to contain quantities of plutonium measured in kilograms, rather than tens of kilograms, spent fuel is not a likely target for terrorists seeking to build weapons; the amounts of plutonium in it are too low.[61]

MOX that has not been irradiated, however, is not difficult to handle, nor is fresh HEU fuel.[62] To exploit either HEU fuel or MOX in a weapon, though, terrorists must first extract the material from the fuel; at that point, the group will have to convert the extracted material either to powder or to metal. The first part of this process—essentially reprocessing, minus the complication of handling radioactive material—adds to the demands on a terrorist plot.[63] Beyond that process, either oxide or metal must be produced. (Carefully assessing how terrorist groups might meet these challenges requires experimentation, not just theoretical analysis. Such assessments have likely been done in nuclear weapons circles.) Additional transportation challenges would be present at least in the earlier stages, since the fuel assemblies containing the nuclear explosive material would increase the weight and bulk that would need to be transported. Although a weapon built using HEU or plutonium from fuel would be no different from one using HEU or plutonium from any other source (assuming the materials had similar isotopic compositions), added difficulties in transporting materials and building a weapon would present more opportunities for failure, discovery, and interdiction.

MOX would present greater radiation signatures than plutonium oxide. It is also well known that its heat would complicate weapon construction, since high explosives surrounding a MOX core would insulate the core, heating the high explosives and possibly leading to their decomposition.[64] A similar problem could occur with shielding, because many typical shielding materials are insulators and have low melting points.

Impure Weapons-Grade Uranium Metal

Although pure weapons-grade uranium metal presents the greatest radiation detection challenge possible, not all weapons-grade uranium is pure. Weapons-grade uranium metal made from used nuclear fuel is fairly common, but it is far easier to detect than weapons-grade material made from fresh uranium. According to one press account, "many [researchers of radiation detection] refer to the possibility of . . . capitalizing on uranium-232 traces present in much of the world's highly enriched uranium."[65]

Weapons-grade uranium made from used nuclear fuel is contaminated with U^{232}. Depending on the material's history, the concentration of U^{232} in weapons-grade uranium might range anywhere from roughly one hundred parts per trillion to ten parts per billion.[66] Fifty kilograms of impure weapons-grade uranium (approximately two reflected critical masses) thus emits between one and one hundred million 2.6 MeV gamma rays each second, far exceeding the strongest distinct emission for uncontaminated weapons-grade uranium.[67] If the material were in a spherical shape, this would be reduced by a factor of three, to between 300,000 and three million gamma rays each second.[68]

Separating this signal from background radiation presents special challenges, since radiation of the same energy is emitted by the element thorium, which is found naturally in the ground.[69] Several approaches have been proposed to differentiate this background, including looking for other gamma rays produced by thorium, or by using detectors that produce a two-dimensional radiation image, allowing a concentrated source (nuclear explosive material) to be distinguished from a distributed one (thorium).[70] The first approach is imperfect but may be much easier to realize; the second could be more effective but is currently very expensive.[71] If the problem of isolating the background from thorium can be solved, the remaining atmospheric background will still need to be contended with, especially if imaging detectors are not used.

If unshielded, the fifty kilograms of material could be detected at a distance of between approximately thirty and three hundred meters (depending on the U^{232} concentration) with one second of observation using a one-square-meter sodium iodide detector with one in a thousand false positives.[72] For portal applications, a two-meter detection distance is more realistic. How much shielding is required to reduce the maximum detection distance to that? Again, it depends on the U^{232} concentration—the radiation emitted would have to be reduced by a factor of between 200 and 20,000. Such a reduction would require approximately 10 to 20 centimeters of lead.[73] Were such a shield to surround a fifty-kilogram sphere, it would weigh between three hundred kilograms and one ton, introducing problems similar to those already discussed for oxide powders. Gamma radiography could also quickly identify the bulky mass.

Border Security beyond Official Points of Entry

Most of the nonideal materials just explored are more vulnerable than pure weapons-grade uranium metal to radiation detection at official border crossings. Terrorists who acquire such materials may therefore choose to work around those detection systems, smuggling materials through more remote territory. Assessing how a broad defense might function thus requires a better understanding of what it would take to circumvent official points of entry.

Although each country faces unique challenges in securing its borders, focus first on the United States, which has the longest undefended borders (both land and sea) in the world and also receives large numbers of airline flights each day. Assessing the potential for securing American borders thus provides, in an important sense, an estimate of the minimum that any other state should be able to achieve. The United States is also a natural candidate for study because of the volume of information publicly available about its borders and border control activities.

Arguments for the fallibility of border controls are often motivated by an analogy with drug interdiction. Indeed the continuing ability of traffickers to move large amounts of drugs into the United States has rightly been taken as evidence that an approach to preventing nuclear terrorism built solely or even primarily on border security is far from a substitute for effective controls over nuclear materials or even an equal to it. But within a systems context, it is important to ask not only whether border controls can provide a defense by themselves, but also whether they can contribute meaningfully to a broader system, a standard that requires far less than perfection. One can examine this question by looking both at the drug trade and at the finer details of border controls.

Focus for now on the case of cocaine, which, like nuclear materials, can pack a lot of material valuable to a smuggler into a small space, meaning that small amounts can be profitably moved. In addition, better data are publicly available for cocaine than for marijuana or heroin (though drug smuggling data are inevitably quite poor). Statistics for cocaine trafficking divide interdictions into those made in the "arrival zone" in the vicinity of the U.S. border and those made in the "transit zone" between those areas where cocaine is typically produced and the arrival zone. The U.S. Drug Enforcement Agency estimates that during 2004, approximately 10–25 percent of the cocaine that reached the arrival zone was seized there. It also estimates that 30–60 percent of the cocaine that departed South America moving toward the United States was lost or seized in the transit zone.[74] The combined probability that cocaine departing South America destined for the United States will actually make it to the United States was estimated to be 35–70 percent. Because nuclear materials moving through the U.S.–Mexico ("southern") border would likely take different routes to the arrival zone than drugs would, one can only estimate that the probability of their being interdicted is somewhere in the range of 10–70 percent. In the context of drug trafficking, this risk may be tolerable for smugglers—prices can be increased to compensate for seizures. But in the context of defense against nuclear terrorism, even the low end of this range may be significant, within a systems framework. Intelligence might, however, play different roles in interdicting drugs and interdicting nuclear explosive materials. This possibility could be explored by institutions with access to details of intelligence and operations. Even if interdiction is targeted through the use of intelligence, terrorist groups with relatively weak operational capabilities would be more likely to use established (drug) smuggling networks and routes, which from a defense perspective would allow drug-related intelligence to help in interdicting nuclear explosive materials.

It would also be valuable to understand whether cocaine traffickers prefer to use official points of entry, where inspections are possible, or to cross the border between official points of entry, where inspections are not possible unless individuals are first spotted and stopped. Substantial disagreement exists over the distribution of cocaine trafficking between these two choices, but what data have been published are illuminating.

According to a study prepared for the U.S. Office of National Drug Control Policy, "conveyance types of choice [for moving through the arrival zone] appear to be commercial vehicle and commercial marine."[75] The same study estimates that the number of border seizures is far greater for noncommercial means than for commercial means.[76] (Commercial transport is always across official points of entry; noncommercial transport also includes smuggling *between* official points of entry.) Taken together, these findings indicate that the probability of cocaine interdiction is much greater for noncommercial than for commercial means. (It still makes sense for smugglers to use noncommercial means in some cases, if such means are considerably less expensive, or if the particular smugglers are simply unskilled at avoiding scrutiny at official crossings.) The study also estimates that 162 metric tons of cocaine were shipped by commercial vehicle during 1999, while 9.4 metric tons were seized, an interdiction rate of 6 percent; for commercial maritime means, it estimates that 203 metric tons were shipped, while 5.1 metric tons were seized, a rate of 3 percent.[77] On the other hand, the study estimates that approximately 25 metric tons were moved by noncommercial vehicles while 9.4 tons were seized, a seizure rate of about 40 percent; for noncommercial marine transport, the corresponding numbers are approximately 10 tons moved and 7 tons seized, a seizure rate of 70 percent. These figures indicate that it may be far more difficult to move drugs—and also nuclear materials—across borders between official points of entry. At the same time, it may be possible to make detection of many nuclear explosive materials at official points of entry much more effective than detection of cocaine at those places, since cocaine can be hidden from sophisticated sensors by hermetic sealing while, as we have just seen, not all nuclear material can be shielded effectively from radiation detectors. This body of data and analysis suggests that the failure to stem the flow of drugs into the United States does not imply that efforts to control nuclear smuggling would fail similarly, especially when viewed as only one component within a broader system.

The authors of the study note, however, that their results estimate that a much greater fraction of cocaine is moved by commercial conveyances than current intelligence estimates suggest.[78] This difference may be in part due to overly simple extrapolation of seizure data to flow information in official estimates, perhaps by assuming that the distribution of flows is roughly the same as the distribution of seizures. It may also be due to flaws in the study's modeling, as the study authors themselves point out. These uncertainties point to a need for further analysis of drug smuggling routes and their difficulties based on detailed intelligence not publicly available, which also might focus on identifying characteristics of various approaches that would change were nuclear materials, rather than cocaine, smuggled.

The cocaine analogy provides useful insight into both the potential and the limits of efforts to control borders. Additional research, however, is needed to understand potential smuggling of nuclear explosive materials, because alternate routes and strategies are likely and because the role of intelligence will be different. A complete understanding of potential smuggling across nonofficial smuggling points will require a team of individuals with a wide range of expertise and with access to government data on border controls. An overview of the problem is still useful, though. It confirms that present border controls can provide some meaningful defense against many potential terrorist groups and that improvement is possible. It also provides a framework for further investigation. Border controls, especially in isolation, are still fundamentally limited. But that is no reason to dismiss their utility outright.

Controls will be particularly effective against failure-averse groups. They may also be useful against tactically conservative groups that prefer to use more familiar official crossing points than to attempt crossings away from official points of entry. In addition, defending against some but not all modes of entry might be effective against groups skilled in one type of entry but not in others.

Terrorist groups might attempt to enter a state by land, air, or sea. Crossing U.S. land borders is more difficult than many suppose. Focus first on the southern border. Precise statistics for successful illegal crossings are difficult to obtain, but estimates are available. The U.S. Immigration and Naturalization Service (INS) estimated that in 1999 (the most recent year for which statistics are available), approximately 968,000 individuals became residents of the United States illegally.[79] (The net increase in illegal residents was smaller, due to departures.) In the same year, 1.56 million apprehensions along the southern border were recorded by the Border Patrol.[80] (The 2004 figure is 1.15 million.) Even if each individual entered at a nonofficial point of entry, these figures would translate to a 60 percent chance of being apprehended; the smaller the fraction that actually used this route, the larger the true percentage caught would be. If the increase in the illegal population had been underestimated by a factor of two, one could still conclude that the probability of being intercepted was 45 percent. (This estimate is, perhaps contrary to intuition, consistent with claims that illegal immigrants can enter the United States with relative ease, since immigrants can make multiple crossing attempts or be released into the United States after being caught.)[81] Such probabilities of apprehension at the border would likely affect the decision making of all but the most risk-hungry terrorist groups, especially when assessed within the broader defensive system. Development and deployment of portable radiation detectors would also ensure that individuals crossing with nuclear materials would not be released after they had been apprehended.

Some groups may, of course, be able to decrease their likelihood of getting caught by using crossing techniques and assistance that are more sophisticated than those used by the typical illegal immigrant. (Intelligence cooperation with Mexico, motivated by the understanding that U.S. immigration policy toward Mexico can be more positive if Mexico polices its border regions for potential terrorists, might help address this problem.) Characteristics specific to particular terrorist groups will likely determine how effectively they can exploit such opportunities. Al Qaeda, for example, has only a "rudimentary presence in Latin America," in contrast with other groups such as Hezbollah (though its operations are generally located far further south than Mexico).[82] Successful smuggling networks catering to Middle Easterners have, however, been established; one network brought hundreds of illegal immigrants into the United States from the Middle East during the 1990s through a mix of crossings at official points of entry and away from them. Many aspects of this operation are not known, however (at least not publicly), such as the mix between the two types of crossings and the limits placed on individuals aided by the smugglers.[83] For example, it is unknown whether the smugglers would have allowed individuals with heavy or bulky baggage to cross using their operations, a detail that would be very relevant to the nuclear smuggling case, though of far less interest to those studying the case purely through an immigration lens. Because the kingpin of the operation, George Tajarian, will be in jail through 2011, that information may be straightforward to obtain.

The northern border (with Canada) is more difficult to police. It requires controlling more rugged, less open terrain (though this will also be a barrier to some terrorist operatives). Even if it were technically possible to police that border with far larger numbers of patrol officers, it would not likely be politically feasible—the large deployments on the southern border are politically possible not because of terrorism, but because of illegal immigration.

Still, it is worth noting that terrorists have had little success at crossing the Canada–U.S. border away from official points of entry. Through the end of 2001, only two individuals who eventually participated in attempted terrorist attacks in the United States were known to have entered through the northern border.[84] The ways they succeeded suggest the potential of simple defensive improvements. Gazi Ibrahim, who was to participate in a plot to bomb a subway in Brooklyn, was caught three times trying to enter the United States between official border crossings. On his fourth attempt, he was caught again, and released into the United States.[85] Whatever this implies for U.S. immigration policy, it suggests that had Ibrahim been carrying nuclear explosive materials, a simple search, possibly aided by radiation detection equipment, could have identified him as a nuclear terrorist. Hakim Tizegha, who took part in the failed Millennium bombing plot, crossed successfully.[86] He did not enter North America through Canada, however, but rather through the United States, by hiding aboard a ship that landed at an official point of entry in Boston.[87] These terrorists could, of course, have used smuggling networks, but chose not to, perhaps out of concerns about operational security.

Yet controls over the northern U.S. border have deep and undeniable weaknesses. For example, one northern border sector estimated in 2000 that it was only "six to seven percent effective at its current staffing level."[88] It is unclear to what extent simple investments could improve that level of effectiveness. For example, the Border Patrol reported in 2002 that it was unable to provide full-time coverage on the northern border, and that continued use of unsecured radios allowed smuggling operations to exploit this weakness by identifying times when borders would be unmonitored. Investments in secure communications might thus have a large impact on effectiveness. Alternatively, such upgrades might simply prompt smugglers to shift to different approaches. Other technological improvements, such as the installation of additional remote cameras and motion sensors, might also improve effectiveness. Only actual deployments and subsequent observations can determine whether particular changes will have a meaningful impact. (Added sensors not only would facilitate interdictions but would also improve statistics by helping identify successful illegal crossings that could not be interdicted.) At a minimum, it is too early to conclude that the U.S. northern border is simply beyond the capabilities of the United States to provide some meaningful security, within the context of a defensive system, at an acceptable cost and without fundamentally changing the Canada-U.S. relationship.

The entire discussion of the northern border also presumes that a terrorist group can move nuclear materials into Canada in the first place at an acceptable risk. Although Canada has immigration policies that are different from those of the United States, there is no reason why technical detection capabilities at its official points of entry cannot be similar to those of the United States. Canada too, of course, has nonofficial points of entry that terrorists might exploit. But no entry point is entirely straightforward.

Covert air entry is limited by NORAD air defense radars, which provide similar coverage to the Canadian borders as they do to those of the United States, though Canadian abilities to intercept aircraft upon warning are likely weaker. (Landings in remote territory would, however, provide extra time for Canadian officials to intercept potential smugglers.)

Canada, unlike the United States, has no short air or sea route to entry from any country other than the United States, with any route requiring either a transatlantic or transpacific crossing. Even were terrorists to land in a remote area, most such areas are in extremely inhospitable terrain, which introduces some not insignificant possibility of failure for many terrorist groups. For example, one group of Chinese boat people, disembarking in the rugged Queen Charlotte Islands off the coast of the western Canadian province of British Columbia in order to evade authorities, quickly found itself having to be rescued by Canadian officials.[89] Nor is it as simple to land a seaworthy boat unnoticed away from an official port of entry in Canada as many might imagine, as evidenced by interceptions of boat people on the Pacific coast and interruption of illegal fishing operations off the northern Atlantic coast.[90] In addition, for terrorist groups to move from remote entry points to the U.S. border, they will almost certainly have to pass through small, remote towns where any stranger would be likely to stand out. None of this implies that smuggling nuclear materials into Canada is anywhere near impossible, whether through official points of entry or away from them, but it does counsel against deeming covert entry entirely straightforward.

Bringing a weapon directly into the United States on a private or charter airplane is not necessarily simple either. If a private airplane is used, it must first be purchased, providing an opportunity for detection, particularly by monitoring financial transactions. If a charter airplane is used, the terrorist group will sacrifice some privacy. This issue may not be important if the group is importing weapons-grade uranium metal, but it may be more problematic for heavier or bulkier materials or equipment, such as many of those just studied.

Aircraft entering the United States without providing notice are likely to be detected by radar and possibly escorted by fighter jets.[91] (The small aircraft many intuitively associate with the cross-border drug trade do not normally attempt to cross the U.S. border, but rather drop their cargoes near the border before those cargoes are carried across by land or sea.)[92] If such an aircraft contains an assembled nuclear weapon, and its operators decide to detonate the weapon in the air rather than landing the airplane and being subjected to what may be a comprehensive inspection, the group will have to drop to a relatively low altitude if the detonation is to cause any appreciable number of casualties. (Alternatively, it might drop its bomb from the aircraft, but this would require a much more sophisticated weapon.) Escorts may not let it do that, though, if only because dropping to a low enough altitude would also allow the airplane to be crashed into a building, a prominent threat that fighter escorts are designed to deal with. For example, the appendix shows that for a ten-kiloton bomb detonated at a height of 1,500 meters, no severe structural damage should be expected on the ground, while for a ten-ton bomb, that required height becomes roughly 100 meters. Escorts able to keep already-suspect aircraft from dropping too low thus could reduce the impact of a terrorist nuclear bomb.

If detonation in the air is impossible, the aircraft will need to land. To land away from an official airport of entry without an escort, aircraft must, at least in theory, go through a preapproval process.[93] Determining the likelihood that any given terrorist group will be able to obtain preapproval without an investigation that would expose its nuclear plot is something that could be studied by a group with expertise in aircraft and related customs operations, intelligence, and financial monitoring (for aircraft purchases). At a minimum, though, many terrorist groups would inevitably lack confidence that they could easily smuggle nuclear materials covertly aboard a private aircraft.

Much if not most of the analysis just outlined makes special reference to geographic and political features of the United States. Any state wishing to improve the security of its borders against terrorist imports of nuclear materials would require its own studies. Consider briefly the United Kingdom and, implicitly, the European Union, to see how analysis might be adapted. As in the American case, far-from-perfect UK (and EU) border controls can still be meaningful in a systems context.

As in the American case, the UK drug trade provides insight not only into flaws in border controls but also into how they might effectively contribute to defense against nuclear terrorism. The UK's National Criminal Intelligence Service estimates that between thirty-five and forty tons of cocaine is transported annually into the United Kingdom.[94] The UK's customs service, meanwhile, reports that it captured roughly six tons in 2001–2002, nine tons in 2003–2004, and twenty tons in 2004–2005.[95] Although the sharp rise in the last figure may be suspect (especially since heroin interdiction dropped during the same year), even eight tons of intercepted cocaine would translate to roughly a 15 percent chance of interdiction, not negligible in a systems context. (If the twenty-ton figure is correct, it would translate to a probability of interdiction over 30 percent.)

The United Kingdom publishes detailed estimates of the routes it believes are used for importing cocaine. It estimates that, by volume, 65 percent is imported "on cross-channel transport, 15% by ship, 15% by air, 4% by rail, and 1% by mail." At the same time, "in terms of numbers [of shipments], most importations arrived by air, on scheduled flights, concealed in baggage or air cargo."[96] Technology presents potentially greater opportunities for detecting nuclear materials smuggled by air than it does for detecting drugs. In contrast, the heavy use of cross-channel transport for importing drugs points to a weakness that nuclear smugglers might also exploit. The main barrier to using that route would likely be in moving contraband (whether drugs or nuclear materials) into the European Union in the first place. That barrier, though, may be low—most cocaine eventually moved through cross-channel transport initially arrives in the European Union by sea, much of it ultimately on small boats.[97]

Statistics for illegal immigration provide further insight into the effectiveness of border controls. One intergovernmental group, reviewing a range of studies, estimates that roughly 50,000 individuals were apprehended at the UK border in 2001, while roughly 100,000 were able to enter illegally.[98] These numbers translate to one-in-three odds of being caught. The report also estimates that roughly 30 percent of those attempting to enter the European Union illegally are caught. Neither of these odds of success is likely to appear encouraging to would-be nuclear smugglers. At the same time, many terrorist groups of concern, such as al Qaeda, have much stronger support in the United Kingdom than in the United States, making it potentially easier for them to use "homegrown" terrorists and thus avoid scrutiny at the border.

As a whole, this analysis emphasizes three conclusions. For Western countries with relatively open borders, border security cannot provide anything close to an ironclad defense against terrorist imports of nuclear materials. At the same time, evidence strongly suggests that border controls can be effective enough to make a difference within the context of a wider defensive system, especially against groups with limited (though still substantial) capabilities, and against those that are tactically conservative or failure-averse. This brief review also points to the need for country-specific analysis. Indeed even from a narrow American perspective, the security of allies, as well of countries that might be transshipment points for nuclear materials, is important.

The Power of Passive Synergies

How can defense *beyond* controls over nuclear materials be improved? An essential part of the emerging answer is, surprisingly, by improving controls over nuclear materials themselves. As obtaining nuclear explosive material becomes more difficult, terrorist groups may settle for less-than-ideal material, which in turn introduces vulnerabilities elsewhere in their plots. Bomb construction becomes harder. Radiation detection becomes easier. Building a bomb is still, to be certain, quite possible, but the potential that a terrorist group will be deterred, or that it will settle for a less powerful weapon, increases, especially if the defense controls or monitors the materials and expertise that a group might seek. Less powerful weapons will, in turn, introduce new consequence management opportunities and increase the value of displacing detonations from population centers. Effective radiation detection does not become inevitable, but investments that might be rejected as too ineffective or costly if measured against the likelihood of detecting weapons-grade uranium metal appear more attractive against plutonium, and even more appealing against other materials or against assembled weapons. Border controls away from official points of entry also become more important, and can have substantial effectiveness. Depending on the type of nuclear explosive materials a group is burdened with, some of the most clandestine options, such as crossing borders on foot, can also become much more difficult to use.

These effects become particularly important in a systems context and against failure-averse terrorist groups; the utility of these measures is also sensitive to specific terrorist capabilities. Moreover, further study might discover other powerful synergies not involving materials protection, control, and accounting (MPC&A). No one should be confident that nuclear terrorism is impossible, but investments that may appear worthless outside a systems context or against the worst case threats become more valuable when studied as part of a system or against less formidable, but still capable, terrorist groups.

The considerations in this chapter are, of course, only part of the picture—among other things, I have deliberately ignored the possibility that one part of the defensive system might alert another part to a developing attack. Incorporating that effect suggests further opportunities for defense.

— 5 —

Warning

Most public discussion of warning in nuclear terrorism has focused on strategic warning, information about the overall likelihood that a terrorist group will initiate a nuclear plot in the future.[1] Observers draw primarily on their understanding of terrorist group motivations and resources as well as on knowing the state of security for nuclear stockpiles worldwide. But it is equally important to understand tactical warning, which, among other things, provides an indication of whether a nuclear terrorist plot has already moved beyond the theft of nuclear materials. Strategic warning informs overall policy and strategy; tactical warning changes more quickly and should be more closely reflected in day-to-day decisions.

Imagine that no nuclear materials had been stolen in the past, that all nuclear materials were protected by heavily armed guards, and that facility employees never conspired to provide materials to outsiders. All thefts of nuclear materials would require the use of massive force, and, with simple monitoring, would be noticed. That would provide warning that a plot might be well under way, and thus could trigger intensified defensive efforts. Conversely, if no thefts were noticed, authorities could have the confidence to reduce their defensive efforts. The net result would be a more efficient use of defensive resources.

Real life is more complicated, but these basic contours often persist. How much a scenario departs from this idealized one depends on how effective real warning systems are and on how much they can be leveraged by a defense. Potential sources of warning are vast—discovery of anything that might possibly be connected to a plot provides at least ambiguous warning that a plot is under way. Solid evidence that a substantial amount of nuclear material has gone missing, however, is decidedly less ambiguous than any other warning. This evidence might come directly from the seizure by authorities of loose nuclear material, but the earliest warning could come from the scene of a theft. As controls over nuclear materials become stronger, it may become harder for thieves to steal materials unnoticed, providing potentially important opportunities for a defense to react or, in the words of one influential study, to "surge" its efforts.[2] Materials protection, control, and accounting may thus be the most powerful source of intelligence and warning in the defensive system. Evaluating this possibility requires exploring how difficult it might be for thieves to steal materials unnoticed, and understanding how effectively a defense might be able to respond.

The Varieties of MPC&A

No single model of how MPC&A provides warning of thefts is possible, since each MPC&A system is unique. Instead of a futile and potentially misleading search for fundamental principles, it is more illuminating to describe a range of possible ways MPC&A systems might provide, or fail to provide, warning. (This approach is similar to what anthropologists call "thick description.")

In each case, the timeliness, precision, and dependability of warning will matter. A long delay between theft and detection will cut into the time the defense has to react. Knowing with precision what has been stolen—for example, knowing whether enough material for a bomb has disappeared—allows a more accurate assessment of whether the theft is the beginning of a credible attempted attack. Precise knowledge of what has been stolen can also help the defense tailor its efforts to recover materials. Dependability—relatively infrequent false alarms and few missed thefts—strengthens a warning-based response, since less money is wasted on reacting to spurious warnings and less effort is required to hedge against warning failures.

These three attributes of a warning system—timeliness, precision, and dependability—are interconnected. There is a direct tradeoff between the rate of false alarms and timeliness of detection: a more sensitive warning system can increase timeliness, but possibly at the cost of increasing the rate of false alarms. (A system might warn of a theft every time a hole is discovered in a facility fence; such warnings would be timely, but they would also generate a false alarm every time a petty thief or an animal broke through the fence.) A synergy also exists between the false alarm rate and the precision of the warning: precise reporting of possible thefts allows the defense to more narrowly target its efforts to search for material, and hence to more quickly resolve whether an alarm is real.

With these attributes in mind, one can examine several of the many possible MPC&A systems. To cover as wide a territory as possible, I will break MPC&A into its building blocks—physical security, materials control, and materials accounting—and study each individually, since any one element might provide evidence that a theft has occurred. The goal here is to understand MPC&A, not to find ways to improve it. Quite the opposite: the goal is to understand how imperfect MPC&A might fit into the broader defensive system. That understanding can help us design defenses that leverage warning generated by MPC&A to boost the effectiveness of their other components. It can also alert us to situations where MPC&A systems may provide inadequate warning, and thus suggest where improvements might be made. To these ends, it is as important to explore examples of weak MPC&A as it is to study best practices.

Before looking at specific examples, though, it is useful to understand how the pieces of MPC&A might ultimately fit back together. For many outsider thefts, effective physical protection or materials control will provide timely warning, because both of these parts of MPC&A are designed to deal with the removal of nuclear material from a facility. Even if one of the layers fails, the system should provide a warning, so long as the other element remains effective. (Some common failures, however, such as an ineffective guard force, would weaken both layers.) Materials accounting can add precision to any warning provided by physical protection or materials control—guards, for example, may know that thieves have entered and escaped, but they may not know precisely what those thieves have taken. Accounting may also provide timely warning even if physical protection and materials control both fail. In addition, accounting can play an important role if outsider theft occurs through deception, such as might be the case if insiders accidentally give nuclear explosive materials to outside thieves, believing incorrectly that those outsiders are authorized to receive the materials.[3]

For insider thefts, most of these conclusions remain the same, except physical protection directed at keeping thieves out of facilities becomes irrelevant. Again, the separation is not entirely clean—for example, strong guards put in place for physical protection might stop insiders from escaping with stolen materials. In this case, though, those guards would be functioning as part of the materials control system. If materials control fails, the entire burden of warning of an insider theft falls on materials accounting. Whether any warning is timely or precise will depend entirely on the details of that system.

Physical Protection

The same attributes that make materials protection effective in preventing outsider theft make it potentially effective in warning that a theft has succeeded. A weak physical protection system might be quietly surmounted, providing no clear and quick warning that it has been breached. As the protection system becomes stronger, any thieves must undermine it from the inside, or attack with greater force, making clear warning, all else being equal, more likely. Between these two possibilities fall likely but delayed warnings: for example, thieves might be forced to cut through poorly monitored fences, creating gaps that might be detected visually only days or weeks later.

RUSSIA IN THE EARLY 1990S. The case of Russia in the early 1990s provides a baseline for considering future (and some past) improvements to MPC&A, and provides insight into whether material might have been stolen in the past without notice. Physical protection at some Russian facilities in the early 1990s was so poor that it was effectively absent. In 1998 it was reported that recent U.S. visitors to Moscow's elite Kurchatov Institute of Atomic Energy found no one guarding a building that held 220 pounds of highly enriched uranium—enough for several bombs—because the cash-strapped institute could not afford to hire a single guard. In other places, U.S. visitors found alarm systems shut down because of unpaid electricity bills, cables cut by guards annoyed by false alarms, and posts abandoned by guards who had left to pick potatoes.[4]

At this extreme, physical protection cannot be expected to provide any alarm following a theft. In a similar but slightly better situation, the physical protection system might provide warning without providing significant protection against theft. This might happen, for example, if budgets were only enough to hire a small number of guards who could easily be overcome but who would provide evidence of a theft, if only, sadly, through the discovery of their dead or disabled bodies.

RUSSIAN FACILITIES WITH "RAPID UPGRADES." The example of Russian facilities that have received "rapid upgrades" provides insight into the current and possible future states of many sites in the former Soviet Union. U.S.–Russian MPC&A cooperation has generally progressed in two stages at any given facility, with the application first of "rapid upgrades," followed later by the completion of "comprehensive upgrades" if deemed necessary. Rapid upgrades, as noted earlier, include such physical protection elements as "bricking up windows in storage buildings" and "installing strengthened doors [and] locks," but do not include "such components as electronic sensors, motion detectors, closed circuit surveillance cameras, [or] central alarm stations to monitor the cameras and alarms."[5] In addition to making thievery more difficult, these simple upgrades might also make a theft more conspicuous—for example, unless insiders cooperate in opening doors, doors might need to be forcibly opened, leaving a trail. Rapid upgrades, however, would not offer the same level of redundancy or automation as the comprehensive upgrades, making the rapid improvements more vulnerable to being undermined from the inside and hence less useful for warning.

MAYAK FISSILE MATERIAL STORAGE FACILITY (FMSF). In addition to being a prominent destination of Western security funding, the Mayak Fissile Material Storage Facility in Russia is important to understand because it boasts one of the most robust physical security systems available. The facility is capable of holding material from approximately eight thousand dismantled nuclear weapons. According to Matthew Bunn, it "is an immense concrete fortress, designed to withstand even artillery fire and armor-piercing bombs dropped from aircraft. The walls are 7 meters (23 feet) thick, and the roof is 8 meters (26 feet) thick. Inside, the facility [is] highly automated, with all of the material canisters under continuous electronic watch. Once nuclear material has been loaded into the facility, it [becomes] some of the most secure material in all of Russia."[6]

Any theft from this facility is thus extremely unlikely. But what would happen if security was nonetheless breached? Theft by brute force from such a heavily fortified facility would be very conspicuous, providing near-instantaneous warning; thus physical security, in this case, is effective as a warning element. Alternatively, thieves might try to undermine security measures by colluding with insiders, or a scheme might involve insiders alone. It is impossible to assess how difficult undermining security from within would be without confidential information about security procedures at Mayak; however, whatever the likelihood of success, if the security system was undermined from the inside, the physical protection system itself would become ineffective as a warning element.

DISASSEMBLED PAKISTANI WEAPONS. The case of Pakistan provides insight into how technically unsophisticated physical security systems might operate. In addition to secrecy, Pakistan likely relies on heavy military force to protect its nuclear weapons, which are thought normally to be stored unassembled.[7] A terrorist group that acquired pieces of a weapon would have to treat them differently from an intact weapon, since the group would still need to manipulate the nuclear material and build a bomb. If a terrorist group seized nuclear materials under stable social conditions, the highest state authorities would almost certainly be made immediately aware.[8] During state collapse or a coup d'état, the situation might differ dramatically. In one possible scenario, the nuclear guardians might not be loyal to the new leadership and might not communicate promptly or truthfully with them. In another, chaos might prevent or disrupt communication, even if the guardians transferred their allegiance to the new regime. In each case, physical protection would be breached, but warning would not reach authorities immediately. Warning is not just a technical matter, but must be embedded within an effective system for communication.

Materials Control

When materials control—measures taken to prevent unauthorized removal of nuclear materials from a facility—is improved in a way that makes theft less likely, it also normally becomes more effective at providing warning during and after successful thefts. (This parallels the case and logic of physical protection.) For example, an employee might surmount use of the two-man rule (two people must always be present when handling sensitive material) by disabling his coworker and escaping with nuclear material. That incident, however, would not long go undetected.

(Were two insiders to collude, though, detection would be less likely.) A portal monitor (a radiation or metal detector) might detect smuggling, but thieves might be able to overwhelm any guards who responded; they would be able to complete their theft, but their action would be quickly known. Many other scenarios are more ambiguous, and would produce delayed warning. For example, if video from surveillance cameras was stored and audited off-site, thieves might still be successful by bribing on-site guards and escaping with nuclear materials, but the theft would be detected later upon review.

CHINESE MATERIALS CONTROL. The Chinese approach to materials control is considered relatively weak by modern standards. Hui Zhang writes that the Chinese system "mainly relies on social controls and the loyalty of workers," and he argues that, given such a system, present trends in Chinese society "would increase the criminal threat and offer more opportunities for [insider] theft and smuggling by criminal elements."[9] Nathan Busch has similarly judged that "to the extent that Chinese nuclear facilities lack systematic MC&A [Materials Control & Accounting] systems, they presumably have a limited ability to detect thefts by insiders."[10] The Chinese system of materials control could thus not be depended on to provide warning following attack by insiders, just as it could not with confidence be expected to stop thefts in the first place.

Primitive MPC&A systems outside of China are generally believed to have similarly weak materials control. For example, "at Building-116 of the Kurchatov Institute [in Russia], no metal detectors were installed to deter theft until 1994. Employees were not searched when they entered and departed the premises." Such descriptions of post-Soviet materials control are common.[11] Again, they suggest that insider thefts not only might succeed but also might not be noticed by materials control systems.

FACILITIES INVOLVED IN HEU BLENDDOWN. Examining the "HEU Purchase Agreement" between the United States and Russia provides insight into possible warning when highly enriched uranium is diverted. Under the agreement, the United States buys power plant fuel produced by diluting HEU from Russian weapons.[12] Since exporting weapons-grade uranium from Russia is not politically acceptable, the material is converted by a large complex within Russia before being exported as uranium with lower enrichment. Oleg Bukharin and Helen Hunt have analyzed extensively the vulnerabilities inherent in the barriers to theft at these facilities. Their analysis provides a foundation for examining the associated vulnerabilities in warning.[13]

They focus on four areas, two of which, visual surveillance and portal monitoring, involve materials control. Visual surveillance "includes observation of process operations and personnel who perform them, and implementation of a two- or three-man rule."[14] The authors report a host of weaknesses, including "susceptibility to collusion," "inability to recognize unauthorized activities," and "attention to completing task." The first two are self-explanatory; the third refers to a worker who is so focused on his task that he does not notice his colleagues' activities. Each flaw weakens the ability of materials control to provide warning as much as it weakens its ability to prevent theft—for example, if an individual is distracted from his colleague, he will not stop that colleague's theft, nor will he even notice the theft. If two colleagues collude to steal material, they will also collude to conceal their theft. Thus in situations where these weaknesses make theft possible, warning from materials control is unlikely.

Bukharin and Hunt also write that "portal monitoring is an essential safeguards measure employed at HEU-handling facilities to deter and detect unauthorized removal of HEU from a material access area or facility."[15] But they argue at length that "detection capabilities of such portal monitoring equipment are subject to serious limitation," namely that small amounts of HEU cannot be reliably detected. Moreover, "portal monitoring by use of non-automated detectors is subject to serious human limitations." As with visual surveillance, the same action that undermines security also undermines warning; if materials are stolen by undermining portal monitoring, portal monitoring is unlikely to provide warning, either.

ROKKASHO PLUTONIUM-REPROCESSING FACILITY. When materials accounting has major limitations, materials control assumes a greater role in providing warning. Such is the case with the plutonium-reprocessing facility in Rokkasho, Japan. Although the finer details of materials control efforts at the facility are not available, the International Atomic Energy Agency experience with establishing safeguards (the term of art for inspections and monitoring) sheds some light on that facility's materials controls, which in turn illuminates the situation at other large reprocessing facilities.

In applying safeguards, the IAEA must be satisfied that it will be able to detect diversion of a "significant quantity" of nuclear material in a "timely" manner with detection likelihood exceeding 95 percent and a false alarm probability of less than 5 percent.[16] This means that if there has been a significant theft during a period covered by twenty inspections, there should be a nineteen-in-twenty chance that it will be discovered, while there should be only one false alarm incorrectly warning that a theft has occurred. Traditional materials accounting cannot provide this level of confidence in detecting bomb-sized losses at Rokkasho (a point argued in detail later). However, expert groups have concluded that a combination of accountancy and containment/surveillance ("C/S") methods could provide the necessary warning that nuclear material has been diverted.[17] Since C/S activities are similar to materials control, this provides insight into how IAEA experts judge the utility of materials control in generating warnings. It suggests that those experts judge the materials control measures at Rokkasho to be highly effective in this regard.

One can infer what IAEA experts believe about the effectiveness of materials control by assuming that the system at Rokkasho must bridge the gap between ineffective materials accounting and the IAEA requirements. For plutonium in used fuel, the IAEA goal for "timely" detection is detection within one to three months, but annual inventories—a typical approach for plutonium reprocessing—cannot provide 95 percent odds of timely detection.[18] Assuming the least taxing timeliness requirement—three months—the likelihood that an annual inventory will occur within three months of a theft, leading to its detection, is no more than 25 percent. (The odds could be considerably worse if a theft were conducted by insiders who knew when inventories were taken.) Moreover, the probability of detecting a diversion of eight kilograms of plutonium—a "significant quantity"—while generating only 5 percent false positives is only 6 percent.[19] This results in an abysmal overall 2 percent likelihood of timely detection.[20]

Other measures are used at Rokkasho to improve accounting, but there is little consensus on their effectiveness. That being the case, the international assessment of materials accounting at Rokkasho most likely did not rely heavily upon them.[21] Materials control measures must thus be able to satisfy the requirement of 95 percent probable timely detection almost entirely on their own. Even without knowing the precise details of the materials control system, we may deduce that the IAEA assessment of Rokkasho finds this system to be highly effective as a warning element, and not simply as part of plant security.

DOE-REGULATED NUCLEAR FACILITIES. The United States Department of Energy (DOE) issues regulations governing materials control for its facilities, which include the U.S. nuclear weapons laboratories, manufacturing and dismantlement plants, and storage areas.[22] The regulations, assuming (perhaps too optimistically) that they are followed, provide insight into the performance of these systems. Rather than issuing overall performance requirements for materials control, or for materials control in combination with materials accounting, the DOE establishes requirements for specific materials control elements.

The DOE requires that tests show that controls for the most sensitive materials are at least 95 percent effective in detecting unauthorized access. These most sensitive materials include four hundred grams or more of plutonium metal, two kilograms or more of plutonium compounds or unirradiated mixtures, sixteen kilograms or more of moderately radioactive plutonium mixtures, one kilogram or more of HEU metal, six kilograms or more of HEU compounds or unirradiated mixtures, and fifty kilograms or more of moderately radioactive HEU mixtures. The guidance also requires that metal detectors and portal monitors designed to detect nuclear materials meet "all applicable tests described in American Society for Testing and Materials [ASTM] guides." These tests are strict—for example, they require that in at least 50 percent of the tests, portal monitors be able to detect ten grams of unshielded weapons-grade uranium metal or one gram of unshielded weapons-grade plutonium metal, small amounts compared with what is needed for a weapon.[23]

These standards refer only to detection, though, and not to the performance needed to actually prevent thefts. Indeed, by not requiring any particular ability to respond to detection, the order provides no basis for determining whether materials control elements will simply detect thefts or will also enable prevention of thefts. Identical measures taken to improve materials control may improve security directly or may improve warning, depending on the defensive response associated with them. The high performance standards in the regulations suggest that the materials control system should provide either security or, if not, then warning, with very high confidence. If poor security allows thefts, those thefts should at least be discovered promptly.

Important limits to these regulations nonetheless still exist, since all the required assessments assume a particular "Design Basis Threat" (DBT) that specifies the expected capabilities of any group of thieves. If the DBT is incorrect, simultaneous failings of both security and warning are possible. For example, if the DBT assumes that only one insider can participate in a plot, while in reality three can, those three insiders may be able to evade access controls unnoticed with far greater consistency than suggested by the regulations. In a "system" twist, the appropriate standard against which to judge a materials control system may be lowered by a more effective broader defense. The more that the broader defense introduces risks throughout a terrorist plot, the group may be less willing to accept the additional risk—compromising operational security—that would result from using more thieves or attempting to recruit facility insiders.

Materials Accounting

Materials accounting does not directly prevent thefts; it is in place to provide warning and, indirectly, to deter theft. It can be part of a warning system in several ways. At one extreme, it provides support to materials protection and control: those elements provide initial warning that a theft has transpired, and materials accounting is then used to confirm the theft and to determine its precise details, such as the amount and type of material stolen. At the other extreme, accounting itself detects thefts by exposing unexpected losses of material. There is also important territory between these two extremes: in particular, ambiguous evidence from physical protection or materials control can be investigated through the use of materials accounting. That evidence might, for example, be a hole in a fence—accounting could be used to determine whether it had been created by thieves (successful or failed), by vandals, or perhaps by animals.

There is also a third possibility: accounting can be used for an investigation following a theft detected not by MPC&A, but by another part of the defensive system. Only one instance of a theft discovered by materials accounting has been reported: Vladimir Orlov notes (following a report in a Russian newspaper) that "in 1996 at the Tomsk Institute of Nuclear Physics of the Tomsk Polytechnic University[,] Gosatomnadzor [the Russian nuclear regulator] discovered loss of one fuel assembly with uranium of 90% enrichment containing 145 [grams] U^{235}."[24] This case is an exception, at least historically; most past nuclear material thefts appear to have been uncovered not at the site of the theft but through discovery of the material later.[25] But it is easy to overstate the relevance of this history. The pattern superficially suggests that thefts are unlikely to be discovered at their origins, but as MPC&A improves, so does the chance that it will provide early warning. Past thefts have also been relatively small, and none appear to have been made by outsiders alone, characteristics that may not be shared by all terrorist attempts to acquire material for a weapon, making the past perhaps a weak predictor of the future.

RUSSIAN FACILITY AFTER "RAPID" SECURITY UPGRADE. Understanding various security upgrades that have been made or are under way in the former Soviet Union provides insight into the state of accounting at many facilities. The more rudimentary rapid upgrades introduced earlier include "counting how many items of nuclear material are present," an accounting measure.[26] Unless paired with regular audits, though, a one-time count of nuclear material does nothing to inform facility operators of thefts—on their own, the accounting elements of a rapid security upgrade should not be expected to produce timely warning. These upgrades should, however, help produce precise warning: if another system element reveals a theft, the old count of material items can be compared with a new count to reveal the extent and nature of material losses. The old count can also be used if authorities must investigate an ambiguous indicator of a theft.

ACCOUNTING AT THE RUSSIAN MINING AND CHEMICAL COMBINE (MCC). More sophisticated comprehensive upgrades include, in addition to the measures just listed, "the installation of complete modern security and accounting systems, designed to be able to protect the facility against at least modest insider and outsider thefts."[27] Such upgrades do not automatically ensure, however, that the new systems will provide useful warning—useless security upgrades have certainly been made before. Moreover, the details and performance of accounting systems installed in comprehensive upgrades are determined facility by facility, making general conclusions about their reliability impossible. One must look instead at each upgrade individually.

The case of the Mining and Chemical Combine (MCC), or Krasnoyarsk-26, provides one such example. The MCC contains several facilities, including one for plutonium oxide storage.[28] As of 1999, the core of the facility's accounting practice was a monthly inventory, which was reconciled with the previous inventory and with an account of materials movements within the previous month.[29] Planned upgrades included a focus on translating this procedure into a near-real-time system, which accounts continuously for materials, by requiring that material movements be initiated through the accounting system, which would make material disappearances more difficult to hide.[30]

Converting from a once-a-month inventory to a near-real-time system would allow the accounting system to contribute not only to precise but also to timely warning. The new accounting system would, in theory, be able to quickly indicate unauthorized movements, though it would not be equipped to prevent them. Of course, were the system undermined from the inside, timely warning might not be provided. Precision and accuracy could also be undermined by manipulating accounting systems, but such subterfuge would require additional effort, which the thieves might judge to be not worthwhile. In all cases, the new accounting system would increase the likelihood of useful warning.

ACCOUNTING AT A PLUTONIUM-REPROCESSING FACILITY. Plutonium-reprocessing facilities are perhaps the most challenging facilities for materials accounting and thus deserve special attention. Many such plants exist, including operating facilities in the United Kingdom, Russia, France, Japan, India, and Israel.[31] Rokkasho, however, is again a useful case to study, since its safeguards have been subject to substantial public scrutiny, providing data for analysis. Moreover, because Rokkasho is a modern facility, its limitations provide insight into the limits of state-of-the-art accounting.

At any given time, operators at any large plutonium-reprocessing plant will not know exactly how much plutonium is in the facility. MIT's Marvin Miller gives perhaps the most accessible of the careful explanations of this problem, including the challenges at Rokkasho.[32] He begins by estimating that the uncertainty in measuring plutonium brought into the Rokkasho facility will be seventy-two kilograms of plutonium per year, in part by asserting that only one or two inventories are possible each year before costs become prohibitive.[33] This uncertainty means that in roughly one of every three measurements, the amount of plutonium observed inside the facility will differ from the amount of plutonium that has actually entered the facility by at least seventy-two kilograms.

This figure is normally input into the IAEA requirement for 95 percent likelihood of discovering a diversion, with 5 percent false alarm probability. In this case, that requirement means that as much as 240 kilograms of plutonium, enough for twenty-four 10-kilogram nuclear weapons, might be diverted without triggering a warning from the accounting system.[34] A detection system used to prevent nuclear terrorism can, however, probably tolerate more false positives. In addition, since simple accounting will never be able to reliably verify that plutonium has not been diverted from a large reprocessing plant, designers might be forced to settle for a secondary goal: deterring, rather than preventing, theft. Deterrence would not require as reliable accounting—but even a reduced level of reliability would be difficult to achieve. With much lower demands on the accounting system—for example, 25 percent false positives and a 50 percent chance of detection—accounting still cannot be confidently expected to warn that enough material for a bomb has been diverted.[35] Accepting 25 percent false positives gives a 30 percent chance of detecting the diversion of enough material for a bomb. Neither timely nor precise warning can be expected from infrequent accounting inspections at a large reprocessing plant, but if operators are willing to accept high levels of false positives, detection might still be useful within the context of a broader system, especially for deterring terrorist groups.

Miller also assesses the potential for near-real-time-accounting (NRTA) methods, in which materials being processed in the facility are continuously monitored. In theory, NRTA should substantially improve the ability to detect diversions or thefts.[36] If thieves steal a large amount of material all at once, NRTA provides a major advantage. If, for example, accounting could be done weekly, a sudden diversion of ten kilograms of plutonium could be detected with over 95 percent confidence and under 5 percent false positives.[37] Similarly, if inventory could be taken monthly, the uncertainty would drop to six kilograms. As a result, ten-kilogram quantities could be detected with 75 percent confidence and 25 percent false positives, with 90 percent confidence and 50 percent false positives, or with 50 percent confidence and 10 percent false positives.

Whether NRTA is effective in detecting protracted diversions, however, is far less clear. In such diversions, only small amounts of material are removed in each measurement period, but they accumulate to large quantities over time. Miller notes that "the sequential tests do not give the operator-diverter credit for diversion strategies which are more sophisticated than simply removing a fixed amount of plutonium during successive material balance periods." The statistical tests used to apply NRTA assume some model of diversion—they guess at what approaches a thief will take. If a diversion scheme not envisaged in the model is used—if the thieves try another approach—the tests almost certainly become less effective. One obvious solution is to use multiple models and multiple tests, but this approach incurs a penalty of increased false alarms. For this among other reasons, the Office of Technology Assessment judged that "there may be considerable uncertainty in the ultimate performance of NRTA methods at large plants for some time."[38]

Thus no strategic warning system can rely on an expectation that NRTA will reveal plutonium thefts at reprocessing centers. This is not to say that installing NRTA systems is not valuable—such systems can only improve detection, and they are often judged to be worth the cost. In addition, the contribution of these systems to international accountancy, not discussed here, must be assessed separately. Yet while accounting may be useful in these contexts, it cannot be expected to produce warning of materials thefts, nor can it be expected to resolve the details of thefts following their discoveries. Still, within a systems context, especially facing a failure-averse terrorist group, NRTA cannot be discounted entirely.

From MPC&A to Real Warning

Before reaction to a warning from MPC&A is possible, the right authorities (those potentially able to react effectively) must receive that warning and translate it from data about missing nuclear materials to information about possible nuclear plots, since not every nuclear plot starts with a terrorist theft, and not every theft leads to a plot. The need for the receipt and translation of a warning by authorities introduces new uncertainty and thus reduces the value of MPC&A for warning. Understanding that uncertainty is essential to optimizing any defense.

Warnings of nuclear thefts and warnings of nuclear plots differ in many ways. Nuclear material may already be in circulation, so terrorists may be able to initiate nuclear plots without first stealing material. As a result, even with the most reliable MPC&A systems, no defense can completely let its guard down simply because it has not noticed any recent thefts. In a slight variation on this theme, terrorists might separate their thefts so widely, geographically or over time, that each theft alone would be weak evidence of a plot. MPC&A systems designed to collect evidence not only of thefts themselves but also of information relevant to identifying thieves could help remedy those gaps, as could follow-up investigations after any thefts. Other simple ways of thinking could also reduce uncertainty: for example, two closely spaced thefts executed with similar tactics may be more likely to be linked than two widely separated thefts. Indeed, if facing a high-quality MPC&A system, a terrorist group may be more likely to stage its thefts in close succession or simultaneously, rather than over a long period of time: its first theft might trigger a response from authorities, and the terrorist group might want to complete all its thefts before authorities are alerted to the first one.

Even if these problems could be solved, warning would still need to reach those capable of adjusting the defense in response. MPC&A, however, provides information first to local facility operators (though some elements, such as video monitoring, might be transmitted offsite.) Upon ambiguous indication of a theft, managers might hesitate to pass information to others, fearing repercussions both in case of real theft and in case of false alarm; instead, they might attempt to resolve the ambiguity by themselves.[39] Even if they decided to pass the information upward within their bureaucracy, it still might not reach those who could best use it. Government officials, for example, might receive information and hoard it, attempting to have elements of government under their control recover the stolen materials; a similar phenomenon might occur within a federal government, as well as internationally between governments. Established protocols and relationships designed for such emergencies might lessen the chance that the information flow would be slowed, but they would provide no guarantees. International monitors might also prevent a state from entirely hiding a theft, but such monitors might also be slow to share information with other states. IAEA inspectors, for example, have proved reluctant to share detailed information about state nuclear activities, citing commercial confidentiality and the need to maintain trust between inspectors and the states being inspected.

After Detection, What?

The ability of MPC&A to generate warning varies widely depending on the types of thefts attempted by terrorist groups, the details of the relevant MPC&A systems, and the way warning of nuclear thefts is translated into warning of nuclear plots. MPC&A's utility, though, also depends on the ways in which a defense can react, since for warning to be truly useful there must be opportunity for response. To see that meaningful options can exist, a return to border controls is illuminating. Here a brief exploration points to the potential utility of using a systems framework to map out a much wider range of responses well beyond border controls, using tools such as law enforcement, intelligence, and emergency response.

Focus on the United States as an example, since we have already learned a fair amount about the potential of U.S. border security. Consider, for example, the possibility of tying container security to warning. The cost of properly inspecting containers for nuclear materials depends heavily on the cost of paying people to operate nuclear detectors; the actual equipment used costs far less.[40] For a wide range of warning systems, container security measures might be substantially improved at a fixed cost by stockpiling detection equipment but only using all of it when the threat of nuclear attack is particularly high. To be certain, this strategy would become weaker if inspections became more automated, reducing labor costs while increasing equipment costs. But labor is currently so much more expensive than detection equipment that there is room both to increase automation and to make better use of warning systems, each of which would reduce costs or improve defenses within fixed budgets.

A surged response in one part of a border security system (such as container security) might have a far more limited effect than expected if a terrorist group could quickly shift its plans for moving nuclear materials. There are at least three reasons, though, to be cautious in overestimating terrorist group flexibility. Many terrorist groups may have limited options simply because of their individual capabilities. Others may theoretically have the potential to be more flexible, but might in practice still be conservative. And even if a broad response by the defense across all entry points was technically feasible but unaffordable, a terrorist group might not be able to predict where border security would be stiffened. The group's lack of prior knowledge of how a defense will be surged would either prompt the group to prepare in advance for several ways of smuggling its material, involving more people and activities in its plot and thus compromising operational security, or force it to alter its approach in the aftermath of a theft, minimizing the size of its conspiracy but introducing delays and additional recruiting and planning activities during a time that not only border security but also law enforcement and intelligence response could be increased by the defense.

How might other elements of border security be strengthened upon warning of a successful theft? The weakest points in American border security are its long remote stretches of coast and its land border with Canada. In a high-threat situation, a defense might have several options. Small boats could be required to give advance notice of arrival. Planes and other resources might be redeployed to improve monitoring for boats that have not declared themselves. (Even if boats were able to land remotely, land-based searches could be better targeted.) Suspect vessels (or, in an extreme situation, most or all vessels) might be required to report to official points of entry to be searched before continuing to their ultimate destinations. (A similar approach might be taken with aircraft.) Intensifying controls over and monitoring of the border with Canada would be more difficult, as we have seen, given the limited utility of an aerial approach in heavily wooded areas and the limited availability of border patrol officers. Canadian police and U.S. National Guard might, however, with the right advance preparations, be quickly deployed to intensify border coverage, though this would likely only be politically possible in an extreme scenario. More reasonably, a similar approach to the one just suggested for U.S. sea security could be applied to Canadian borders, with U.S. surveillance assets supplementing Canadian equipment and personnel. In addition, it takes weeks to cross either the Atlantic or the Pacific Ocean with a relatively small and stealthy craft, a passage that makes a surged response possibly useful even if warning is substantially delayed.[41] This short list of options should not alone make anyone confident that nuclear smuggling can always or even often be stopped. But it should make clear that true systems analysis, targeted at finding ways to respond to strong warning of nuclear attack, is valuable.

Warning beyond MPC&A

We have just seen that one of the best warnings of a developing nuclear plot is the discovery that nuclear materials have been stolen. MPC&A provides one way of exploiting that insight. But interception of nuclear materials later in a plot could also be leveraged effectively with the right preparations and the right strategy.

Border Security as a Warning System

Consider one concrete and suggestive illustration. Imagine that a scheme has been developed that allows radiation detectors to spot material at a border crossing. A terrorist group imagines that by moving smaller pieces of material, it can evade the detectors. On its surface, this plan seems like a foolproof strategy. But looking at the defense as a system shows why this strategy could be far less useful than some might imagine.

Why? Subdividing material into smaller pieces makes each shipment easier to hide, but increases the number of shipments required. Increasing the number of shipments multiplies the number of opportunities both for direct detection of materials and for infiltration of a potentially expanded plot. If the interception of a single significant shipment of materials, or the discovery of a new thread in a conspiracy, can be used to tighten borders or to cue a broader law enforcement and intelligence response, this terrorist tactic begins to lose effectiveness. In many situations that effect can quickly outweigh any narrow advantage of dividing materials into smaller pieces.

Consider a simple model. A terrorist group must smuggle some quantity of nuclear material, and to reach its destination, the group must pass the material through a radiation detector. (This model is far from a universal one, but it is suggestive of many easy-to-imagine cases. The total amount of material smuggled is irrelevant in this discussion.) How do the detector and the defense react? The detector senses background radiation as well as radiation emitted by the material. The defense sets a threshold: if in an inspection the detector registers a radiation level above the threshold, the material is detected. If, despite the presence of material, it registers a radiation level below the threshold, a false negative, or failure to detect the material, occurs. If nuclear material is absent, but the background radiation still exceeds the threshold, a "background positive" is obtained. This term makes more sense than the traditional "false positive," since it can occur even when there is nuclear material present.

Subdividing material can also lead to an expanded and thus less secure conspiracy. One might imagine that a group could avoid expanding its conspiracy by using the same couriers and entry points for repeated smuggling attempts, but doing so would, at a minimum, slow down its plot. I will not model this additional vulnerability here, thus potentially underestimating the power of the defensive system.

Once nuclear material is divided into many pieces, two sets of odds change. The odds that any piece will be detected become smaller, since less nuclear material emits less radiation. More crossings, though, are required, while the odds of a background positive remain the same for each crossing. The group's total chance of being caught by a background positive thus increases, even if its material cannot be detected directly. Initially, as material is subdivided, the first effect dominates, and the terrorist group gains an advantage. But eventually the odds of a background positive catch up, and the terrorist group begins to become more vulnerable. This gradual increase naturally imposes limits on how much a group can reduce its vulnerability through this type of strategy.[42]

Figure 5.1 shows crudely how the probability of detection varies as material is subdivided in this caricatured model. In all cases in Figure 5.1, the background positive rate is set at 10 percent; the probability of detecting the undivided material shipment varies between 10 and 90 percent. The graph, perhaps surprisingly, shows that a terrorist group cannot reduce its detection probability at a portal by more than 25 percent by subdividing its material. If the rate of background positives is substantially lower, as it likely must be in some important places such as truck crossings, where too many follow-up inspections would slow down traffic unacceptably, this effect will be weaker. Consider the case where the background positive rate is 1 percent rather than 10 percent, as shown in Figure 5.2. Before, if a terrorist group began with a 90 percent probability of being detected, it could re-

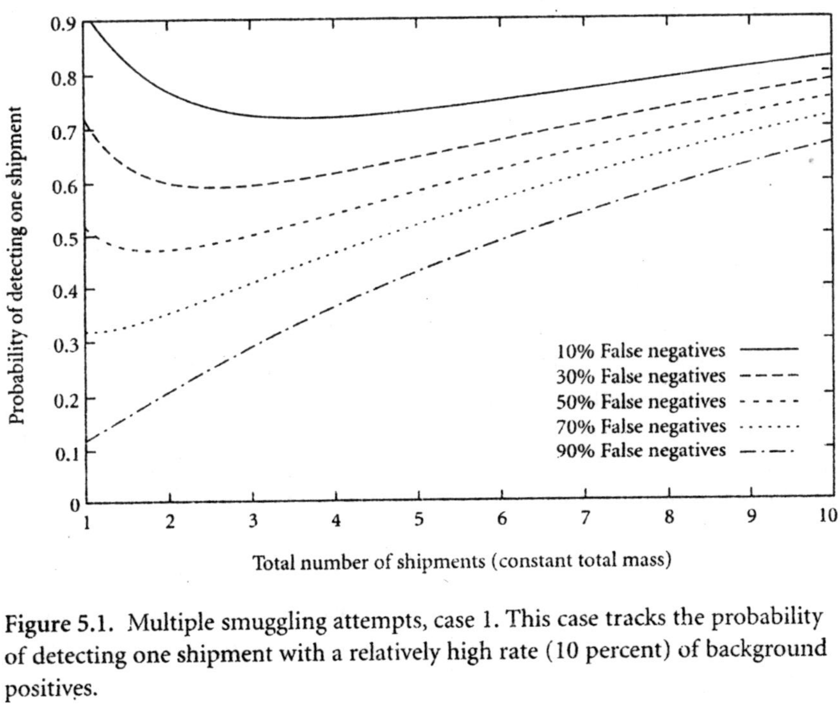

Figure 5.1. Multiple smuggling attempts, case 1. This case tracks the probability of detecting one shipment with a relatively high rate (10 percent) of background positives.

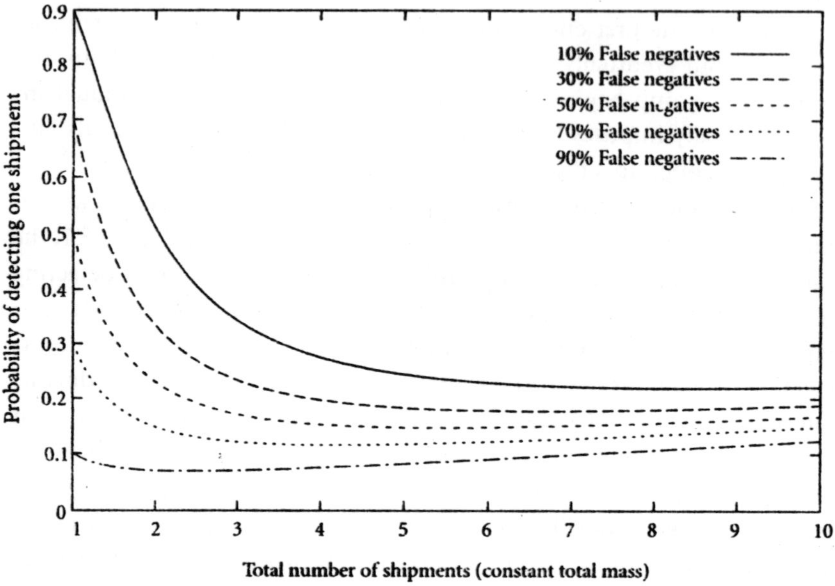

Figure 5.2. Multiple smuggling attempts, case 2. This case tracks the probability of detecting one shipment with a relatively low rate (1 percent) of background positives.

duce that at most to 75 percent by subdividing its material. Now, for the same initial scenario, it can potentially reduce its chances of detection to 22 percent, substantially lower, though far from negligible in a systems context.

This analysis implicitly assumes that given a single interception, some combination of tightening the border and broader law enforcement efforts will ensure that the terrorist plot is defeated—that is, it assumes a very effectively integrated defensive system. What if the defense is less effective?

Imagine that a single interception, rather than leading to the end of a terrorist plot, does nothing more than capture the intercepted material. To fully succeed in its plot, following a single detection, a terrorist group would need to begin with extra nuclear material. Because nuclear material is normally difficult to obtain, this requirement could be onerous. Consider a case in which a terrorist group must smuggle fifty kilograms of weapons-grade uranium, and in which it faces a 50 percent chance of detection if it moves the material in one shipment. Assume that the defense also chooses to accept a background positive rate of 5 percent. Shipping five twelve-kilogram pieces—any four of which are roughly sufficient to meet the terrorists' maximum goals—yields a 15 percent chance of two detections (one detection would not defeat this plot), the minimum probability of defeat achievable with this strategy. (Two losses would not, however, immediately end a terrorist plot, since a lower-yield or more complex weapon might still be built with the remaining material.) To employ this strategy, the terrorist group will still need to acquire at least an extra twelve kilograms of weapons-grade uranium. Doing so will, however, substantially reduce its vulnerability to later detection.

Reality is likely to be somewhere between the last two cases. Imagine that law enforcement and stepped-up border security attempt to terminate a terrorist plot following a significant interception, but assume that they will only have a 75 percent chance of terminating the plot. If the background positive rate is 5 percent and the probability of detecting a single fifty-kilogram shipment is 50 percent, the group can reduce its probability of defeat to at best 35 percent, a surprisingly high number.[43] As in the previous example, a lower rate of background positives makes the strategy more attractive to a terrorist group. If the group faces a background positive rate of only 1 percent, it can reduce its probability of defeat to just over 20 percent. These odds are certainly not the stuff of a perfect defense, but they are potentially valuable within a broader system.

Subdividing material may provide advantages to the smuggler beyond a simple reduction in radioactive signal. In particular, by reducing material bulk, the group might be able to fit more shielding within a given space and weight limit, reducing the radioactive signal further. In any scenario where radiography is effective in detecting shielding, though, more space for shielding will not be worth much, neutralizing this potential advantage. High enough rates of background positives would similarly undermine any benefit arising from new shielding.

A numerical example helps illuminate what happens when radiography and background positives do not impose significant constraints. Imagine that splitting a piece of nuclear material in half makes room for enough shielding to reduce radioactive emissions tenfold. (This would require about three or more centimeters of lead for a typical case involving gamma ray detection.)[44] Then this terrorist strategy can reduce the likelihood of detection by at most 70 percent, assuming that the initial detection probability is in the range of 10 to 90 percent. This reduction is substantial, but it still keeps the detection probability well above zero. Such scenarios are probably not important in the case of large containers, since the amount of space gained for shielding is very small compared with the size of the container. In contrast, they may be of more concern for hand-carried or vehicle-transported material, where space and weight constraints are tighter and where radiography is more difficult to use. In the latter cases, though, the added number of conspirators adds a much more significant vulnerability, since each terrorist may be directly detected at a border crossing without nuclear material first being detected. Container shipping is much more anonymous.

Overall, if the defense can capitalize on the capture of nuclear material, a single interdiction can have a far greater effect than its immediate impact would suggest. The possible gains from such a detection provide more evidence that an integrated system can be more effective than one composed of disjointed pieces. They also indicate the value of looking for further synergies of this sort.

Deliberate Warning

Terrorists might also provide warning intentionally, declaring that they have a nuclear weapon and threatening to detonate it unless their demands are met.[45] This was the prevailing theoretical model for nuclear terrorism before the September 11, 2001, terrorist attacks shifted attention to terrorist groups that, it was believed, sought to kill rather than to extort concessions.[46] Like the other forms of warning just explored, even deliberate warning is ambiguous. A terrorist group might be bluffing. It may be mistaken in assessing its own capabilities, believing that it has developed a working weapon from stolen materials or cracked the codes on a complete bomb when it in fact has a device that will not work. Yet the group also might be telling the truth.

The United States in particular has long experience dealing with nuclear threats and has established procedures for vetting them. Every claim faced so far has been a hoax, though, and none have forced the U.S. government into concessions or even into major public reactions. But if a terrorist group genuinely had a nuclear weapon, could it realistically use it to extort significant concessions?

The answer depends on the risks that governments are willing to take. Past patterns suggest that the burden of proof placed on a terrorist group would be high, yet substantiating a threat without providing information that could be used to defeat it would, while possible, be challenging. A terrorist group would almost certainly need to show that it had acquired appropriate nuclear materials, which reinforces the value of MPC&A systems that provide effective warning, since those systems might be used to audit terrorist claims (and to provide leads for tracking down the missing material). Most assume the group would have to provide a material sample—yet forensic techniques might be used to trace that sample to its origin, providing even more information to those attempting to track the remaining material down. The group might also need to provide evidence that it had the technical capabilities to build a bomb or operate a stolen weapon, something that might be done by identifying missing individuals with the appropriate technical skills. Doing that, though, would again provide new clues to help locate the stolen material or weapon. None of this comes close to guaranteeing that a plot would be defeated, but it adds additional uncertainty to terrorist calculations.

A terrorist group might also expose itself through the demands it makes. If a group simply demanded money or other goods, it would run great risks when it attempted to collect its payment. (An early nuclear hoax was discovered to be a fraud when no one showed up to collect the ransom.)[47] A group might, alternatively, demand broad concessions, such as military withdrawals or other substantial political actions, that would not require it to interact closely with the government it was threatening. Yet it would likely take a long time for any government to deliver on such concessions, providing an extended opportunity to penetrate and defeat the nuclear plot. And some demands, such as permanent withdrawal from designated territories, could only be enforced by indefinite possession of nuclear weapons or indefinite perpetration of a hoax, neither of which would be easy. This all adds to the uncertainty involved for any terrorist group contemplating using stolen nuclear materials for extortion, beyond the difficulties involved in acquiring and delivering a nuclear weapon in the first place.

Stepping Back to the Broader System

Two basic themes connecting materials protection, control, and accounting to the broader defensive system have emerged over the last two chapters. Depending on how MPC&A performs in securing nuclear materials—depending on what types of materials it fails to secure—a broader defense against a subsequent terrorist plot may be more effective than one might expect from looking only at the worst case. And depending on how MPC&A performs as a warning system—depending on the warning it provides when security fails—subsequent defense against an ensuing terrorist plot can become more effective in response to that warning. Because both these effects have their roots in the same MPC&A systems, it is natural to ask whether these two sets complement or reinforce each other. (They cannot cancel each other, since both sets of effects strengthen the defense.)

If states deliberately calibrate their security approaches according to the dangers posed by particular nuclear materials (as is typically the case), materials security will be more effective, all else being equal, for those materials that enable more effective terrorist plots. This approach has clear implications for warning. If materials security is bolstered by improving physical protection, greater force may be needed for an outsider theft, making any attack more conspicuous and increasing the likelihood of timely warning. Larger attacks would also be more difficult to organize, and thus more likely to fail on their own.[48] If security is improved by strengthening materials control, then the same systems that would detect thefts in progress, in the hopes that those thefts could then be stopped, would also provide warning if those thefts succeeded. And if rather than improving security directly, accounting was enhanced (to deter potential thefts), warning would automatically improve. Here the two types of synergies between MPC&A and the broader defensive system reinforce each other.

Different materials also lend themselves differently to surreptitious theft. The same materials characteristics that make more effective physical protection and materials control possible often make broader defense more effective too. Bulkier materials are harder to hide from law enforcement and border security and are also harder for insider thieves to remove inconspicuously from nuclear facilities. Heavier materials are more difficult to transport, and are also harder for any fixed team of thieves to remove from a facility without special equipment. Materials that emit more intense radiation are easier for defenses to detect, and for the same reason, they are more easily detected by portal monitors at nuclear facilities. To be sure, this pattern, while common, is not universal. The relative ease of converting various materials into weapons, the weight and bulk of resulting weapons, and the expected yield of a weapon made from a given quantity of material are relevant to the broader defense but irrelevant to the effectiveness of MPC&A.

The main pattern, where the synergies studied so far reinforce each other, extends to materials accounting. Thefts of larger quantities of materials make terrorist plots more effective and are also more likely to be detected by an accounting system. The use of metal, rather than powder, generally makes a terrorist plot more likely to succeed and more likely to achieve a high yield, but metal lends itself more easily to effective accounting—pieces of metal are easily counted, and thus accounted for, but measuring small losses of powder is more difficult. One exception is important: plutonium, while in processing, is harder to account for than uranium, and thus less likely to generate warning upon theft—yet plutonium is also less useful to a terrorist group.

In still other cases, the nature of the material stolen is of only marginal importance to the issue of warning. If a theft is executed simply through brute force, warning will result regardless of the materials targeted. If a theft succeeds by undermining security from the inside, the difficulty of the terrorists' main hurdle in undermining both security and warning—organizing the appropriate group of insiders—will not depend principally on the material in question.

This discussion of warning must be read with caution. The possibility of undetected thefts or thefts detected late, combined with the costs of responding to false alarms, will constrain the extent to which any defense can exploit warning. The bottom line, though, is becoming familiar. As controls over materials (and other sources of warning) improve, many tools for strengthening the broader system become more useful as well. More synergies that do not include MPC&A might also exist. But if potential synergies are ignored at the planning stage, those opportunities might never be realized.

— 6 —

A Wider Universe of Nuclear Plots and Defenses

I have focused so far on terrorist plots involving stolen nuclear materials and improvised nuclear devices, but the guiding principles laid out at the start of this book can be applied to the rest of nuclear terrorism as well. My goal in this brief and selective tour through that territory is to show how useful and interesting further analysis might be and to generate new questions, reinforcing our framework for thinking about nuclear terrorism.

Nuclear Weapons

If a terrorist group acquired a complete nuclear weapon rather than nuclear materials, it might gain two advantages. Most obviously, it would have a whole weapon, which could in principle be detonated as-is, rather than just one part of a bomb that would still need to be built. The weapon might also be much more powerful than one built by a terrorist group—advanced state arsenals contain weapons with explosive powers measured in megatons, hundreds of times larger than the most powerful weapons that terrorists might build.[1] Possession of such a weapon could allow terrorists to inflict more death and destruction, or allow them to detonate their bomb from a more remote location while still killing hundreds of thousands. And while many whole weapons would be heavy, some can be very light—for example, one U.S. warhead "had a weight of 114–135 kg, a diameter of 0.40m, and a length of 0.94m."[2]

Yet just as materials other than pure weapons-grade uranium metal introduce a mix of opportunities and challenges for would-be nuclear terrorists, the advantages of acquiring a whole weapon would often come at a price. Although a stolen weapon might be complete in a strict sense, it might also have sophisticated security measures that a terrorist group would find difficult to overcome. Analysts' attention has focused on permissive action links (PALs), systems that protect most nuclear weapons from unauthorized use by requiring that secret security codes be entered before a weapon can be detonated.[3] Charles Ferguson and William Potter point out that so-called SAFF (Safing, Arming, Fusing, and Firing) procedures may pose another important barrier for terrorists seeking to use stolen weapons, writing that "the arming sequence for a warhead may require changes in altitude, acceleration, or other parameters verified by sensors built into the weapon, designed to ensure that the warhead can be used only according to a specific mission profile."[4] Might a terrorist group work around these measures? This question can only be answered with access to detailed information about safety mechanisms, something that for good reason is not public. But the amounts of money invested in these security measures, and the reliance placed upon them, suggest that governments believe that they provide substantial barriers to use. At a minimum, it is hard to see how a terrorist group could be confident of success absent, at a minimum, significant insider cooperation. Even if such assistance was potentially available, it would add complications to a terrorist plot—no sensible security system would entrust the same individuals with providing security over weapons and with holding the secrets that make those weapons work.

A group might instead choose to extract the nuclear explosive material from a stolen weapon. But it might not find enough material for it to build its own bomb—modern weapons are far more sophisticated than earlier ones, permitting them to use less nuclear material than a group making a crude bomb would need.[5] Moreover, while many weapons in state arsenals are more powerful than the most effective terrorist-built weapons, others are less powerful than those bombs. U.S. nuclear weapons have had explosive yields ranging from tons to megatons, and Russian nuclear weapons likely cover a similar range.[6] In particular, battlefield nuclear weapons, which are probably less secure than warheads for missiles, likely have the lowest yields.[7]

States also naturally provide greater security over complete weapons than they do over nuclear materials—in particular, all weapons are in military rather than civilian custody, unlike some nuclear materials. Weapons thefts are also easier to identify—while nuclear material may be difficult to count or measure and might in theory be removed from a facility in many small, hard-to-spot batches, whole weapons are more easily accounted for and cannot be removed in pieces.

Early-generation weapons designed to be delivered by missile—those most likely to be found in states with immature security systems, as well in some states, like Pakistan, that might become unstable—will likely weigh one ton or more.[8] For example, the Chinese warhead whose design was likely exported to Pakistan weighed roughly 1.3 tons.[9] The first American gun-type nuclear weapon, Little Boy, weighed 4 tons, while South Africa's first bomb, a major improvement, weighed roughly a ton.[10] If terrorist groups are restricted in what they are able to acquire, either because they want to seize an opportunity that presents itself or because they face significant defenses, they may become saddled with difficult-to-handle weapons.

Unable to tailor the details of their weapons, terrorists with whole weapons might also have difficulty hiding them from radiation detectors. Steve Fetter and his colleagues, for example, have sharply contrasted the radiation emissions and detectability of nuclear cruise missiles that use tungsten tampers and those that use depleted uranium tampers: depleted uranium tampers greatly increase the ease of detection and the challenges involved in shielding.[11] An opportunistic terrorist group may not have the luxury of choosing which type to acquire.

States have also used depleted or natural uranium in thermonuclear weapons in order to boost their yields.[12] That uranium could contribute to strong high-energy radiation signatures. Shielding a large weapon would also require far heavier material than shielding the nuclear material needed to make it. For example, a fifteen-centimeter-thick shield placed around a weapon fifty centimeters in radius would weigh twenty times more than one placed around a fissile material core that was five centimeters in radius.[13]

Many nuclear weapons also use plutonium rather than (only) uranium, presenting opportunities for neutron detection. And most nuclear weapons incorporate explosives, presenting another detection opportunity. Each of these variations is only suggestive—coupled with intelligence on weapons stockpiles, precise calculations may become possible regarding what weapons and weapon characteristics a terrorist group might deal with, leading to greater insights into detection possibilities.

The constraints that terrorist groups that acquire early-generation nuclear weapons may face suggest that another major set of policy tools could be influential, in a novel way, in combating nuclear terrorism. As central pieces of any strategy for preventing nuclear terrorism, many analysts and policymakers have rightly focused on measures that prevent new states from acquiring nuclear weapons. Yet this brief review suggests that measures aimed at constraining certain qualitative developments in state arsenals may also be valuable, if they prevent states from miniaturizing their weapons or from moving to designs that involve less heavy material, either of which would make weapons stolen from their arsenals more valuable to terrorists.

Although whole weapons carry a mix of advantages and disadvantages compared with improvised nuclear devices, plots involving them would also have many properties in common with plots that begin with only nuclear explosive materials. Whole weapons would place similar demands on operational, financial, and, perhaps to a lesser extent, technical expertise. Most important, just as in the case of stolen nuclear materials, the terrorists' need to balance effectiveness and operational security would be unavoidable.

Deterring Transfers

Theft is not the only way to acquire nuclear weapons or materials—states or their senior officials might deliberately transfer nuclear weapons or materials to terrorist groups. Different defensive tools might be brought to bear here—most obviously, traditional and familiar diplomatic tools aimed at dissuading states and terrorist groups from cooperating would become important.[14] In recent years, analysts and policymakers have also begun to pay attention to another potentially powerful nuclear-specific tool: the ability to attribute nuclear attacks to those states where nuclear materials originate. By threatening states with retaliation should a nuclear terrorist attack be traced back to them, it may be possible to deter them from transferring nuclear materials in the first place.[15]

Nuclear forensics—the science and art of linking nuclear materials to their sources—has been developed to enable better law enforcement and nuclear safeguards. In the first case, the goal is to trace the flow of nuclear material from its original source to its final recipient in order to prosecute intermediaries and rectify security gaps. In the second case, analysts have been interested in understanding proliferation pathways and in determining the truth of state claims about the origins of their nuclear materials.[16] Techniques range from those drawn from traditional forensics, such as fingerprinting individuals, to measures that are more nuclear specific, such as determining the mix of plutonium and uranium isotopes in nuclear material as well as microscopic material properties.[17] Were forensics applied in the case of whole nuclear weapons, the designs of those weapons would also provide clues about their origins.

It is easier to identify nuclear weapons or materials, of course, if they are captured before a nuclear attack, which would wipe out many clues, like fingerprints, and obscure others, like the microscopic properties of the nuclear materials involved and the design of the terrorist weapon.[18] But much can still be learned about a terrorist weapon even after it is detonated. Comprehensive descriptions of the process by which (though not all the fine details of how) the original details of a nuclear weapon could be inferred following its detonation have been published by several former government officials and advisors.[19] They show that many details, including isotopic composition of weapons materials, weapon design, and trace contaminants in weapons material, might be reconstructed from weapon debris. Initial assessments of isotopic compositions and weapon designs could be made within hours, with proper preparation. More detailed characterizations, including assessments of trace-element impurities, could be completed within days.

Although the methods used to perform attribution analyses are complex (and partly unknown beyond classified circles), some basic understanding is useful, given how unintuitive these capabilities might seem. Simple studies show that even without releasing sensitive details of U.S. or other attribution capabilities, it should be relatively straightforward to convince other states that a nuclear detonation will not necessarily hide the details of their materials or bombs.

Consider a specific example that many worry about: the use of a gun-type weapon incorporating weapons-grade uranium. (Most states use implosion weapons in their own arsenal, but subversive officials might want to hide their "fingerprints" by not using their standard designs.) During detonation, atoms of uranium change primarily by fission or by capturing neutrons.[20] The details of this process imply that, for this weapon (and for most weapons studied in this book), roughly 99 percent or more of the original material is preserved in the postdetonation debris.

The amounts of different isotopes present will not each be reduced by the same fraction.[21] For gun-type or powder-based weapons, though, ratios of the amounts of different isotopes—for example, the ratio of U^{235} to

U^{238}—will not change by more than about 5 percent between pre- and postdetonation.[22] (For plutonium, the change would be no more than about 1 percent.) This simple approach leads to less promising results for more sophisticated weapons, as terrorists might obtain if a state provided a complete implosion weapon, or if terrorists developed an implosion weapon themselves.[23] Yet states have developed more sophisticated methods to infer the initial composition of any nuclear weapon from its debris, capabilities that may have substantially greater potential against more sophisticated weapons, as several authoritative publications suggest.[24]

Once the original isotopic composition has been estimated, it must still be matched to its origin. This attribution poses the greatest challenge. Because particular reactor types and particular nuclear fuels produce plutonium with distinct isotopic details, creating a "fingerprint" is relatively straightforward for many cases involving plutonium. Indeed several unclassified studies have shown how different reactors and reactor histories produce different fingerprints, though more could be learned from direct access to materials in suspect states, which might be obtained through international inspections or through covert intelligence action.[25] More careful study of how material details can be inferred from reactor histories, or at least more public access to careful study, would still be useful. And while more has likely been done within classified circles than in unclassified studies, publicly demonstrated attribution capabilities are more likely to deter potential state sponsors than are secret capabilities that those states know little about.

Predicting differences in the isotopic details of uranium is more difficult, since most states (with the notable exceptions of the United States and France) depend (or have depended in the past) on the same technology—gas centrifuge enrichment—to produce weapons-grade uranium.[26] The limits of techniques similar to those available for identifying sources of plutonium—for example, distinguishing isotopic signatures on the basis of operating histories—is poorly understood, at least at the public level. Direct knowledge of the isotopic composition of a state's materials may be necessary for developing a fingerprint. In some cases, this information might be obtained through routine IAEA inspections, but in others that might be impossible, either because the site where the materials originate is not subject to IAEA inspections or because the material had been covertly produced. One simple exception is the distinction between reprocessed, re-enriched uranium, which contains U^{232}, and uranium that has never been reprocessed, which does not. The isotopic composition of re-enriched uranium may also provide clues regarding the type of reactor where it was irradiated, allowing states to leverage their understanding of differences between plutonium production reactors. Although these tools alone are unlikely to identify the origin of uranium, they might be effective in combination with other, more traditional, forensic tools.

In both the plutonium and the uranium cases, a state would at a minimum consider altering its nuclear materials before transferring them, in order to make them harder to trace. Mixing different samples of nuclear explosive material to produce another sample with unfamiliar characteristics is one possible method of alteration. The ease with which such mixing could be done—and hence its attractiveness as a countermeasure—would vary from case to case. States holding fairly uniform stocks of nuclear explosive material would only be able to create combinations that were again similar to each other and to the original stock. This limitation would impose a greater constraint on younger nuclear programs, which may be less likely to have used different technologies or to have many different production histories, and hence may be less likely to have a wide variety of materials. (An exception might arise if a new nuclear state experimented extensively with technical alternatives.) Fortunately, those states, such as North Korea, or perhaps a future Iran, are also more likely to be deliberate sources of terrorist material. Research in classified circles could shed important light on the limits to manipulation (and may already have done so).

States may be able to address shortfalls in their ability to attribute attacks in any of several ways. In the aftermath of a nuclear attack that killed tens or hundreds of thousands, political dynamics would change. Both nuclear and non-nuclear evidence, while perhaps not conclusive, might narrow down the set of potential state sources for the material used. The international community, a limited coalition, or even an individual state could then attempt to coerce suspect states into submitting to intrusive inspections. There are precedents for such action, most notably the inspections in Iraq between 2002 and 2003; more aggressive steps, such as inspections forced by military action, might also be considered, though the robustness of the line between such action and forcible regime change is questionable.[27]

Another related point of leverage would be states' interest in exonerating themselves, which might lead many to come forth with information after an attack that they would not otherwise provide. The desire for exoneration might also be used in advance of any theft or attack: states could tag their own materials so that they could determine whether their own materials had been used in an attack.[28] Although many states could not be trusted to reliably tag their materials, the ability to eliminate some states as possible sources would still help focus the search for the origins of any nuclear material.

The combined evidence suggests that attribution can be effective. More sophisticated analyses, including those based on classified or proprietary data, can substantially improve the assessment of attribution given here.

Attribution technology must still be matched to a broader strategy if it is to deter nuclear transfers effectively. This may be quite challenging. For concreteness, focus on American strategy; a similar analysis would work for any state. What should the United States threaten to do if the material used in a nuclear attack can be traced back to a specific state? I will not propose a precise strategy here, but rather will outline some of the many questions that should be thought through in crafting one.

Some have argued that the United States should threaten to retaliate against any state that leaks nuclear materials, whether deliberately or inadvertently. These analysts imagine that the threat will deter deliberate transfers and will compel states to secure their weapons and materials against inadvertent leakage.[29] There are severe problems, however, with this approach. A threat to retaliate against Moscow for the inadvertent loss of nuclear weapons or materials has no credibility—could anyone believe that the United States would attack Russia in any circumstance? The thought of threatening similar retaliation against Pakistan, a frontline partner of the United States and a nuclear-armed nation, strains credulity as well. Meanwhile, delivering either threat would hurt diplomatic relations, making it even more difficult for any of the states to cooperate on nuclear security than it is now. Rather than making meaningless threats, it makes more sense to focus on cooperating with states like Russia and Pakistan, while preparing to exploit the political opportunity to massively step up those efforts if a leak of nuclear weapons or materials is discovered.[30]

Finding the right approach to a state like North Korea is in some ways more straightforward, but in others more difficult. North Korea has poor relations with most of the world already, does not cooperate in securing its nuclear weapons and materials, and cannot retaliate against the United States in the same ways that Russia, or even Pakistan, can. Threatening to retaliate against North Korea should materials used in a nuclear attack be traced back to it would thus be relatively cost-free. It therefore makes sense to issue such a threat, as U.S. president George W. Bush did (albeit vaguely) in October 2006, asserting that "the transfer of nuclear weapons or material by North Korea to states or non-state entities would be considered a grave threat to the United States, and we would hold North Korea fully accountable for the consequences of such action."

To deter effectively, though, threats must not only be made, but be credible. In deterring North Korea, two problems arise. Would the United States be willing to retaliate if it was not completely confident that a transfer was intentional? This problem would almost certainly present itself, as at least some ambiguity would be unavoidable. And even if the United States made no distinction in its policy between an intentional and an inadvertent transfer, would it itself be deterred from action by the prospect of North Korean retaliation? Neither answer would need to be unequivocal for deterrence to be effective—North Korea would only need to believe that it was not worth testing whether the United States would make good on its threats—but uncertainty could still be problematic.

To think through these problems, it is useful to divide possible responses into two categories. The United States could take punitive action (not necessarily with nuclear weapons) against North Korea. Alternatively, it could take military action to directly prevent further transfers of weapons or materials, most likely overthrowing the North Korean regime.

Simple punitive action would have one advantage over regime change: if the United States followed through with it, the North Korean leadership would still be left with something to lose. By holding out the threat of even greater consequences, the United States might, following a first nuclear terrorist attack, be able to deter North Korea from future nuclear transfers (or compel it to lock down its weapons and materials). If, in contrast, the United States clearly intended to overthrow the North Korean regime, that regime would have little to lose by lashing out, potentially killing hundreds of thousands in South Korea and Japan. It would be essentially impossible to quickly destroy North Korea's ability to respond.[31] In this sense, a threat of simple but restrained retaliation is the most credible.

Yet the threat of regime change is, in another dimension, more believable. If the United States were to retaliate punitively against North Korea, what would it hit? Threatening to retaliate against the North Korean people would probably be ineffective in deterring the North Korean leadership, which does not appear to care much about its citizens. It would also, arguably, be immoral, leading North Korea to believe that the U.S. public would not countenance it. Threatening to retaliate against military and economic installations would probably be more effective since such a threat would be more believable, but it is difficult to know whether it would substantially affect North Korean decision making. In contrast, the prospect of regime change would, if credible, certainly deter North Korean leaders. Its credibility would be boosted by the fact that regime change would allow the world to directly secure North Korean nuclear assets (making it an appropriate response even for inadvertent leaks) and to assist, rather than to harm, the North Korean people.

A final twist further complicates planning: the United States need not necessarily follow through with its threats. It could, for example, threaten regime change, but in the aftermath of what it believed was an unauthorized transfer, it might decide that simple punishment, combined with a demand that North Korea secure its arsenal, would be more prudent. Or it could threaten simple punishment, but, following what it believed to be an intentional transfer, decide that regime change was the only responsible course.

As strategists and diplomats develop a deterrence policy, they should think through all these questions and possibilities. Ultimately, states have three options: they can threaten to punish North Korea for any attacks; they can threaten regime change in response to any attacks; or they can leave their threats more ambiguous. Even the last choice, though, should be deliberate, rather than the result of negligence by strategists.

When Nuclear States Collapse

When states oppose all nuclear terrorism, they can be helped in strengthening their controls over nuclear materials and weapons. States that might potentially support nuclear terrorism can, at least in part, be dealt with through deterrence. But what happens when a state collapses outright—when it ceases to exist? (This question is not directed at cases where central control persists despite a radical change in governance, or when a state simply fractures, both of which characterized the collapse of the Soviet Union.) This scenario is one that analysts and policymakers often fret about publicly, although unclassified analyses of possible responses are few.[32]

The complete collapse of a nuclear state could offer terrorists an opportunity to acquire nuclear weapons or materials with relative ease and potentially without being noticed. Of course, state collapse itself would be easy to see—it is the nuclear dimension that would be far more difficult to monitor. In the face of this possibility, defensive options fall into three categories. States may attempt to prevent the collapse of others. They may take measures in cooperation with vulnerable states that would decrease the nuclear-related impact of any state collapse. And they might make independent preparations for dealing with the collapse of weak nuclear-armed states.

Strategies for preventing state failure have been widely discussed and are largely independent of whether the state concerned holds nuclear assets.[33] Analysis of this challenge is thus best left largely to strategists focused on non-nuclear issues. (Better understanding of how to prevent state failure in general would be valuable both here and for cases where state collapse could provide terrorist sanctuary.) Pakistan and North Korea are the most obvious nuclear-armed candidates for collapse, though states with nuclear materials, not just those with nuclear arms, also deserve attention.

The collapse of a nuclear state can be prevented in two ways—by ensuring that no nuclear state collapses, and by ensuring that no state that might collapse has nuclear materials or weapons. The second challenge is the target of nonproliferation and denuclearization, the latter of which might still be possible with North Korea (though this is admittedly a remote possibility). Although North Korea already has nuclear arms, it might, in theory, be disarmed through a mix of incentives and threats. Strategies to disarm North Korea have been widely discussed, though pessimism predominates.[34] No similar hopes exist for disarming Pakistan.[35]

Each case presents a similar paradox. Disarming North Korea may require pressure, but that pressure may induce state collapse rather than concessions. Those who believe that North Korea can be made to give up its nuclear arms will thus focus on disarmament rather than on preventing collapse. Those who are less optimistic divide into two camps. Some believe that North Korean collapse, even if not accompanied by disarmament, would be desirable.[36] Others view collapse less positively: worried that pressure would induce undesirable collapse, while at the same time concerned that it would not bring about disarmament, they are inclined to counsel against applying too much pressure on the North Korean regime.[37] This dimension of defense against nuclear terrorism deserves more attention.

Pakistan, while unlikely to come under pressure to disarm, will still be pushed to improve its nuclear security.[38] Here we again see a tension between strengthening current controls over nuclear weapons and preventing a much worse future situation. The case of A. Q. Khan, who ran Pakistan's sales of nuclear technologies, is illuminating. Stronger Pakistani action against Khan and his associates after they were exposed, and greater access to Khan by foreign intelligence agencies, would likely help the world improve controls over nuclear materials and weapons, including in Pakistan.[39] At the same time, Pakistan has reasonably protested that too much action against Khan, a national hero, could destabilize its government and exacerbate terrorism more generally.[40] This type of tension is unavoidable.

Cooperative steps might also be taken in advance of state collapse that would enable a more effective response if the worst happened.[41] But several major barriers impede the available options. Few leaders are willing to acknowledge that their states are vulnerable to collapse—not only might they judge that such steps would undermine them politically, but they might fear that sending signals of weakness would, perversely, make collapse even more likely. Leaders of insecure states also tend to be even more wary than others about interference, even if cooperative, in their nuclear affairs (though this problem may be less pronounced for states with civil nuclear material stockpiles but without nuclear weapons). Those states where dangers are most acute, such as North Korea, often will not have cooperative relationships with states that might provide appropriate assistance, such as the United States (though North Korea might work with China). States that might provide assistance will fear that cooperating with unstable nuclear states will be seen as legitimizing their arsenals and undermining nonproliferation efforts.[42] As a result, cooperation with India, for example, is more likely than cooperation with Pakistan, which in turn is far more likely than cooperation with North Korea.

That said, what can be done? These issues require new and careful thinking, but a few basic ideas are suggestive of the possibilities. Assistance in screening security personnel can increase the odds that even after state collapse, nuclear guardians will continue to protect nuclear assets; reliable guards will also help other states identify and secure nuclear materials or weapons so that terrorist or criminal groups cannot move in.[43] In nuclear-armed states, cooperation in developing systems such as permissive action links would contribute to postcollapse security. Cooperative efforts might also encourage states at risk to develop or improve systems that secure weapons components rather than complete weapons, as has been suggested for Pakistan.[44] Other, far more sensitive tools might be contemplated as well. For example, a state such as Pakistan might be persuaded to outfit its nuclear weapons with GPS locators that transmit encrypted position information. In the immediate aftermath of state collapse, deposed leaders might be able to provide decryption information to a second, trusted state. Choosing to do this would, without doubt, be difficult, not least because a state might worry that its encryption might be broken by an adversary, allowing that adversary to locate parts of its arsenal and to mount a preemptive strike. Nonetheless, this example suggests the broad range of possibilities that might be examined.

Regardless of what cooperative steps might be taken, states would be imprudent not to prepare for, or at least explore options for, managing the collapse of a nuclear-armed state with a vulnerable arsenal. There have been occasional reports of planning for such cases, most notably for a Pakistani collapse, though the credibility of these reports has been disputed.[45] But overall relatively little public study has been devoted to such cases, though more has likely taken place (and should take place) within military circles. Open study is essential, however, if policymakers and the public are to help decide how much weight this part of the defensive system should be given. The most important exception to the lack of analysis is a brief working paper by Michael O'Hanlon, focused on the Pakistani and North Korean cases, whose conclusions provide useful insight and a starting point for more in-depth study.[46] O'Hanlon begins with the pessimistic yet reasonable observation that outside forces are unlikely to know the locations of vulnerable weapons, thus making the seizure of weapons in the aftermath of a collapse very difficult. He therefore focuses on the much broader challenge of stabilizing a nuclear-armed state, following collapse, in order to provide more manageable territory within which to search for loose weapons or materials. This goal drives him toward recommendations for rapidly deployable stabilization forces, which would also contribute to objectives well beyond the immediate case.

This assessment is pessimistic, and other opportunities for partially managing nuclear collapse may be found. In Pakistan in particular, facilities that store nuclear materials would likely be much easier to locate than actual weapons, and hence could be useful targets for rapid security operations. Such operations would still leave holes, but could be valuable in that terrorist groups are, just like outside forces, likely to know much more about the locations of fixed facilities than about where to find actual weapons. It would also let states use many of the defenses discussed earlier in this book. (In states with only nuclear materials in known facilities, but with no nuclear weapons, such operations could be even more valuable.) In North Korea, terrorists are extraordinarily unlikely to acquire weapons directly, since no terrorist groups operate within North Korea, making measures aimed at disrupting nuclear sales particularly relevant and important.

In both cases, and particularly in North Korea, it may be possible, at least with appropriate preparation, to impose a partial quarantine for a limited period, buying time for stabilization operations and for locating nuclear weapons and materials. Both sea and land borders would need to be secured. In both cases, preventing the leakage of nuclear materials by sea would be the easier task—ships could be stopped offshore, inspected, and turned back if there was any suspicion of nuclear smuggling. In both the North Korean and the Pakistani examples, access to offshore areas would be straightforward.[47] Specialized radiation detection systems might be developed for such circumstances—for example, in the aftermath of the collapse of a nuclear-armed state, inspections with powerful active interrogation systems that might pose substantial radiation hazards would become far more acceptable, at least to the state conducting inspections. Such technologies would have to be developed in advance with this special scenario in mind.

Land borders are more challenging. North Korean land borders are primarily with China and South Korea (in addition to a very short border with Russia), both of which have effective armies that might provide security, though Chinese worries about refugee flows following a North Korean collapse suggest that their ability to seal the northern border is quite limited. (They may, however, be more able to prevent people, including those potentially seeking nuclear materials, from entering, rather than leaving, North Korea.) Pakistan is an even more difficult challenge—in addition to having much longer borders, it shares those borders with states including Tajikistan and Iran, which have less capable militaries. (It also shares a border with Afghanistan, where NATO troops are present as of 2007 yet unable to secure the border.) More analysis of the military capabilities needed to interdict and inspect traffic leaving a collapsed state is desirable. Beyond helping prepare for a catastrophe, such investigations would help inform decisions regarding broader strategies that have the potential to destabilize nuclear-armed states.

— 7 —

The Way Forward

At the outset of this book I presented three pairs of alternatives. Defense against nuclear terrorism can be designed against a wide range of terrorist capabilities, or it can be designed against a worst-case threat. Defenses can be studied as systems, or they can be studied as something narrower and less integrated—as series of independent layers, as sets of individual components, or as single defensive elements. Strategists can supplement efforts to prevent nuclear terrorism with attempts to reduce the consequences of any attacks that might occur, or they can focus singularly on prevention.

We have seen many cases where the interplay between a terrorist group and a given defense depended in a critical way not only on the overall strength of the group but also on that group's particular capabilities. Some defensive tools showed substantially more promise as analysis moved from materials security to a layered defense and then to an actively integrated defensive system. Meanwhile, many defensive options that might not prevent terrorist attacks but that might lessen their consequences (and perhaps by doing so deter attacks in the first place) have surfaced.

The essential role of ostensibly non-nuclear tools in preventing nuclear terrorism is implicit in the portrait I have painted. We have frequently encountered situations where basic intelligence or law enforcement might play a critical role in monitoring finances, recruiting, procurement, and weapons testing, among other targets; where sanctuary, both from states and from publics, is of central importance to the defense; where border security against nuclear smuggling is as much about controlling terrorists as about controlling nuclear materials; and even where military preparedness for stabilizing and securing failed states might play an important role. One advantage of a strategy that leverages non-nuclear activities is that it can benefit from the large body of experience and scholarship having nothing explicitly to do with nuclear terrorism. Overall improvements in counter-terrorism and homeland security will benefit defense against nuclear terrorism, even if those improvements are not made with nuclear terrorism in mind.

The test of a framework for understanding any complex challenge is as much in the questions it generates as in the answers it gives. This book has just begun to scratch the surface of what we might learn about defense against improvised nuclear devices, and it has only taken a quick tour through the rest of the territory worth exploring. Further questions include ones about technology, about defensive operations, about vulnerabilities, about terrorist mindsets, and about the connections between these dimensions. As those questions are asked and answered, the framework developed here can help piece them together into a big-picture understanding of nuclear terrorism and defense.

Reforming Defense

Nuclear terrorism is, of course, not just something to be studied—it demands the most effective possible response from leaders and policymakers. That response will need to be international, but the United States, as the country most concerned about the threat of nuclear terrorism, will likely need to take the lead. It has already invested heavily (though still inadequately) in securing vulnerable nuclear weapons and materials, the core of any effective defense, and equally important, it has been able to lead other states to step up their own contributions. It has also been a leader in generating smart ideas about how best to implement these efforts. The United States now has a similar opportunity to follow the growing interest in broader defenses with serious thinking about how to craft them and with leadership in implementing them. So much confusion exists about how defenses might work, though, that it is far from inevitable that this opportunity will be seized.

Disabusing policymakers of some basic myths about nuclear terrorism would be an important first step. Making clear that materials and weapons security, while potentially very effective, cannot be perfected opens the door to more realistic discussion of broader defenses. Realizing that there may be no such thing as a true nuclear black market (where nuclear materials are freely traded) is the first step toward crafting policies aimed at stopping a more robust and genuine one from emerging. Understanding that building a nuclear weapon is not as simple as surfing the Internet may prompt more interest in detecting terrorist attempts to build bombs. Explaining how smuggling nuclear materials is different from smuggling drugs can promote more careful attention to tools for thwarting nuclear smuggling. Emphasizing that testing defensive tools only in isolation and only against worst-case threats distorts how we judge our overall defense may make policymakers more inclined to evaluate defenses as genuine systems and against more realistic threats.

Helping those focused on nuclear terrorism better understand the actual terrorist groups and plots we might face could also transform their ways of approaching nuclear terrorism. It has never been easy to dislodge images of an infallible ten-foot-tall enemy, but doing that is essential to understanding the best ways to design broad defenses. Worst-case estimates have their place, but the possible failure-averse, conservative, resource-limited five-foot-tall nuclear terrorist, who is subject not only to the laws of physics but also to Murphy's Law of nuclear terrorism, needs to become just as central to our evaluation of strategies.

Perhaps most difficult will be getting policymakers to accept goals that fall short of completely preventing nuclear terrorism, despite the fact that perfect defense is impossible. Talk of minimizing the number of deaths from any nuclear terrorist attack even while reinforcing the centrality of prevention was hard to sell politically during the Cold War, and is unlikely to be much more acceptable today. That doesn't mean that minimizing the effects of a nuclear attack shouldn't be one of many objectives—more and more analysts are talking about emergency response in the aftermath of any nuclear attack, and other tactics that might save lives or ameliorate additional consequences could gain traction too. Even if these goals are not spoken of much in public, they could (and may already) be emphasized in classified guidance.

Getting top policymakers to take the full spectrum of defensive tools more seriously doesn't mean anyone should want them to micromanage a broad defense. The goal of reshaping how leaders look at nuclear terrorism should be twofold: to spark a handful of big-picture initiatives that would institutionalize smart approaches to nuclear terrorism and spur activity throughout government, and to enable intelligent and effective oversight of whatever programs are pursued.

Policymakers should focus on five goals:

1. Support the strongest possible efforts to improve controls over nuclear weapons and materials and to prevent their further spread.
2. Place special emphasis on defensive measures that address nuclear terrorism at the same time that they address other terrorist threats.
3. Mandate a strategic intelligence assessment of the nuclear terrorist threat that emphasizes the full range of possibilities rather than the worst possible case, and have as much of that assessment as possible declassified.
4. Bring together the defensive system by mandating a plan that would define the responsibilities of each part of government in combating the nuclear terrorist threat, by breaking down barriers to sharing information regarding nuclear terrorism, and by promoting international cooperation well beyond security for nuclear weapons and materials.
5. Implement approaches to auditing defensive efforts that reflect a range of possible threats, rather than overemphasizing the worst possible cases, and that test the defensive system as a whole.

Improve Security for Weapons and Materials

Vigorous efforts to secure nuclear weapons and materials as well as possible must always be at the center of any smart strategy for preventing nuclear terrorism. Perhaps paradoxically, this book's case for broader defenses against nuclear terrorism strengthens this fundamental point. The link is clear: systems that secure nuclear weapons and materials not only prevent nuclear terrorism directly—they also make broader defenses more effective when the initial defenses fail. There is a wealth of writing on the wide spectrum and finer details of options for improving materials and weapons security that policymakers would be wise to consult. The annual report on nuclear terrorism published by the Nuclear Threat Initiative and Harvard University provides invaluable updates on the status of security efforts as well as careful policy recommendations.[1] Other clear and useful guides to policy options include Graham Allison's *Nuclear Terrorism: The Ultimate Preventable Catastrophe* and Charles Ferguson's *Preventing Catastrophic Nuclear Terrorism*.[2]

Emphasize Non-Nuclear Tools

When policymakers discuss defenses against nuclear terrorism, they tend to focus on nuclear-specific tools such as nuclear materials security, radiation detection, and nuclear forensics. But we have seen that beyond the core of materials and weapons security, defense against nuclear terrorism is as much about bread-and-butter counterterrorism and homeland security as it is about nuclear-specific measures. Interdicting nuclear smuggling, for example, is as much about detecting terrorists as it is about detecting plutonium; disrupting any nuclear black market may be as much about constraining terrorist financing as it is about nuclear stings; stopping terrorist groups from converting nuclear materials to a nuclear weapon may be as much about denying sanctuary as it is about controlling specialized machine tools or potential bomb components.

Investing in non-nuclear tools would also have the benefit of strengthening security well beyond *nuclear* terrorism. Conversely, by becoming more involved in the broader counterterrorism and homeland security discussion, those focused on nuclear threats can help shape those wider investments in a way that has the greatest value for preventing nuclear terrorism.

Integrating nuclear-specific strategy with non-nuclear defenses will not come without its share of challenges. Cost comparisons will become more complicated. It is relatively easy to compare the utility of various measures for securing nuclear material, and while it is more difficult to compare the value of expenditures on different nuclear-specific tools like materials security and radiation detection, they can at least be evaluated against the same goal: defending against nuclear terrorism. It is much harder to compare a measure such as increased materials security, which has clear value but only against nuclear terrorism, with, for example, stepped-up border patrols, which have value well beyond preventing nuclear terrorism. Even if those border patrols will do less to prevent nuclear terrorism than increased materials security will, it is not always clear which is the more worthwhile investment—that decision depends on how important preventing nuclear terrorism is compared with other counterterrorism (and immigration policy) goals. No simple solution to this challenge exists; it will require high-level guidance to address. Simply acknowledging the tension, though, is an important first step.

Incorporating the full range of possible tools into any nuclear terrorism strategy will unfortunately but inevitably drag those who focus on nuclear terrorism into a host of bureaucratic and organizational nightmares that plague the broader counterterrorism and homeland security world. From coordinating counterterrorism across departments and agencies to figuring out how to make the Department of Homeland Security work, these problems are relatively easy to identify and immeasurably harder to solve.[3] People focused on nuclear issues have largely been able to stay away from these thorny issues, but if they are to promote a genuinely comprehensive approach to nuclear terrorism, they will have to become more actively involved.

A Strategic Intelligence Assessment

Getting our understanding of nuclear terrorism right through a carefully constructed strategic intelligence assessment would contribute immensely to improving our defenses. It would help explicitly guide the design of broad defensive strategy, and also inform less formal development of any defense.

It is impossible to know what classified assessments of the nuclear terrorist threat look like—they may look like what I propose below. If they do look similar, policymakers need to pay far more attention to them than they apparently do—their public assessments, at least, consistently focus on the worst case. But if big-picture intelligence estimates suffer from some of the same flaws that public judgments do, an overhaul is in order. It is unhelpful to dictate what the conclusions of such an assessment should be, but the patterns of analysis applied in this book suggest guidelines.

Nuclear experts often hold intuitive assumptions about terrorism that are not borne out in the study of actual terrorist groups. At the same time, it is impossible to adapt traditional counterterrorism strategies to the nuclear problem without accounting for the many special properties of nuclear weapons. Thus any assessment should interweave expertise on nuclear weapons with expertise on terrorism, something that has not always occurred in past analyses.[4] Because so many ideas about nuclear terrorism are deeply ingrained, any effort should also take pains to include analysts who have had little or no exposure to the study of nuclear terrorism.

Along similar lines, a new intelligence assessment should be structured in a way that grounds the creativity and imagination needed for the uncharted waters of nuclear terrorism in the wisdom on terrorist behavior that has been accumulated over many years. The review should catalogue even small potential opportunities for terrorist failure, and include judgments of how such possibilities may influence and contribute to deterrence against terrorists' pursuit of nuclear plots.

Rather than only developing a single model (or a small number of models) for what a nuclear terrorist plot might look like, the analysis should identify a wide range of possible and credible variations, just as strategic intelligence underlying defense planning identifies a wide range of contingencies and capabilities that might be addressed. Although the analysis should evaluate the likelihood of the different possibilities, it should err on the side of including too many rather than too few possibilities, leaving triage to those charged with designing defensive strategy. In each case, the analysis should identify resource requirements, both material and human, as well as potential timelines for particular plots. It should also devote particular attention to preparations that might be made *before* a group attempts to acquire a nuclear weapon or nuclear explosive material, which would help strengthen efforts to detect such preparations, something that could be leveraged to strengthen security over weapons and materials. This should all be supplemented with focused analyses of how particular high-threat groups might consider and carry out nuclear plots. This last approach diverges slightly from one that is capabilities based, but it may serve as a useful supplement if good intelligence is available.

The intelligence community, in improving its understanding of nuclear terrorism, should go beyond passive collection and reasoning by analogy to active operations designed to understand terrorist approaches to nuclear plots. To better understand terrorist behavior, for example, sting operations involving sales of nuclear material could be supplemented with offers to sell nuclear material aimed not at apprehending terrorists but at understanding their behavior. Similar tactics could be used to understand how terrorist groups might recruit technical expertise or acquire non-nuclear materials, and in other areas that operators and analysts could collectively identify.

An intelligence assessment should also explore not only how terrorists might behave, but how others might respond to their actions. If an optimal strategy for confronting nuclear terrorism is to include measures that address the consequences of an attack, an intelligence assessment must examine potential reactions to a nuclear terrorist event, including to a publicized but failed plot. Such an assessment should at a minimum ask how the wider effects of a nuclear attack will depend on its finer physical details, which would help policymakers decide what value to place on defensive measures that would cut fatalities but not prevent attacks.

Policymakers should also attempt to have as much of this intelligence assessment made public as is possible without handing terrorist groups any meaningful advantage. To the extent that the public better understands the real nuclear terrorist threat, support for a strategy designed against that threat, rather than against the worst-case caricatures that dominate much popular thinking, is more likely to be sustainable.

Bring the Defensive System Together

Any broad defense against nuclear terrorism will involve too many parts and, perhaps more important, too many bureaucratic interests for it to be actively managed from above. And with effective defense demanding contributions at the local, state, federal, and international levels, no single manager is even theoretically possible at the highest levels. Instead, federal policymakers should emphasize three goals. They should develop a plan that defines the responsibilities of each part of the federal, state, and local governments in preventing nuclear terrorism. They should break down classification barriers that perversely prevent many potentially critical players in the defense from receiving information they need to do their jobs most effectively, such as those that prevent many law enforcement workers from learning how to identify nuclear materials or weapons components. And they should promote international efforts to coordinate defenses and share information.

Past experience strongly suggests that appointing a so-called czar for nuclear terrorism would be bureaucratically all but impossible. Before the radiation-detection-focused Domestic Nuclear Detection Office (DNDO) was created in 2005, there was an effort within the federal government to designate a high-level coordinator for defending against nuclear terrorism using the full spectrum of possible tools. That coordinator, who would have headed a National Domestic Nuclear Defense Office, would have reported directly to the president.[5] Intense resistance from agencies that would have fallen under the new office led to major limits on both its scope and its power. The result was DNDO, whose director reports to the secretary of homeland security rather than to the president. It is unlikely that another attempt at appointing a top-level leader would fare any better—the very characteristics that would make such a leader attractive to strategists would again doom the effort bureaucratically.

The best alternative is for departments and agencies to collaboratively develop a framework that allows policymakers and those implementing policy to see how many small pieces fit together to produce an effective defense. Such a framework would be accomplished not through a short directive, like the one establishing DNDO that set out each department's responsibilities in the broadest possible terms, but through a plan that drilled down into specific programs and showed how they would fit into an overarching strategy, much as the 2006 *National Strategy to Combat Terrorist Travel* did. Rather than forcing coordination from the top down, the plan would provide departments and agencies with a framework within which to plan their activities, and with a tool to use in justifying and seeking funding for those programs. The plan could also be used by the Executive Office of the President and by Congress to measure progress toward an integrated strategy.

This sort of planning is most naturally done by individual countries. (The U.S.-specific outline just given could easily be adapted to other states.) But only coordinating strategy within governments would miss valuable opportunities, since those states that will naturally invest the most in combating nuclear terrorism may not be the only ones from which important contributions are needed. Those governments most intimately involved in defense against nuclear terrorism should work with foreign counterparts to strengthen those counterparts' capabilities, exploiting the landmark UN Security Council Resolution 1540, which mandates all states to strengthen defenses against the spread of nuclear weapons to nonstate actors. States should also collectively plan for joint operations should nuclear explosive material or a nuclear weapon be discovered missing. Without advance preparation, taking radical steps during an emergency may be exceedingly and unnecessarily difficult.

Cooperation between local, state, and federal levels, as well as among countries, may be hurt by stringent controls over any information related to nuclear weapons. There is considerable apprehension about sharing nuclear-weapons-related information with local and state officials, who will not have high-level nuclear security clearances, and with international partners that do not already have nuclear weapons. But such restrictions can lead to problems. Many law enforcement officers, for example, may not learn how to spot telltale signs of nuclear plots; many border officials may not be properly trained to recognize nuclear weapons or their components in cross-border traffic. The United States should continually reassess its balance between secrecy and the need to empower those at many nontraditional lines of defense, actively looking for opportunities to improve defense by sharing information while still retaining prudent controls over genuinely sensitive material.

Evaluate Defensive Efforts Wisely

How governments assess the effectiveness of their defenses can be a major factor in determining how those defenses evolve. An effective program that appears useless in the face of a poorly designed audit might come under heavy pressure to be canceled, while a useless program evaluated by a similarly ill-thought-out test might actually appear effective and, rather than being reformed or terminated, could become untouchable. Smart evaluations of defensive programs are thus as critical as intelligence assessments or strategic plans to build and improve an effective defense.

Three approaches can complement one another. Traditional audits should verify that the tasks prescribed in any integrated strategy are being carried out as intended. Large-scale military-style exercises should be conducted to improve decision makers' understanding of the broader system and to identify unexpected synergies and weaknesses. Careful red-teaming—subjecting defenses to teams that play the role of an adversary—should also be used to identify realistic weaknesses.

Government audits of individual programs are an essential component of assessment, but are not enough by themselves. They identify whether a strategy is being implemented, but do not deeply test whether it is effective. With the exception of materials and weapons security and elimination, which have been subjected to sophisticated analyses, most public assessments of broader defenses against nuclear terrorism have been audits of this type. The U.S. Government Accountability Office, for example, normally focuses more (though not exclusive) attention on measuring how many radiation detectors have been installed at all ports than on carefully examining whether those deployments will be effective.[6]

It is not enough, however, to simply check that a system is being implemented as designed. After all, the system may not have been designed well, or there may not even be an overall plan against which the system can be audited. Assessment thus requires measures that evaluate whether the system, even if properly implemented, is as effective as possible. Exercises and red-teaming should be used to address this need.

Exercising aims to make sure a defense works the same way in practice as in theory, and to understand any differences. The enemy in any exercises should be based on the sort of intelligence assessment recommended earlier—exercises against unrealistic threats can be worse than none at all. Reflecting the approach to the proposed intelligence assessment, exercises should engage the full defensive system against multiple variations on the possible threat. Some of those exercises should include several countries, since nuclear terrorism is inevitably a transnational problem. Large-scale exercises can also increase the deterrent effect of the defense by visibly demonstrating the strength of defensive activities, and can help build valuable networks among those who participate. Such networks may be particularly useful at the international level, where top-down coordination is extremely difficult.

Red-teaming is an essential complement to exercises. While exercising aims to confirm system performance against expected threats, red-teaming challenges defensive assumptions about the very nature of the threat. The technique is already widely used in assessing defense against nuclear terrorism.[7] But it tends (and is often explicitly designed) to drive defensive planners toward a focus on worst-case scenarios, distorting defensive strategy. Indeed a 2003 Defense Science Board study noted approvingly that "in some cases the red team is not explicitly constrained to think and behave as an adversary might, but is given wider latitudes to discover technological counters to US systems."[8] Such an approach would drive defensive planners in a direction opposite to the one they should be heading in, since terrorist decision making is as important a constraint on potential nuclear plots as is technology. The challenge is to constrain red teams in realistic ways without draining them of their value.

Efforts to simulate realistic technological constraints have many precedents. These usually involve employing recent PhDs without access to classified materials in developing threat technologies. One prominent instance of this was the Nth Country experiment, which as we saw earlier shed light on potential adversary capabilities (and which at the same time provides a cautionary tale about wrongly interpreting red-teaming). A more effective example is the constrained red-teaming used by the Strategic Defense Initiative (SDI) in its pursuit of missile defenses during the 1980s. As in the

Nth Country Experiment, SDI used recent PhDs without access to classified information; in this case, their task was to design countermeasures to ballistic missile defenses. (Such countermeasures have been discussed for as long as missile defense has been an issue.)[9] Since most debate had focused on the theoretical difficulty of designing such countermeasures (it is now widely agreed that in theory the design is easy), the red-teaming was used to explore engineering challenges as well. Thus red-team participants were required not only to design but also to build and fly their countermeasures. Such an approach cannot be replicated directly in exploring nuclear terrorism—not only would it be inappropriate to test potential nuclear weapons, but even building them would entail large dangers. However, creative ways of learning from constrained red-teams could be developed. For example, "amateurs" with different levels of technical training could be told to perform tasks involved in nuclear weapons engineering, such as casting uranium or plutonium, without access to support staff or classified information. It is possible, of course, that such activities have already been conducted. If they have been, but not recently, it would be valuable to repeat them in the current scientific and technological environment.

Setting up scenarios for the red team that are realistically constraining is more difficult, but would not be entirely impossible. Teams of physicists working on simulated weapons, for example, might be guided by teams of terrorism and regional experts who would be empowered to stop them from taking steps that a particularly conservative or failure-averse group might avoid. (Had such a group supervised the Nth Country Experiment, it might have told the participants to focus on the easier gun-type design.) Similar approaches could be used with red-team members attempting to evade border security or to procure manufacturing equipment.

The Bottom Line

Exactly how much can defense against nuclear terrorism be improved by applying the principles set forth in this book? The answer is perhaps surprising. Although the principles guide us toward better defensive strategies, they do not tell us precisely how effective such strategies can be—indeed, they help explain why precision is impossible.

Why? To start, it is trickier to separate controls at the source of nuclear weapons and materials from the broader defense than many suppose it is. Sometimes a broader defense will affect a terrorist plot directly—it will break up a nuclear transaction or detect radioactive materials at a port. But sometimes it will convince a group that nuclear terrorism is not worth trying, and controls at the source will never be tested. Other times it might have an intermediate effect. Faced with increased risks in the rest of its plot, a terrorist group may use a smaller force to attack a facility, or be more cautious in attempting to co-opt insiders, implicitly increasing the effectiveness of controls at the source. To ask for independent assessments of these different parts of a system is to discard at some level the fact that it is a system at all.

The effectiveness of a given defense also depends strongly on the terrorist group with which it is matched—that is, on whether it faces a ten-foot-tall or a five-foot-tall nuclear terrorist (and on what sort of five-foot-tall nuclear terrorist it faces). A defense that makes nuclear terrorism impossible for one group may have essentially no effect on another. Groups cannot even necessarily be ranked—a technically capable but operationally weak group may be vulnerable to one defensive system, while a technically weak but otherwise capable group may be vulnerable to another. It is not unreasonable to judge that a defense might reduce the risk of nuclear terrorism by a factor between ten percent and a thousand, or by an even wider range—these distinctions may simply reflect the degree to which effectiveness depends on terrorist opponents, who are difficult to understand and hard to predict.

The value of a broader system also depends on how we measure effectiveness. Those who place little value on reducing the consequences of any nuclear terrorist plot that at least partially succeeds will measure the utility of broader defenses differently from those who value that secondary objective.

Then there is the matter of luck. Luck has been invoked as the magic factor that explains why less-than-perfect security over nuclear materials has not brought us nuclear terrorism. But luck plays a much deeper role. We gravitate toward worst-case scenarios, but we need to pay as much attention to Murphy's Law of nuclear terrorism as we do to the laws of physics. What can go wrong might go wrong, and when it comes to nuclear terrorism, a broader, integrated defense, just like controls at the source of weapons and materials, can multiply, intensify, and compound the possibilities of terrorist failure, possibly driving terrorist groups to reject nuclear terrorism altogether. No defense can eliminate nuclear terrorism: as long as we continue to live with nuclear weapons and materials, eradicating nuclear terrorism will not be an option. But the right strategy can keep our gambling to a minimum, and tilt the odds in our favor.

Appendix

Glossary

Notes

Acknowledgments

Index

APPENDIX

Radiation Detection and Weapons Effects Calculations

How can we understand radiation mathematically? Steve Fetter and his colleagues give a clear review of the subject that this book uses throughout for describing detection.[1] By discussing notional detectors rather than the specific detectors that are deployed, the discussion of Fetter et al. allows a basic understanding of detection that can underpin policy and strategy analysis without providing specific instruction to terrorist groups. That discussion estimates the distance at which a source of nuclear radiation can be detected as $r = (A_s \varepsilon_s t / 16\text{m}^2\pi^2 b)^{1/4} S^{1/2}$, where A_s is the detector area, ε_s is the detector efficiency (the fraction of particles incident on the detector that are actually detected), b is the well-known background radiation density, S is the signal strength, and t is the observation time. The number of standard deviations above background a signal must be for it to register is denoted by m—larger m implies fewer false positives.

Fetter and his colleagues describe four notional detectors, two of which detect neutrons and two of which detect gamma rays. Their properties are described in Table A.1. The detector area can be varied—the number in the table is simply a typical size, and gives some indication of what size detectors might be affordable.

The neutron background given in the table, however, reflects assumptions that will often not hold for counterterrorism applications. In many situations, radiation must be detected in the presence of an uncertain background. It is useful to understand how that affects calculations, something not addressed in the above-referenced paper.

Let $B \in [L, U]$, where B is the (possibly unknown) background neutron detection rate at a detector, L is the lowest possible value for B (normally the atmospheric background), and U is the greatest possible value for B. Let m be defined by setting the false positive rate equal to $1 - N(\text{m})$, where $N(\text{x})$ is the cumulative normal distribution. Similarly, let n be defined by

Table A.1 Detector characteristics

Detector type	Gamma energy (MeV)	Detector area (m^2)	Detector efficiency	Background (counts/m^2-s)
Large neutron		0.3	0.14	50
NaI(Tl) gamma[a]	1.0	0.3	0.16	860
NaI(Tl) gamma	1.6	0.3	0.10	320
HPGe gamma[b]	1.0	0.003	0.57	17
HPGe gamma	1.6	0.003	0.43	4.4

Source: Adapted from Steve Fetter et al., "Detecting Nuclear Warheads," *Science and Global Security* 1 (1990): 234, table 5.

a. Energy resolution is 10 percent.

b. Energy resolution is 2 keV.

setting the false negative rate equal to $1 - N(\mathrm{n})$. Given a detection rate threshold D (the rate of neutrons detected above which an event is registered), we want to determine the minimum signal S_o (the rate of neutrons emitted by the source and later detected) that can be reliably detected. The efficiency and area of the detector are implicitly included in D, B, L, U, and S_o.

A false positive is registered when there is no source present and when the observed detection rate is at least m standard deviations above the background rate. Were B known, the detection threshold, Dt, would be set at $Bt + \mathrm{m}(Bt)^{1/2}$, where t is the observation time. We thus can place a lower bound on m: $\mathrm{m} = (D - B)t^{1/2}/B^{1/2} \geq (D - U)t^{1/2}/U^{1/2}$.

A false negative is registered when there is a source present but when the observed detection rate is less than the detection threshold. We then have $Bt - \mathrm{n}(Bt)^{1/2} + S_o t = Dt$. Rearranging, we find $\mathrm{n} = (Bt + S_o t - Dt)/(Bt)^{1/2} \geq (L + S_o - D)t^{1/2}/U^{1/2}$. Equivalently, we have $S_o \leq \mathrm{n}U^{1/2}t^{-1/2} - L + D$.

The inequality for m can be solved to give $D \leq \mathrm{m}U^{1/2}t^{-1/2} + U$. Substituting into the inequality for S_o, we find $S_o \leq \mathrm{n}U^{1/2}t^{-1/2} - L + \mathrm{m}U^{1/2}t^{-1/2} + U = (\mathrm{n} + \mathrm{m})(U/t)^{1/2} + (U - L)$.

For well-known B, $U = B$, $U - L = 0$, and the expression for the minimum reliably detectable signal, S_o, is reduced to the usual expression for a known background. S_o is always bounded from below by $U - L$, the uncertainty in the background signal.

What sorts of backgrounds might be expected? The neutron background (50 n/m^2 – s) given earlier is the average terrestrial atmospheric background. The actual atmospheric background at sea level can be as high as 150 $n/m^2 - s$, depending on latitude.[2]

In the presence of heavy cargo, the interaction of cosmic ray protons with cargo materials produces more neutrons through spallation; depending on the particular scenario, this source of neutrons may be larger than the atmospheric background.[3] For the scenarios of interest in this book, the number of neutrons produced in this way depends linearly on the mass of cargo material present, as well as (more weakly) on the molar mass of that cargo. (The number of neutrons produced also varies with altitude; this variation is neglected here, since we are primarily interested in sea-level detection.) To estimate this effect, consider the case of container cargo, as well as two cases for smaller cargoes.

Shipping containers may hold at most thirty tons of material.[4] Then pessimistically assuming a cargo consisting entirely of lead (neutron production increases with molar mass), a cargo will produce at most approximately four thousand neutrons per second (at the same latitude at which atmospheric background is 150 $n/m^2 - s$).[5] Since the surface area of a twenty-foot container is approximately forty square meters, this results in a flux of at most 100 $n/m^2 - s$ at the container surface. (The flux is at most half that for a forty-foot container.) The total background is thus at most twice the atmospheric background.[6]

Now consider lighter shipments that are not containerized. For a given mass of material, the worst case occurs when that material is lead.[7] Then 100 kg of the material produces 15 n/s, while 1 ton of the material produces 150 n/s. If the material is distributed uniformly throughout a sphere, the corresponding fluxes at the surface of the sphere are 70 $n/m^2 - s$ and 150 $n/m^2 - s$, respectively; for other shapes, those fluxes are lower. At a distance of two meters from the center of either sphere, the fluxes due to spallation in the lead are 0.3 and 3 $n/m^2 - s$.

Effects of Nuclear Weapons

Weapons with yields of ten kilotons or less kill primarily through neutron radiation and blast. The precise effects of any weapon differ on the basis of the type of weapon used (gun or implosion), by the degree of blast and neutron shielding in the area where the bomb explodes, and by the fact that people on high floors of tall buildings will be more protected from neutron radiation than they are protected from the blast.

To get a feel for how fatalities might depend on yield, consider four caricatured scenarios: a gun-type weapon and no neutron shielding; a gun-type weapon and tenfold neutron shielding; a crude implosion weapon with no neutron shielding; and a crude implosion weapon and tenfold neutron shielding.[8] Unless otherwise noted, I will use formulae published by the Defense Intelligence Agency and the Defense Nuclear Agency and reprinted by the Natural Resources Defense Council (NRDC) to assess these.[9]

The number of fatalities from the blast effect in an area with uniform population density can be estimated as the population density multiplied by the area over which the blast exceeds 5 psi.[10] This area is equal to 3 km^2, 0.6 km^2, and 0.1 km^2 for yields of 10, 1, and 0.1 kilotons respectively. To estimate the effect of neutron radiation, first estimate the neutron doses at various distances from the bomb using the NRDC formulae and then relate those to probabilities of death using a lognormal distribution with LD_{50} = 620 rem and geometric standard deviation 1.4.[11] This probability of death due to neutron radiation is approximated well by a "cookie-cutter" (or step) function that is equal to one within some radius and to zero outside.

Assuming that the fatality area for any weapon type, yield, and shielding scenario is equal to the greater of the blast and radiation areas, one finds the fatality areas shown in Table A.2. (Treating the probabilities of death from the blast and from radiation as independent gives similar results.) Depending on the type of weapon used and on the ambient shielding, the reduction in fatalities as one drops from ten kilotons to one hundred tons can be anywhere from a factor of five to a factor of twenty.

For convenience, the remaining analyses in this appendix assume a gun-type weapon with a shielding factor of ten, an intermediate case that is also plausible for a terrorist attack. Unless the weapon is detonated in an infinite area of uniform population density, the number of resulting deaths depends on the population distribution and on the point where the weapon is detonated. NRDC reports that the relationship between the distance from the bomb and the fraction of targets with a specified level of blast damage can be described by a cumulative lognormal function. Combining this with the rule of thumb that 50 percent of blast fatalities will occur within the 5 psi ring, one can fit a unique cumulative lognormal function to these data. Comparing this function with the one describing deaths due to neutron radiation shows that the fraction of people killed is approxi-

Table A.2 Fatality areas of nuclear weapons (km^2)

	Neutron radiation				
	No shielding		10X shielding		
Yield	Gun	Implosion	Gun	Implosion	Blast (any)
10 kT	5	3	2	1	3
1 kT	2	1	1	0.5	0.6
100 T	1	0.5	0.3	0.1	0.1

mated well by a step function. For one-hundred-ton and one-kiloton detonations, fatalities are dominated by radiation, and the radii of the step functions are four hundred and seven hundred meters respectively. For a ten-kiloton detonation, fatalities are dominated by the blast, and the radius of the step function is one kilometer.

To predict the number of fatalities caused by a detonation that is displaced from a population center, integrate the product of the population distribution and of the fraction of people killed at any distance from the detonation over all space. The population distribution can be modeled as the Gaussian $P(x,y) = (P_o/2\pi R^2)\exp(-(x^2 + y^2)/2R^2)$, where P_o is the total population and R describes how quickly the population concentration drops off away from the center. (R is the radius that contains 70 percent of the population; larger R corresponding to a slower drop-off.)[12] Consider three cases: a uniform population distribution, a population distribution in which $R = 2000$ m, and one in which $R = 500$ m. Figure A.1 shows the results.

A detonation can also be displaced vertically, altering its effects on the ground. Focus on the blast: increasing the height-of-burst for a nuclear weapon can substantially reduce the pressure, and hence damage, that it generates at ground level. (Increasing the height would also reduce or eliminate intense local nuclear fallout.) At a detonation height of 500 meters, a ten-kiloton nuclear bomb will produce ground-level overpressures of at least 5 psi over an area of roughly 6 square kilometers; at 1,000 meters, that area decreases to roughly 1.5 square kilometers; at 1,500 meters, that area becomes zero. The effect is even more pronounced for lower-yield weapons: a nuclear weapon with a ten-ton yield detonated at a height of 500 meters will not even produce a 1 psi overpressure anywhere on the ground; to produce a 5 psi overpressure over even a nearly vanishing

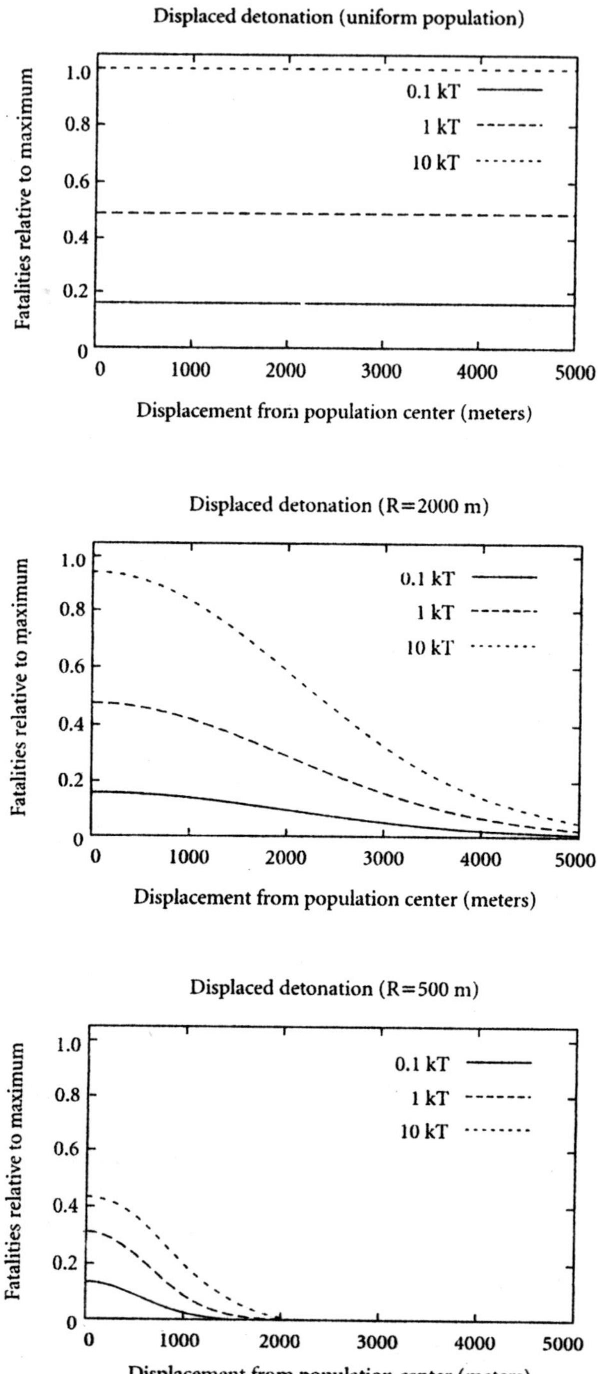

Figure A.1. Expected fatalities.

area would require that the bomb be detonated at a height of roughly 100 meters.

Fallout and Emergency Response

These results ignore delayed radioactive fallout, whose effects depend on emergency response. Assume a 10 kT weapon, a wind speed of 4.5 m/s (ten miles per hour), and uniform population density, and compare two simple response strategies, along with a maximum-casualty baseline that assumes all individuals are exposed to fallout as if they were standing in the open for twenty-four hours. In the first response strategy, individuals are told to flee the fallout zone; in the second, individuals are told to head to the interiors of their buildings, where protection from fallout is greatest, and shelter in place for twenty-four hours.[13]

Estimate the area of deadly fallout by calculating the area where the expected radiation dose exceeds the LD-50, itself estimated as 500 rem.[14] For the baseline case, this area, zone 1 in Figure A.2a, is 11 km^2, extending approximately 15 km downwind, and is approximately 1 km wide at its widest point.[15] In contrast, assume that by staying inside, each person can shield himself by a factor of twenty; this estimate is pessimistic for an area dominated by multistory buildings, where shielding factors as great as one hundred might be achieved.[16] The area receiving a fallout dose greater than the LD-50, zone 2 in Figure A.2a, is now 1 km^2; the fallout zone extends 3 km downwind, and is approximately 400 m wide at its widest point. Since most people within the 5 psi ring will already die as a result of the blast, one finds that only 0.7 km^2, zone 2 in Figure A.2b, are predominantly affected by fallout. The sheltering strategy thus appears to reduce fallout casualties to approximately 6 percent of the number in the baseline case.[17]

This estimate, though, may overstate the value of sheltering if a substantial amount of fallout falls on areas where population densities are much smaller than those near where the bomb is detonated. As one proceeds downwind, along the direction of the fallout cloud, the population density will decline. Thus much of the area "saved" by using a sheltering strategy may be in far less densely populated areas than the areas near ground zero that still receive lethal doses. One way to estimate this effect is to consider the reduction in width, rather than in area, of the radioactive plume, which has the effect of ignoring the length of the plume. Using this approach, but keeping the other details from the previous calculation, one can esti-

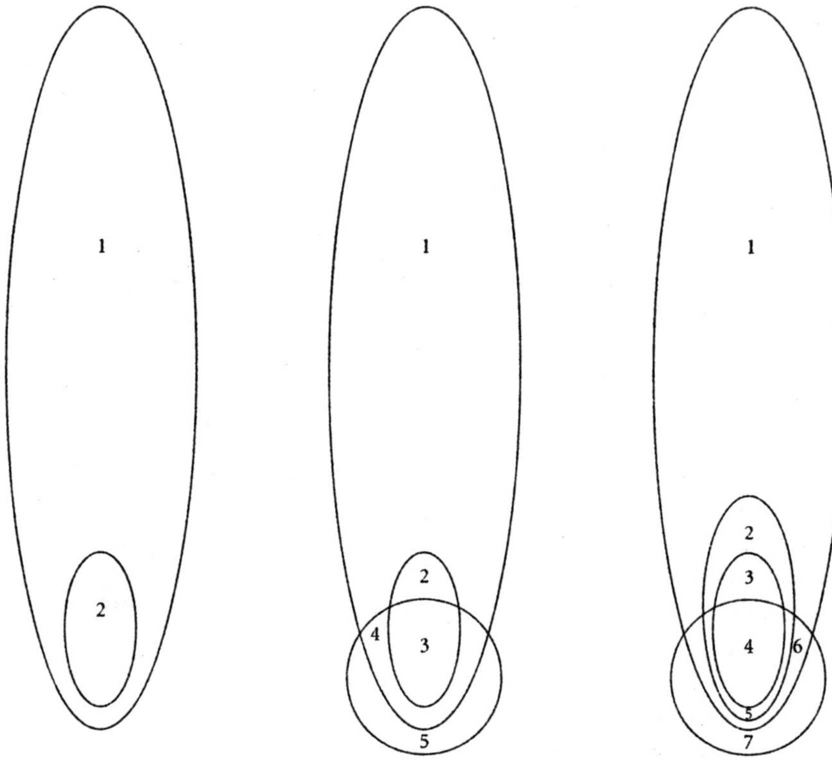

(a) (b) (c)

Figure A.2. Emergency response scenarios. The rings are not drawn to scale.

mate a reduction in fallout deaths to 40 percent of the otherwise expected number.

In either case, simple planning for postattack response can have a large impact on the number of deaths resulting from a full-scale nuclear attack. The destructive radius for a ten-kiloton blast is one kilometer; thus the destructive area is roughly 3 km^2. In contrast, the area where a 500-rem dose could be expected should everyone be exposed to fallout without shielding was roughly 10 km^2. Thus even using the pessimistic estimate of the effectiveness of shielding, the simple sheltering approach just described could reduce the number of deaths from fallout roughly in half.[18]

Compare this with another simple strategy, where everyone attempts to evacuate. One can then determine the area over which people trapped outside for at least one hour while evacuating are guaranteed to receive a 500-

rem dose. Multiplying that area by the fraction of people unable to evacuate within one hour yields an "effective area" than can be compared with the areas calculated above.[19] That area, the combination of zones 2–5 in Figure A.2c, is approximately 2 km^2. Excluding the area within which people will die anyhow due to the blast effects, this becomes the combination of zones 2–3 in Figure A.2c, which is still roughly 2 km^2. To achieve the same effective fallout area as with the sheltering approach described above (0.7 km^2), over 60 percent evacuation must be achieved within one hour. If the evacuation time is extended to six hours, nearly 90 percent evacuation is required for the strategy to be as effective as sheltering in place.

The effectiveness of emergency response also depends on weapon yield and detonation point. Repeat the above assessments but for a one-hundred-ton nuclear explosion, again assuming a gun-type weapon and tenfold neutron radiation shielding. The worst-case baseline used above—the area over which people exposed without shielding for one day would receive an LD-50 dose—is now 0.3 km^2, the same as the area over which people are killed by the initial radiation. The two zones, however, are not coincident, and a shelter-in-place strategy now all but reduces fallout-related casualties to zero, since almost the entire zone over which sheltered individuals receive an LD-50 dose from fallout is contained within the area where people receive an immediate lethal dose of radiation. In contrast, the area over which people fleeing but unable to escape the fallout zone within an hour would receive an LD-50 dose would extend beyond that area. In the case of a hundred-ton weapon, the shelter-in-place strategy appears to be decisively more effective than an evacuation strategy, although the details of any specific scenario might change that.

Synergies between emergency response and displacing the detonation point can be powerful too. If, for example, a nuclear bomb is detonated in a low-density area upwind from a more highly populated area, the initial number of expected deaths may be small, but the potential for deaths from downwind fallout may be high. In that case, reducing fallout deaths downwind through appropriate emergency response will effect even greater fractional reductions in total casualties than if the bomb were detonated in a high-density area.

Glossary

Active interrogation. A detection method that penetrates shielded cargo using nuclear radiation and stimulates a unique radiation signature from cargo contents in order to identify nuclear material.

Alloy. The combination of a metal with a second metal. The new material usually has desirable engineering properties that the original metal did not have.

Alpha particle (α). Helium nuclei ejected from unstable atoms. The particles interact with light elements to produce neutrons.

Attribution, nuclear. Using information or physical evidence from smuggled or detonated nuclear material to identify the source of the material.

Background positive (BP). Occurs when a detector registers a warning because radiation from natural sources exceeds the minimum amount of radiation set by the defense to trigger a warning.

Background radiation. Radiation that comes from natural sources, such as cosmic radiation and radioactive elements in the ground.

Baseline count of materials. Quantity of material measured at the beginning of a time period against which future changes are measured.

Beryllium, Beryllium oxide. Light material that can be used as a reflector in a nuclear weapon.

Black market. A market where substances or products are bought and sold illegally.

Border Patrol. Former U.S. agency charged with controlling American borders.

Chain reaction. A process within an atomic bomb or nuclear reactor. A nucleus splits and releases neutrons and energy; the neutrons induce more splitting of nuclei, release more energy, and form a chain of repeated events.

Chemical, biological, radiological, nuclear (CBRN). Chemical, biological, radiological, and nuclear materials.

Comprehensive upgrades. Security and accounting equipment upgrades installed in Russia with international assistance to protect nuclear weapons and materials facilities against both insider and outsider theft.

Consequence management. Actions taken in the aftermath of a disaster resulting from a nuclear, chemical, or biological weapon attack or other destructive event.

Containment/Surveillance (C/S). Features used to establish physical security, detect movements, and maintain continuity of knowledge of an area or item. Containment can include storage structures or seals. Surveillance can include information from inspectors or measuring instruments.

Cooperative threat reduction. A program initiated by the United States in 1991 to assist the states of the former Soviet Union to control and protect their nuclear weapons and associated materials and human capital, and to dismantle and destroy nuclear weapons delivery systems and chemical weapons.

Countermeasure. An action taken to offset any opponent's action or to reduce one's vulnerability.

Critical. The state of a system wherein fission generates just enough neutrons to offset the loss of neutrons through capture and escape.

Critical mass. The minimum amount of fissionable material required to sustain a chain reaction.

Curie (Ci). A measure of material radioactivity, equal to 3.7×10^{10} disintegrations per second.

Department of Energy (DOE). The U.S. government department responsible for the national nuclear weapons complex.

Department of Homeland Security (DHS). The U.S. government department created in 2002 to secure the United States from terrorist attacks and to respond to domestic emergencies.

Design Basis Threat (DBT). The characteristics of an adversary who might attempt theft of nuclear material against which a defensive system is designed and evaluated.

Deterrence. The strategy of discouraging an enemy from using force, through threats to retaliate.

Diagnostics. Tests performed on a device to ensure proper operation.

Domestic Nuclear Detection Office (DNDO). An office within the Department of Homeland Security established in April 2005 to address domestic and global nuclear detection.

Explosive lens. The explosives in an implosion weapon that focus waves from the detonation into a single converging wave and that compress the core of the weapon, causing it to be supercritical.

Facility insider. Individual granted access to restricted areas in or confidential information about a facility.

Facility outsider. Anyone who has not been granted access to restricted areas in or confidential information about a facility.

Failure-averse. An individual or group is failure-averse if he or it is acutely sensitive to the possibility of failure.

False alarm rate. The frequency with which a detection device will detect an illicit substance when the substance is not actually present.

False positive. A false alarm.

Fat Man bomb. Code name of the plutonium implosion weapon detonated over Nagasaki by the United States Army Air Forces in August 1945. It had an explosive yield of about twenty kilotons.

Fissile material. Material whose nuclei can be split by high-energy neutrons. Includes U^{235} and Pu^{239}.

Flash X-ray. A device that produces intense bursts of radiation to penetrate and image a rapid event, such as the implosion of a nuclear weapon.

Fuel cycle, nuclear. The steps to produce and use nuclear fuel, such as mining uranium ore, milling the ore into powder, converting the powder into gas, separating different isotopes within the gas, converting the gas into fuel for a power reactor, transporting the fuel to and from the power reactor, storing the waste and reprocessing the remaining material into new fuel.

Full crystal density. The maximum ratio of mass per unit of volume in an assembly of crystalline powder.

G-8. The Group of Eight nations consists of Canada, France, Germany, Italy, Japan, Russia, the United Kingdom, and the United States.

G-8 Partnership against the Spread of Weapons of Mass Destruction (Global Partnership). A commitment made by the Group of Eight nations in June 2002 to prevent terrorists or those that harbor them from acquiring or developing nuclear, chemical, radiological, and biological weapons, missiles, and related materials, equipment, and technology.

Gamma radiography. A detection method that fires gamma rays at an object to create an image of heavier materials, such as shielding or nuclear material, that block gamma rays.

Gamma ray. Radiation emitted by a nucleus when it transitions to a lower energy level.

Gas centrifuge enrichment. Process that uses rotating cylinders filled with gas to separate heavier uranium molecules from lighter uranium molecules.

Gilmore Commission. Advisory panel established by the United States Congress in 1999 to assess the ability of the United States to respond to domestic terrorist attacks using weapons of mass destruction.

Government Accountability Office (GAO). An arm of Congress established in 1921 that performs financial and performance audits and program evaluations of U.S. government programs.

Gun-type weapon. A fission weapon that can explode when one subcritical mass of fissionable material is shot at another within the weapon in order to form a supercritical mass.

Handheld germanium-based detector. Portable tool used to detect radioactive materials and to identify the type of radioactive isotope present, through detection of gamma rays.

HEU Purchase Agreement. Agreement between the United States and Russia to blend down highly enriched uranium from dismantled Russian nuclear weapons and to use the product in power plants.

Hezbollah. A Lebanese umbrella organization of Shiite groups that was founded in 1982 as a response to the Israeli invasion of Lebanon.

Highly enriched uranium (HEU). Uranium that contains a concentration of 20 percent or more of the U^{235} isotope.

Hiroshima-type yield. An explosion with a yield of about ten kilotons, similar to that of the weapon used over Hiroshima, Japan.

HMX or high melting explosive, RDX or research department explosive. Explosive chemical powders that can detonate a nuclear weapon.

Immigration and Naturalization Service (INS). Transitioned into the U.S. Citizenship and Immigration Services in 2003, this agency administered immigration and naturalization and enforced immigration laws, including border controls.

Implosion weapon. A weapon that can explode when an arrangement of explosives rapidly compresses one or more pieces of fissile material into a supercritical mass.

Improvised Nuclear Device (IND). A nuclear bomb assembled by a terrorist group.

Inertial tamper. Component of a nuclear weapon that slows down expansion of the weapon core, increasing the weapon's yield.

Initiator. In a nuclear weapon design, a source of neutrons that triggers a nuclear explosion.

Insulator. A material that conducts heat poorly.

International Atomic Energy Agency (IAEA). An independent intergovernmental organization created in 1957 that is related to the United Nations system. It promotes the peaceful use of nuclear energy, verifies state compliance with nonproliferation agreements, and promotes nuclear safety.

Isotopes. Atoms of the same element that have the same number of protons but a different number of neutrons and thus different atomic masses, such as U^{235} and U^{238}. Isotopes of the same element often display different attributes.

Isotopic signature. The fingerprint of an element characterized by the types and amounts of isotopes it contains.

Khan, Abdul Qadeer (A. Q.). Founder of the Pakistani nuclear weapons program; known for his involvement in the nuclear black market.

Kiloton. An explosive force equal to that of 1,000 tons of TNT explosive.

LASCAR. Large-scale reprocessing plant safeguards process. A multinational forum established in 1987 to assist the International Atomic Energy Agency in developing safeguards for fuel reprocessing plants.

Lawrence Livermore National Laboratory (LLNL). A research and development institution for the U.S. Department of Energy, which focuses on the design, development, and stewardship of nuclear weapons as well as on arms control and homeland security technologies.

Lithium hydride. A material composed of lithium and hydrogen that can be used to shield a neutron-emitting material from detection.

Little Boy. Code name of the gun-type fission weapon detonated over Hiroshima by the United States Army Air Forces in August 1945. It had an explosive yield of about fifteen kilotons.

Low-enriched uranium (LEU). Uranium that contains a concentration of greater than 0.7 percent and less than 20 percent of the U^{235} isotope.

Materials Accountability Systems. Systems associated with MPC&A that ensure that all material is accounted for, enable the measurement of losses, and provide information for investigations of irregularities.

Materials Control Systems. Systems associated with MPC&A that prevent unauthorized movement of materials and detect theft or diversion of material. These should control exit of material from storage sites and verify the material's location and condition.

Materials Protection, Control, and Accounting (MPC&A). Arrangements that secure and account for nuclear materials.

Medium-enriched uranium. Uranium that contains a concentration of between 20 and 80 percent of the U^{235} isotope.

Megaton. An explosive power equivalent to one million tons of TNT.

Metallurgy. The science and technology underlying the manipulation of metals.

Millennium bombing plot. Attacks planned by al Qaeda to occur around January 1, 2000.

Mixed oxide fuel or MOX fuel. A nuclear power reactor fuel that includes plutonium from spent reactor fuel or dismantled weapons. It is a mixture of uranium oxide and plutonium oxide.

Muon. A naturally occurring elementary particle produced when cosmic rays strike air molecules in the upper atmosphere.

Muon radiography. System that uses detectors to monitor the change in muon trajectory before and after muons interact with cargo, therby constructing a three-dimensional image of the dense cargo.

Murphy's Law. An adage, named after Air Force engineer Edward A. Murphy, Jr., that is commonly stated as "Whatever can go wrong, will go wrong."

Mutually assured destruction. A doctrine of military strategy in which the use of nuclear weapons by one nuclear-armed state against another inevitably results in the destruction of both the attacker and the defender.

National Academy of Sciences (NAS). An organization created in 1863 whose members serve voluntarily and without fee as advisors on science and technology for the United States government.

Near-real-time-accounting (NRTA). An accounting system that takes frequent measurements of material without disrupting processing of the material.

Neutron. A basic, neutral particle.

Neutron radiography. A nondestructive detection technology that uses a neutron beam to penetrate an object and, by measuring how the neutrons are affected, gathers information about its interior structure and composition.

Neutron reflector. Surrounds the core of a nuclear weapon and creates more fission reactions by redirecting neutrons, which would otherwise be lost, back into the core.

9/11 Commission. An independent, bipartisan commission created in 2002 to prepare a complete account of the September 11, 2001, terrorist attacks and provide recommendations designed to guard against future attacks.

Noncommercial transport. A vehicle used exclusively for private transportation of passengers or cargo for purposes unrelated to a business or commercial enterprise.

North American Aerospace Defense Command (NORAD). A joint organization of the United States and Canada founded in 1958 to monitor man-made objects in space, to ensure North American air sovereignty and air defense, and to detect, validate, and warn of air or space attack against North America.

Nuclear forensics. Methods that analyze radioactive debris or intercepted nuclear material to trace its origins, transportation route, and possible applications.

Nuclear proliferation. The spread of nuclear technologies to parties that do not already possess them.

Nuclear Suppliers Group (NSG). A multinational body of nuclear supplier countries founded in 1975 that seeks to contribute to nonproliferation of nuclear weapons by implementing guidelines for nuclear exports.

Office of Technology Assessment (OTA). An office of the United States Congress in operation from 1972 to 1995 that analyzed public policies related to science and technology.

Official point of entry. A place where travelers or goods enter or leave a country under official supervision.

Operational conservatism. The tendency to adhere to a circumscribed set of tactics that minimizes risk of failure and maximizes success.

Organizational learning. A process by which a group obtains knowledge that is used to improve tactics and decision making, or to increase the likelihood of successful operations.

PAL. Permissive action link. Device that prevents arming of a weapon unless certain steps are taken.

Partially quarantine. To restrict movement of some, but not all, vehicles, persons, or materials.

Passive gamma ray detection. A method that detects nuclear material by spotting its naturally emitted gamma radiation.

Physical Protection Systems. Systems associated with MPC&A that detect unauthorized penetration of barriers and portals and trigger the use of force if necessary.

Pin method. Used to determine the changing dimensions and positions of nuclear weapon components during implosion.

Plutonium. A heavy, radioactive, metallic element produced artificially in a reactor by bombarding uranium with neutrons. It is used primarily in nuclear weapons.

Radioactive. Describes an unstable nucleus that decays spontaneously and emits particles.

Radioactive fallout. The dangerous release of radioactive particles into the ground and atmosphere from nuclear power plants or nuclear explosions.

Rapid security upgrades. Security and accounting upgrades undertaken in Russia with international assistance to increase survivability of response forces, decrease response time, and place more guards closer to possible targets.

RDX. *See* HMX.

Red-teaming. A simulation designed to identify weaknesses, test security, and anticipate modes of attack by taking an attacker-like approach.

Reprocessing. The process used to separate useful products, such as uranium and plutonium, from spent nuclear fuel, for reuse in reactor fuel or for the core of a nuclear weapon.

Risk-averse. Describes one who chooses an option with less risk of failure or of retaliation over an option with more risk of failure or retaliation.

Rokkasho Plutonium Reprocessing Facility. A Japanese facility commissioned in 2006 to produce plutonium and mixed oxide fuel from spent nuclear reactor fuel.

Safing, Arming, Fusing, and Firing (SAFF). A complex set of requirements intended to ensure that a nuclear weapon will detonate at the intended time and place, and that it will not detonate at any other time or place.

Sanctuary. A place that provides protection and refuge for a terrorist group or its associated activities.

Sarin gas. A colorless and odorless gas that interferes with the transmission of nerve impulses and can spread quickly through the air.

Self-shielding. In a nuclear device, a decrease in the rate of flow per unit area of gamma rays from the inner layers of the core because of their absorption in the outer layers. A weapon with greater self-shielding is more difficult to detect.

Shielding. Material that surrounds a radiation source and decreases the amount of radiation ultimately emitted.

Signal-to-background ratio, signal-to-noise ratio. A comparison of the radiation emitted from nuclear material to the radiation emitted from natural sources, such as cosmic radiation.

Sodium iodide detector. A common radiation detector.

Special nuclear material (SNM). Plutonium or uranium that is enriched in U^{233} or U^{235}. In concentrated form, these can be the primary ingredients of nuclear explosives.

Spent fuel or spent fuel assembly. Radioactive fuel that has been used in a nuclear reactor.

Spontaneous fission. A process in which a nucleus splits spontaneously, generating neutrons and gamma rays.

Strategic Defense Initiative (SDI). A U.S. government program that functioned from 1984 to 1993 in order to develop national defense against nuclear ballistic missile attack.

Strategic warning. Warning to policy officials of change in the character or level of a national security threat before the enemy initiates hostilities.

Strategic weapons. Weapons that are long or medium-range, equipped with a nuclear warhead.

Supercritical or supercriticality. When the quantity of fissionable material becomes large enough to sustain a runaway chain reaction it is supercritical. Supercriticality is necessary for the explosion of a nuclear weapon.

Surge. A sudden increase in defensive efforts after a warning or a first attack by an enemy.

Synergy effects. The interaction of forces that results in a combined effect greater than the sum of the individual parts.

Tactical nuclear weapons. Weapons that have shorter range, lower yield, and smaller size than strategic weapons and are intended for battlefield targets.

Tactical warning. Warning to officials that the enemy has initiated hostilities.

Tamper. In a nuclear weapon design, an optional layer of dense material that surrounds the active material to retard expansion of the nuclear material.

Tungsten, tungsten carbide. Very dense material that can be used as a tamper in a nuclear weapon.

Two-man rule. Used to prevent theft of nuclear material by insiders, this rule ensures that there are at least two qualified workers who must act together in order to perform some action.

United Nations Security Council Resolution 1540. Resolution adopted by the United Nations Security Council in 2004 requiring all states to adopt appropriate effective measures to prevent nonstate actors from acquiring biological, chemical, and nuclear weapons, and associated delivery systems.

Warning threshold. The minimum level at which warning begins. A threshold that is too low may overwhelm the detection system with false alarms; a threshold that is too high may lead to thefts going unreported.

Yield of a weapon. The energy released by detonation of a nuclear weapon.

Notes

Prologue

1. This story is based on Brian Ross et al., "Customs Fails to Detect Depleted Uranium," *ABC News*, September 11, 2002.

1. Principles for Defense

1. Fred Kaplan, *The Wizards of Armageddon* (Palo Alto, CA: Stanford University Press, 1991), 9–10.
2. Sharon Ghamari-Tabrizi, *The Worlds of Herman Kahn* (Cambridge, MA: Harvard University Press, 2005), 48.
3. Terrorism is restricted to nonstate actors for the purposes of this book; state terrorism—that is, terrorism that does not involve subnational groups—is of a fundamentally different character.
4. For a review of the basic categories of counterterrorism tools, see Audrey Kurth Cronin and James M. Ludes, eds., *Attacking Terrorism: Elements of a Grand Strategy* (Washington, DC: Georgetown University Press, 2004).
5. Richard G. Lugar, *The Lugar Survey on Proliferation Threats and Responses*, Office of Senator Richard Lugar, Washington, DC, 2005, 30–31. For a sampling of past writing, see Mason Willrich and Theodore B. Taylor, *Nuclear Theft: Risks and Safeguards* (Cambridge, MA: Ballinger Publishing Company, 1974); Paul Leventhal and Yonah Alexander, eds., *Nuclear Terrorism: Defining the Threat* (Washington, DC: Pergamon-Brassey's, 1986); Richard Falkenrath et al., *America's Achilles' Heel* (Cambridge, MA: MIT Press, 1998); Ashton B. Carter and William J. Perry, *Preventive Defense* (Washington, DC: Brookings Institution Press, 1999; Matthew Bunn et al., *Controlling Nuclear Warheads and Materials* (Cambridge, MA: Belfer Center for Science and International Affairs, Kennedy School, Harvard University, 2003); Graham Allison, *Nuclear Terrorism* (New York: Times Books, 2004); Charles Ferguson and William Potter, *The Four Faces of Nuclear Terrorism* (Washington, DC: Monterey Institute for In-

ternational Studies, 2004).

6. National Research Council, *Making the Nation Safer: The Role of Science and Technology in Countering Terrorism* (Washington, DC: National Academies Press, 2002), 55–56; Bunn et al., *Controlling Nuclear Warheads;* Defense Science Board, *Preventing and Defending against Clandestine Nuclear Attack* (Washington, DC: Office of the Undersecretary of Defense of Acquisition, Technology, and Logistics, 2004); Ferguson and Potter, *Four Faces;* Michael M. May et al., "Detecting Nuclear Material in International Container Shipping," *Journal of Physical Security* 1 (Fall 2004): 1–28; Matthew Bunn, "Designing a Multi-Layered Defense against Nuclear Terror," presentation for Homeland Security Advisory Council Task Force on Weapons of Mass Effect, June 12, 2005; Michael V. Hynes et al., "Denying Armageddon: Preventing Terrorist Use of Nuclear Weapons," *Annals of the American Academy of Political and Social Science* [hereafter AAPSS] 607 (2006): 150–161.
7. Philip B. Heymann, "Dealing with Terrorism: An Overview," *International Security* 26 (Winter 2001/2): 24–38; National Research Council, *Making the Nation Safer,* 287–312; Stephen Flynn, *America the Vulnerable: How Our Government Is Failing to Protect Us from Terrorism* (New York: HarperCollins, 2004).
8. Michael Lewis, *Moneyball: The Art of Winning an Unfair Game* (New York: W. W. Norton & Co., 2003).
9. This analysis assumes that the steps are independent.
10. Henry Kyburg, *Probability and the Logic of Rational Belief* (Middletown, CT: Wesleyan University Press, 1961).
11. Matthew Brzezinski, "Bust and Boom," *Washington Post Magazine,* December 30, 2001.
12. National Commission on Terrorist Attacks, *The 9/11 Commission Report* (New York: W. W. Norton & Company, 2004), 182.
13. Ibid., 273.
14. One notable exception is Matthew Bunn, "A Mathematical Model of the Risk of Nuclear Terrorism," *Annals of the AAPSS* 607 (2006): 103–120.
15. For an introduction to qualitative systems dynamics, see E. F. Wolstenholme, "Qualitative vs. Quantitative Modeling: The Evolving Balance," *Journal of the Operational Research Society* 50 (1999): 422–428.
16. Arthur Brooks, *Weapon Mix and Exploratory Analysis: A Case Study* (Santa Monica, CA: RAND, 1997).
17. Les Aspin, *Report on the Bottom-Up Review* (Washington, DC: U.S. Department of Defense, 1993).
18. Ibid.
19. Paul K. Davis, *Analytic Architecture for Capabilities-Based Planning, Mission-System Analysis, and Transformation* (Santa Monica, CA: RAND, 2002).

20. This example is loosely based on one in ibid., xviii–xxii.
21. John Parachini, "Putting WMD Terrorism into Perspective," *Washington Quarterly*, Autumn 2003, 43.
22. Wyn K. Bowen, "Deterring Mass-Casualty Terrorism," *Joint Forces Quarterly*, Summer 2002, 25–29.
23. Paul K. Davis and Brian Michael Jenkins, *Deterrence and Influence in Counterterrorism* (Santa Monica, CA: RAND, 2002), 16.
24. Gavin Cameron, *Nuclear Terrorism: A Threat Assessment for the 21st Century* (New York: Palgrave Macmillan, 1999), 60–61.
25. Brian Michael Jenkins, *Unconquerable Nation: Knowing Our Enemy, Strengthening Ourselves* (Santa Monica, CA: RAND, 2006), 81.
26. I will use the male pronoun for simplicity throughout.
27. Bruce Hoffman, *Inside Terrorism* (New York: Columbia University Press, 1998), 178.
28. This preference is demonstrated throughout the account of the 9/11 attacks in National Commission on Terrorist Attacks, *The 9/11 Commission Report.*
29. Lawrence Freedman, *The Evolution of Nuclear Strategy* (Basingstoke, England: Palgrave Macmillan, 2003).
30. See the appendix.

2. Security at the Source

1. Charles Ferguson and William Potter, *The Four Faces of Nuclear Terrorism* (Washington, DC: Monterey Institute for International Studies, 2004), 119–120.
2. HEU figures derived from "Civil HEU Watch," Institute for Science and International Security, www.isis-online.org (accessed June 25, 2006).
3. Plutonium figures derived from "Separated Civil Plutonium Inventories," Institute for Science and International Security, www.isis-online.org (accessed June 25, 2006).
4. The history recounted here follows Kenneth N. Luongo and William E. Hoehn III, "Reform and Expansion of Threat Reduction," *Arms Control Today* 33 (June 2003), and *The Nunn-Lugar Vision: 1992–2002* (Washington, DC: Nuclear Threat Initiative, 2003).
5. Up-to-date analyses of the Global Partnership can be found at www.sgpproject.org.
6. Matthew Bunn and Anthony Weir, *Securing the Bomb 2006* (Washington, DC: Nuclear Threat Initiative/Belfer Center for Science and International Affairs, 2006), 54.
7. *Weapons of Mass Destruction: Additional Russian Cooperation Needed to Facili-*

tate U.S. Efforts to Improve Security at Russian Sites (Washington, DC: General Accounting Office, 2003), 24; and Bunn and Weir, *Securing the Bomb 2006*, 54.

8. Thomas Kean, interview on "Meet the Press," NBC, May 29, 2005.
9. Bernard T. Feld, presentation to Nuclear Control Institute–SUNY conference, June 1985, in Paul Leventhal and Yonah Alexander, eds., *Nuclear Terrorism: Defining the Threat* (Washington, DC: Pergamon-Brassey's, 1986), 139.
10. Books that advocate a fairly even balance include Graham Allison, *Nuclear Terrorism* (New York: Times Books, 2004); Michael Levi and Michael O'Hanlon, *The Future of Arms Control* (Washington, DC: Brookings Institution Press, 2005); and George Perkovich et al., *Universal Compliance: A Strategy for Nuclear Security* (Washington, DC: Carnegie Endowment for International Peace, 2005).
11. For a review, see Levi and O'Hanlon, *Future of Arms Control.*
12. John F. Kennedy at the third Kennedy-Nixon presidential debate, October 13, 1960, in Sidney Kraus, ed., *The Great Debates: Kennedy vs. Nixon, 1960* (Bloomington: Indiana University Press, 1962), 394.
13. Other arguments aimed specifically at showing this fallibility can be found in Siegfried S. Hecker, "Toward a Comprehensive Safeguards System: Keeping Fissile Materials out of Terrorists' Hands," *Annals of the AAPSS* 607 (2006): 121–132; Ronald F. Lehman III, prepared statement, Hearing on Terrorist Efforts to Build a Nuclear Bomb, House Select Committee on Homeland Security, May 26, 2005.
14. U.S. Department of the Treasury, "Fun Facts about the United States Mint," www.usmint.gov (accessed August 4, 2005).
15. U.S. Army, "Fort Knox—Home of Cavalry and Armor," www.knox.army.mil (accessed August 4, 2005).
16. Office of International Affairs, National Research Council, *Protecting Nuclear Weapons and Material in Russia* (Washington, DC: National Academies Press, 1999), 12.
17. George Bunn and Chaim Braun, "Study on New Terrorist Threats to Research Reactors: Preliminary Results," presentation, August 23, 2002, Stanford, CA.
18. Allison, *Nuclear Terrorism*, 148.
19. Ibid., 154.
20. Office of International Affairs, *Protecting Nuclear Weapons*, 13.
21. Ronald H. Auguston and John R. Phillips, "Russian-American MPC&A," *Los Alamos Science*, no. 24 (1996).
22. Chaim Braun and Christopher F. Chyba, "Proliferation Rings: New Challenges to the Nuclear Nonproliferation Regime," *International Security* 29 (Fall 2004): 5–49.
23. David Albright, "Securing Pakistan's Nuclear Weapons Complex," Institute for

Science and International Security, www.isis-online.org (accessed April 21, 2005).

24. Richard A. Clarke et al., *Defeating the Jihadists: A Blueprint for Action* (Washington, DC: Century Foundation Press, 2004), 137.
25. For a careful discussion of this scenario, see Kenneth Pollack, *The Persian Puzzle* (New York: Random House, 2004), 419–420.
26. Ibid.
27. Michael E. O'Hanlon and Mike Mochizuki, *Crisis on the Korean Peninsula* (New York: McGraw-Hill, 2003), 40.
28. For example, Richard K. Betts, "Suicide from Fear of Death?" *Foreign Affairs*, January/February 2003.
29. Matthew Bunn et al., *Securing Nuclear Warheads and Materials: Seven Steps for Immediate Action* (Cambridge, MA: Belfer Center for Science and International Affairs, Kennedy School, Harvard University, 2002).
30. Betts, "Suicide from Fear of Death?"
31. For the first U.S. threat, see Joel S. Wit et al., *Going Critical: The First North Korean Nuclear Crisis* (Washington, DC: Brookings Institution Press, 2004).
32. "N Korea 'Reprocesses' Nuclear Rods," *BBC News*, July 13, 2003.
33. For Pakistan, see Stephen P. Cohen, "The Jihadist Threat to Pakistan," *Washington Quarterly*, Summer 2003. On North Korea, see Ashton B. Carter, "Alternatives to Letting North Korea Go Nuclear," testimony before the U.S. Senate Committee on Foreign Relations, March 6, 2003.
34. William C. Potter and Elena Sokova, "Illicit Nuclear Trafficking in the NIS: What's New? What's True?" *Nonproliferation Review*, Summer 2002, 112–120.
35. National Research Council, *Making the Nation Safer: The Role of Science and Technology in Countering Terrorism* (Washington, DC: National Academies Press, 2002), 42.
36. Matthew Bunn et al., *Controlling Nuclear Warheads and Materials* (Cambridge, MA: Belfer Center for Science and International Affairs, Kennedy School, Harvard University, 2003), 116.
37. Richard Lugar, *The Lugar Survey on Proliferation Threats and Responses*, lugar.senate.gov (accessed December 1, 2006), 17.
38. Ibid., 16.

3. Building Blocks

1. This description is based primarily on Charles Ferguson and William Potter, *The Four Faces of Nuclear Terrorism* (Washington, DC: MIIS, 2004), 113.
2. Ibid.
3. International Atomic Energy Agency, "IAEA Illicit Trafficking Database," www.iaea.org (accessed October 24, 2005).

4. Kimberly McCloud and Matthew Osborne, *WMD Terrorism and Usama Bin Laden*, Center for Nonproliferation Studies/Monterey Institute for International Studies Report, 2001, cns.miis.edu (accessed October 24, 2005).
5. *Sunday Times* (London), January 4, 2004. Cited in "Libya Purchased Nuclear Weapons Plans from Pakistan, Qadhafi's Son Says," *Global Security Newswire*, January 5, 2004.
6. For a general discussion of efforts to counter terrorist financing, see Maurice R. Greenberg et al., *Terrorist Financing* (New York: Council on Foreign Relations, 2002).
7. National Commission on Terrorist Attacks, *The 9/11 Commission Report* (New York: W. W. Norton & Company, 2004), 170.
8. John Roth et al., *Monograph on Terrorist Financing* (Washington, DC: USG, 2004), 28.
9. Ibid..
10. Ibid., 27–28.
11. Mark Kleiman, private communication, November 17, 2005.
12. R. T. Naylor, *Wages of Crime: Black Markets, Illegal Finance, and the Underworld Economy* (Ithaca, NY: Cornell University Press, 2002), 117.
13. Ibid., 116.
14. Ibid.
15. For al Qaeda, see Michael Scheuer, *Through Our Enemies' Eyes* (Washington, DC: Potomac Books, 2006), 167–170. For Hezbollah, see Kenneth Pollack, *The Persian Puzzle* (New York: Random House, 2004), 201.
16. Stephen P. Cohen, "The Jihadist Threat to Pakistan," *Washington Quarterly*, Summer 2003.
17. Robert I. Rotberg, ed., *State Failure and State Weakness in a Time of Terror* (Washington, DC: Brookings Institution Press, 2003).
18. Kim Cragin, "Hizballah, the Party of God," in Brian A. Jackson et al., *Aptitude for Destruction*, vol. 2 (Santa Monica, CA: RAND, 2005), 50.
19. Ferguson and Potter review several assertions along these lines (with which they concur). Ferguson and Potter, *Four Faces*, 132–133. I assume weapons-grade uranium has 93% U^{235}, 6% U^{238}, and 1% U^{234}.
20. This assertion is made in Jeffrey Lewis and Peter Zimmerman, "The Bomb in the Backyard," *Foreign Policy*, November/December 2006. They assume a three- or four-person team working on the gun, including one "familiar with the interior ballistics of guns in the appropriate size range."
21. Luis W. Alvarez, *Adventures of a Physicist* (New York: Basic Books, 1988), 125.
22. Matthew L. Wald, "Suicidal Nuclear Threat Is Seen at Weapons Plants," *New York Times*, January 23, 2003.
23. Carson Mark et al., "Can Terrorists Build Nuclear Weapons?" in Paul Leventhal and Yonah Alexander, eds., *Preventing Nuclear Terrorism: The Report and*

Papers of the International Task Force on Prevention of Nuclear Terrorism (Lexington, MA: Lexington Books, 1987).

24. John E. Daugherty, *A Summary of Indicators of Nth Country Weapon Development Programs* (Los Alamos, NM: Los Alamos National Laboratory, 1978), 6.
25. Andrew Bird and Simon Anthony, "Casting Uranium: Experimental and Modeling Capabilities," *Discovery,* July 5, 2002.
26. U.S. Department of Energy, *DOE Handbook: Primer on Spontaneous Heating and Pyrophoricity* (Washington, DC: U.S. Department of Energy, 1994), 36–38, 52.
27. Matthew Brzezinski, "Bust and Boom," *Washington Post Magazine,* December 30, 2001.
28. H. E. Pearson, *1954—AEC Uranium Fire Experience* (Richland, WA: Hanford, 1954; HAN-64841), cited in M. G. Plys and D. R. Duncan, *Uranium Pyrophoricity Phenomena and Prediction* (Richland, WA: Fluor Hanford, 2000), 5-1.
29. Steven van Evera, "Assessing U.S. Strategy in the War on Terror," *Annals of the AAPSS* 607 (2006): 10–26.
30. Charles Duelfer, *Comprehensive Report of the Special Advisor to the DCI on Iraq's WMD with Addendums,* vol. 2 (Washington, DC: Government Printing Office, 2004), 8 (Nuclear).
31. Ibid., 59 (Nuclear).
32. "Iraq's primary focus was a basic implosion fission design." Iraq Nuclear Verification Office, "Fact Sheet: Iraq's Nuclear Weapons Program," www.iaea.org (accessed June 12, 2005).
33. Mark et al., "Can Terrorists Build Nuclear Weapons?"
34. David Albright, *South Africa's Secret Nuclear Weapons* (Washington, DC: Institute for Science and International Security Report, 1994).
35. Albright notes that the weapons each contained 55 kilograms of 90 percent U^{235}, which corresponds to a neutron output of approximately 120 neutrons each second. Robert Serber, *The Los Alamos Primer* (Berkeley, CA: University of California Press, 1992), estimates the time from first to maximum criticality would be on the order of one hundred microseconds, during which there would be less than a 1 percent probability that a neutron would be emitted. These are at best order of magnitude estimates.
36. Thomas Cochran, private communication, August 3, 2005.
37. For example, to achieve a 90 percent chance of detonation before full assembly was reached, the group would have to accept a 40 percent chance of a tenfold or greater reduction in yield. Based on Serber, *Los Alamos Primer,* 49.
38. Richard Rhodes, *The Making of the Atomic Bomb* (New York: Simon and Schuster, 1986), 578.
39. Richard Rhodes, *Dark Sun* (New York: Simon and Schuster, 1996), 168.
40. Implosion speeds are on the order of eight kilometers per second, between one

and two orders of magnitude greater than in the gun-weapon case, which suggests that fewer neutrons per second might be required in the latter. On the other hand, different shock dynamics will produce different mixing of the alpha and neutron emitters, meaning that the relationship between Po^{210} quantity and neutron emissions will not translate directly.

41. R. R. Paternoster, *Nuclear Weapons Proliferation Indicators and Observables* (Los Alamos, NM: Los Alamos National Laboratory, 1992), 21.
42. 9 CFR 110.23 (2005) (U.S. NRC Rules for Export and Import of Nuclear Equipment).
43. U.S. Department of Commerce, *Commerce Control List: Supplement No. 1 to Part 774* (Washington, DC: U.S. Government Printing Office, 2005); U.S. Department of Commerce, *Commerce Control List Overview and the Country Chart* (Washington, DC: USG, 2005), category 1, p. 48.
44. Environmental Science Division, "Polonium," Argonne National Laboratory, 2005.
45. The precise change in yield is unknown publicly.
46. Mark et al., "Could Terrorists Build Nuclear Weapons?"
47. I thank Peter D. Zimmerman for this observation.
48. Thomas Cochran, private communication, October 2005.
49. Robert B. Ross, *Metallic Materials Specification Handbook*, 3rd ed. (London: E. & F. N. Spon, 1980), 612.
50. Department of Commerce, *Commerce Control List.*
51. For densities, see Ross, *Metallic Materials Specification Handbook.* For performance as reflectors, see William C. Rask, *Beryllium* (Albuquerque, NM: Office of Strategic Planning and Analysis, Albuquerque Operations Office, Department of Energy, 1983), 3.
52. P. Greenfield, *Engineering Applications of Beryllium* (London: Mills & Boon Limited, 1971), 11.
53. John A. McPhee, *The Curve of Binding Energy* (New York: Farrar, Straus and Giroux, 1974), 66.
54. Peter D. Zimmerman, private communication, September 2005.
55. Agency for Toxic Substances and Disease Registry, *Beryllium* (Atlanta: Centers for Disease Control, 2002).
56. For details of the calculations substantiating these statements, please contact the author.
57. Brian A. Jackson, *Organizational Learning and Terrorist Groups* (Santa Monica, CA: RAND, 2004), 3.
58. Ibid., 13–17.
59. Brian A. Jackson et al., *Aptitude for Destruction*, vol. 2 (Santa Monica, CA: RAND, 2005).
60. National Commission on Terrorist Attacks, *The 9/11 Commission Report.*

61. John Parachini, "Aum Shinrikyo," in Jackson, *Aptitude for Destruction,* 18.
62. Ibid., in Jackson, *Aptitude for Destruction,* 19.
63. Ibid., in Jackson, *Aptitude for Destruction,* 23, 26, 27.
64. National Commission on Terrorist Attacks, *The 9/11 Commission Report,* 155.
65. Ibid., 160.
66. Ibid., 255–256.
67. Steve Coll, "What Bin Laden Sees in Hiroshima," *Washington Post,* February 6, 2005.
68. This is found by first simulating a uranium sphere emitting a uniformly distributed 186 keV gamma ray (from U^{235}) in TART, a Monte-Carlo simulation code published by the United States government that simulates neutron and photon transport. Its results are accurate enough to inform qualitative policy and strategy judgments, but not precise enough for terrorists to use the results presented here as a substitute for experimentation or far more careful calculation. The code gives the flux at the uranium surface in energy bins; 0.5 percent of the gamma rays escape with energies within 2 keV (the detector resolution) of the original energy. From that and from the specific activity of U^{235}, one can estimate that approximately 3.5 million such gamma rays are emitted each second. Steve Fetter et al., "Detecting Nuclear Warheads," *Science and Global Security* 1 (1990), write that a surface emitting 70,000 186 keV gamma rays can be detected at a distance of 6 meters in one minute; scaling using the equations in the appendix gives the distance provided. An introduction to TART is given in Dermott E. Cullen et al., *TART95: A Coupled Neutron-Photon Monte Carlo Transport Code* (Livermore, CA: Lawrence Livermore National Laboratory, 1995).
69. The dominant emission is at 1.001 MeV from U^{238}, at a rate of 73/g-s. The sphere of uranium thus emits 74,000 1.001 MeV gamma rays per second, 2,400 of which escape each second with energies within 1 keV of the original energy. The latter figure is derived by simulating the assembly of uranium and lead in TART. The detection distances are calculated using the formulae in the appendix.
70. ASTM International, *Standard Guide for Laboratory Evaluation of Automatic Pedestrian SNM Monitor Performance,* introduction at www.astm.org (accessed November 21, 2006).
71. The simulation and calculation are the same as in the previous example.
72. The background of 90 neutrons is due to neutron production in the atmosphere. The number may be higher if the container also contains substantial amounts of other high atomic number materials, due to neutron production through cosmic ray proton spallation.
73. "The Intermodal Container FAQ," www.rob1.w1.com (accessed May 9, 2005).
74. Office of Economic and Statistical Analysis, *Vessel Calls at U.S. Ports, 2003*

(Washington, DC: U.S. Department of Transportation, Maritime Administration, 2004), 1.

75. For an example of such criticism, see Randall Larsen, "70–20–10," *Wall Street Journal*, May 25, 2006.
76. Stephen Flynn, *America the Vulnerable* (New York: HarperCollins, 2004), 83–84.
77. Stephen Flynn, personal communication, June 2006.
78. For example, Stanford Study Group, *Container Security Study* (Stanford, CA: Center for International Security and Cooperation, Stanford University, 2002); Devabhaktuni Srikrishna et al., "Deterrence of Nuclear Terrorism with Mobile Radiation Detectors," *Nonproliferation Review* 12 (Fall/Winter 2005).
79. For a discussion of detection against nonconstant backgrounds, see the appendix. It shows that, for container voyages, an uncertainty on the order of 100 n/m^2-s in the neutron background is likely to be unavoidable.
80. For example, see Stanford Study Group, *Container Security Study*, 5.
81. Dennis Slaughter et al., *Detection of Special Nuclear Material in Cargo Containers Using Neutron Interrogation*, UCRL-ID-155315 (Livermore, CA: Lawrence Livermore National Laboratory, 2003).
82. For example, Richard L. Garwin, "The Technology of Megaterror," *Technology Review*, September 2002.
83. J. L. Jones et al., *Proof-of-concept Assessment of a Photofission-based Interrogation System for the Detection of Shielded Nuclear Material* (Idaho Falls: Idaho National Engineering and Environmental Laboratory, 2000).
84. Slaughter et al., *Detection of Special Nuclear Material.*
85. Ibid., 15.
86. Ibid., 16.
87. The basics of neutron radiography in cargo scanning are discussed in J. M. Moss et al., "Applications of Antineutrino Detector Technology to Counterterrorism," in *Research Highlights from Physics Activity Report 2003* (Los Alamos, NM: Los Alamos National Laboratory, 2003), 97–100. The description of neutron radiography there does not depend specifically on the antineutrino detector technology, but rather on the availability of relatively low cost, large-area thermal neutron detectors. An alternative option for a low-cost, large-area detector, based on a boron-rich semiconductor, is described in P. A. Dowben et al., "Interdiction of Cross-Border Transport of Fissile Materials," paper for the Project on Nuclear Issues, 2004. See also Roger C. Byrd et al., "Nuclear Detection to Prevent or Defeat Clandestine Nuclear Attack," *IEEE Sensors Journal* 5 (August 2005): 601–602.
88. Moss et al., "Applications of Antineutrino Detector Technology to Counterterrorism." The study in the reference refers to weapons-grade plutonium, and leverages the fact that shielding there against passive interrogation will span a

diameter on the order of at least 50 cm. This is replicated here for active interrogation—the shielding in the first case has a thickness of 30 cm, while in the second case, assuming the hydrogenous material is water, the shielding has a thickness of 120 cm. The low required resolution allows a low-intensity and hence safe and relatively inexpensive neutron source to be used.

89. For a technical review of the most prominent results, see K. N. Borozdin et al., "Radiographic Imaging with Cosmic Ray Muons," *Nature* 422, no. 277 (2003). For a nonspecialist summary, see Brian Fishbine, "Muon Radiography: Detecting Nuclear Contraband," *Los Alamos Research Quarterly*, Spring 2003.
90. Byrd et al., "Nuclear Detection," 597–599.
91. The most expensive component of the VACIS radiography system, widely in use already, is the NaI(Tl) detectors. Victor V. Verbinski et al., *U.S. Patent No. 6507025* (Washington, DC: U.S. Patent and Trademark Office, 2003). These cost less than $100,000 at current Na(Tl) prices, while the VACIS costs over $1,000,000. "Laredo Gets New Rail Inspection Building and Upgraded Equipment," *Customs and Border Protection Today*, October/November 2003. This difference is likely accounted for by R&D costs (amortized over all units), assembly costs, costs of other components, and profit. Each could be substantially reduced for large volumes.
92. Byrd et al., "Nuclear Detection," 593–609.
93. For recent studies that credit the utility of emergency response without delving into much detail, see "A Mathematical Model of the Risk of Nuclear Terrorism," *Annals of the AAPSS* 607 (2006): 117; Siegfried S. Hecker, "Toward a Comprehensive Safeguards System: Keeping Fissile Materials out of Terrorists' Hands," *Annals of the AAPSS* 607 (2006): 128.
94. Stephen Flynn, personal communication, September 2006.
95. A description of this challenge, and of possible countermeasures specific to the American case, can be found in Continuity of Government Commission, *Preserving Our Institutions—The First Report of the Continuity of Government Commission* (Washington, DC: American Enterprise Institute, 2003).
96. Lynn E. Davis et al., *Individual Preparedness and Response to Chemical, Radiological, Nuclear, and Biological Terrorist Attacks* (Santa Monica, CA: RAND, 2003).
97. Ferguson and Potter, *Four Faces*, 86–91. Some argue that sending first responders into the inner part of this zone would be sacrificing their lives without significantly reducing casualties; certainly, more research in this area would be valuable. Peter D. Zimmerman, personal communication, August 2005.
98. The Advisory Panel to Assess Domestic Response Capabilities for Terrorism Involving Weapons of Mass Destruction (Gilmore Commission), *Third Annual Report to the President and the Congress* (Arlington, VA: RAND Corporation, 2001), G-2-16–G-2-23.

4. The Beginnings of a True System

1. Oleg Bukharin, "Analysis of the Size and Quality of Uranium Inventories in Russia," *Science and Gobal Security* 4 (1996): 59–71.
2. All figures in the paragraph are from Robert L. Civiak, *Closing the Gaps: Securing Highly-Enriched Uranium in the Former Soviet Union* (Washington, DC: Federation of American Scientists, 2002).
3. Oleg Bukharin, private communication, February 2004.
4. Interview with former senior U.S. nonproliferation official, May 2005.
5. As of the end of 2003. David Albright, "Global Fissile Material Inventories," www.isis-online.org (accessed May 17, 2005).
6. For a review of weapons programs, see Joseph Cirincione et al., *Deadly Arsenals: Nuclear, Biological, and Chemical Threats,* 2nd ed. (Washington, DC: Carnegie Endowment for International Peace, 2005).
7. Albright, "Global Fissile Material Inventories."
8. Oleg Bukharin, "Understanding Russia's Uranium Enrichment Complex," *Science and Global Security* 12 (2004): 193–214.
9. Oleg Bukharin, "Making Fuel Less Tempting," *Bulletin of the Atomic Scientists,* July/August 2002, 44–49.
10. Allison Macfarlane et al., "Plutonium Disposal: The Third Way," *Bulletin of the Atomic Scientists,* May/June 2001, 53–57.
11. Anatoly S. Diakov, "Disposition of Weapons-Grade Plutonium in Russia: Evaluation of Different Options," in Nancy Turtle Schulte, ed., *Dismantlement and Destruction of Chemical, Nuclear and Conventional Weapons* (Brussels: NATO, 1996), 171–180.
12. Reviewing the main yield equation in Robert Serber, *The Los Alamos Primer* (Berkeley, CA: University of California Press, 1992), one can see that the only variables that differ between cases here are Δ and M. For two spherical systems with yields Y_1 and Y_2, then, $Y_1/Y_2 = (M_1/M_2)\Delta_1^3/\Delta_2^3 = (M_1/M_2)(M_1^{1/3} - M_C^{1/3})^3/(M_2^{1/3} - M_C^{1/3})^3$, where M_C is the critical mass. Strictly speaking, the estimate in Serber applies only to unreflected systems, since Serber uses an estimate for α valid only for unreflected systems. However, inspecting the figure in Serber, *Los Alamos Primer,* 44, one sees that the deviation is likely to be small.
13. Figures in this paragraph are from Alexander Glaser, "On the Proliferation Potential of Uranium Fuel for Research Reactors at Various Enrichment Levels," *Science and Global Security* 14, no. 1 (2006): 1–24.
14. The bare critical mass of 36 percent enriched uranium is approximately 300 kg, while α at full assembly for two critical masses is approximately $13/\mu s$. For a system reflected by 15 cm of beryllium, the critical mass becomes 70 kg, and α becomes $2/\mu s$. The yield follows from the same calculation as used for this scenario in Chapter 3.

15. To request details of the calculations underlying these assessments, including specific figures, please contact the author. The estimates are very pessimistic, since they make idealized assumptions about gun performance.
16. For capacities of various cranes, see Department of the Army, *Engineering and Design of Military Ports* (Washington, DC: Department of the Army, 1983), 12–13. The weight limit in the United States for a forty-foot container is 65,000 pounds, indicating an upper bound on the physical capacity for a container. Lawrence Wein et al., "Preventing the Importation of Illicit Nuclear Materials in Shipping Containers," draft, 10.
17. Barry Rosenberg, "Gulfstream Brings New Visions Here: Of Runways and Product Nomenclature," *Aviation Week*, www.aviationweek.com (accessed June 3, 2005).
18. Office of Technology Assessment, *Technologies Underlying Weapons of Mass Destruction* (Washington, DC: OTA, 1994), 74.
19. The description here generally follows Dan Stober, "No Experience Necessary," *Bulletin of the Atomic Scientists*, March/April 2003, 56–63.
20. Charles Ferguson and William Potter, "Improvised Nuclear Devices and Nuclear Terrorism," WMD Commission Paper no. 2, 16.
21. Morten Braemer Maerli, *Crude Nukes on the Loose?* Norwegian Institute of International Affairs (NUPI) paper no. 664, 2004.
22. F. S. Eby and L. S. Germain, "Critique of the Nth Country Weapon Design," in W. J. Frank, ed., *Summary Report of the Nth Country Experiment—Extract*, UCRL-50249, March 1967, 24.
23. Frank, *Summary Report*, 37.
24. A. J. Hudgins, "The Operating Rules for the Nth Country Project", in ibid., 34.
25. Lillian Hoddeson et al., *Critical Assembly: A Technical History of Los Alamos during the Oppenheimer Years, 1943–1945* (Cambridge: Cambridge University Press, 1993), 267–292, 268.
26. International Atomic Energy Agency, INFCIRC/254/Rev.4/Part 2, *Communications Received from Certain Member States Regarding Guidelines for Transfers of Nuclear Related Dual-Use Equipment, Materials, Software and Related Technology*, March 9, 2000, 5-1.
27. International Atomic Energy Agency, *Al-Athir [Al-Atheer] Plant Progress Report for the period 1 January 1990 to 31 May 1990*, as translated in *Annex to the First Report on the On-site Inspection in Iraq under Security Council Resolution 687*, 1991. Although Iraq did procure a 160 kV flash X-ray system, the NSG finds only systems over 500 kV worthy of control.
28. Hoddeson et al., *Critical Assembly*, 272.
29. International Atomic Energy Agency, INFCIRC/254, 6-3.
30. James Glanz et al., "Huge Cache of Explosives Vanished from Site in Iraq," *New York Times*, October 24, 2004.

31. Voids in an explosive lens will distort the explosive shock in that lens, in turn perturbing the imploding shock wave from its ideal spherical shape. Peter D. Zimmerman, personal communication, October 2004.
32. Committee on International Security and Arms Control, *Monitoring Nuclear Weapons and Nuclear-Explosive Materials: An Assessment of Methods and Capabilities* (Washington, DC: National Academies Press, 2005), 224; J. Carson Mark, "Explosive Properties of Reactor-Grade Plutonium," *Science and Global Security* 4, no. 1 (1993): 119.
33. Stanislav Rodionov, "Could Terrorists Produce Low-Yield Nuclear Weapons?" in *High-Impact Terrorism: Proceedings of a Russian-American Workshop* (Washington, DC: National Academies Press, 2002).
34. For an overview of plutonium metallurgy, see "Challenges in Plutonium Science," *Los Alamos Science*, no. 26 (2000).
35. PU^{238} might seem to be an option, but it is strictly controlled and melts if gathered together in significant quantities. I thank an anonymous reviewer for the first observation.
36. Carson Mark et al., "Can Terrorists Build Nuclear Weapons?" in Paul Leventhal and Yonah Alexander, eds., *Preventing Nuclear Terrorism: The Report and Papers of the International Task Force on Prevention of Nuclear Terrorism* (Lexington, MA: Lexington Books, 1987).
37. David Fishlock, "The Drama of Plutonium," *Nuclear Energy International*, July 2005.
38. This amount is half of an IAEA "significant quantity," 8 kilograms.
39. One kilogram of weapons-grade plutonium emits roughly 56,000 neutrons each second; four kilograms thus emit roughly 6×10^5 neutrons each second, accounting also for neutron multiplication in the plutonium, assuming a spherical shape. All radiological data in this paragraph are from Steve Fetter et al., "Detecting Nuclear Warheads," *Science and Global Security* 1 (1990), and from Monte-Carlo simulations using TART.
40. These are neutron-induced gamma rays in the plutonium. Approximately 70,000 gamma rays are emitted with energies between 100 keV and 1 MeV; approximately 60,000 are emitted with energies between 1 MeV and 2 MeV; and approximately 30,000 are emitted with energies between 2 MeV and 3 MeV. Figures were obtained using TART simulation. Smuggling plutonium in non-spherical shapes would decrease neutron multiplication but would also decrease self-shielding of gamma rays.
41. Simulated using TART. This includes 2,300 photons with energies between 1 and 2 MeV, and 1,500 with energies between 2 and 3 MeV.
42. I assume an NaI(Tl) detector as described in Fetter, searching for photons near 1.6 MeV with the background shielded by a factor of 10. The number of pho-

tons within that window is determined by TART simulation, and the detection distance and time is then calculated using the formulae in the appendix.

43. Based on TART simulation. The worst-case threshold assumes detection in intermodal containers at high latitude. Detection in the presence of less massive cargoes and at lower latitudes would reduce the detection threshold.
44. For example, J. L. Jones et al., *Proof-of-concept Assessment of a Photofission-based Interrogation System for the Detection of Shielded Nuclear Material* (Idaho Falls: Idaho National Engineering and Environmental Laboratory, 2000), and Wein et al., "Preventing the Importation of Illicit Nuclear Materials."
45. I assume that the lithium hydride is at full crystal density (a pessimistic assumption for the defense) and that the borated polyethylene is 7.5 percent boron by weight. All figures obtained through simulation in TART.
46. For a review of border security, see Michael E. O'Hanlon et al., *Protecting the American Homeland: One Year On* (Washington, DC: Brookings Institution Press, 2003), 13–34.
47. For example, Assistant U.S. Attorney Marina Marmolejo, in Ralph Vartabedian et al., "Rise in Bribery Tests Integrity of U.S. Border," *Los Angeles Times*, October 23, 2006.
48. John A. McPhee, *The Curve of Binding Energy* (New York: Farrar, Straus and Giroux, 1974).
49. Gunnar Arbman et al., *Eliminating Stockpiles of Highly Enriched Uranium* (Stockholm: SKI, 2004).
50. Mark et al., "Can Terrorists Build Nuclear Weapons?"
51. International Atomic Energy Agency, *Report on the Twenty-Eighth IAEA On-Site Inspection in Iraq under Security Council Resolution 687* (New York: United Nations, 1995).
52. Mark et al., "Can Terrorists Build Nuclear Weapons?"; McPhee, *Curve of Binding Energy*, 113.
53. Further details related to this paragraph may be requested from the author.
54. Fetter gives background contributions for both alpha-induced neutrons and spontaneous fission, assuming 0.2 percent oxygen impurities (by weight), which is equivalent to 3 percent by atom. For weapons-grade uranium metal, this is dominated by U^{238}, which contributes 14 n/kg-s from spontaneous fission, and by U^{234}, which contributes 56 n/kg-s, primarily due to the interaction of alpha particles with oxygen impurities. In the oxide, however, there are 2 oxygen atoms for every uranium atom, not 0.03 as in the metal. Since most alpha particles will be absorbed by uranium, the oxygen presence may be treated as a small perturbation: as a result, one can simply scale up the production of neutrons from alpha particles with the oxygen concentration. Figures from Fetter et al., "Detecting Nuclear Warheads," Appendix. A.

55. B. D. Geelhood et al., *Gamma Ray Spectroscopy of Partially Oxidized Plutonium Metal* (Richland, WA: Pacific Northwest National Laboratory, 2001). Several specifics of their setup are important. First, their sample contains 81 percent Pu^{239} and 17 percent Pu^{240}; weapons-grade plutonium contains more Pu^{239} and less Pu^{240}. One can show that correcting this leads to an increased gamma production rate of roughly 25 percent. Second, the authors study a 2.2 kg mass of PuO_2, but do not account for self-shielding in determining their emission rate. However, since the authors describe their material as being the typical output of a reprocessing plant, it can be assumed that the material is at low density, roughly 3 g/cc. Self-shielding at that density and for that mass would not be significant.
56. Determined by simulation in TART.
57. Calculation using formulae in the appendix.
58. Based on TART simulation and formulae in the appendix.
59. National Academy of Sciences, "Steps Must Be Taken to Reduce Plutonium Risks," press release, January 24, 1994.
60. National Academy of Sciences, Board on Radioactive Waste Management, *Safety and Security of Commercial Spent Nuclear Fuel Storage: Public Report* (Washington, DC: National Academies Press, 2005), 33.
61. Edwin S. Lyman, "Can the Proliferation Risks of Nuclear Power Be Made Acceptable?," paper presented at the Nuclear Control Institute twentieth anniversary conference, April 9, 2001.
62. National Academy of Sciences, *The Spent-Fuel Standard for Disposition of Excess Weapon Plutonium: Application to Current DOE Options* (Washington, DC: National Academies Press, 2000).
63. The demands involved in extracting fissile material from either MOX or HEU fuel are discussed in R. R. Paternoster, *Nuclear Weapons Proliferation Indicators and Observables* (Los Alamos, NM: Los Alamos National Laboratory, 1992), 7–9.
64. Mark, "Explosive Properties of Reactor-Grade Plutonium."
65. Joe Fiorill, "Experts Question U.S. Emphasis on Nuclear Weapon Detection," *Global Security Newswire*, June 8, 2005.
66. For an example of the former, see the measurements of a Soviet warhead in Steve Fetter et al., "Gamma-ray Measurements of a Soviet Cruise-Missile Warhead," *Science* 248, May 18, 1990, 828–834. For an example of the latter, see the description of "off-spec" HEU in Gary W. Fox and John Matheson, "Dealing with the Legacy of US and Russian Nuclear Defense Programmes—AREVA's Contributions," World Nuclear Association annual symposium, 2003.
67. This calculation is based on a U^{232} emission of 2.7×10^{11} n/g-s. Fetter et al., "Gamma-Ray Measurements." That emission rate, in turn, assumes an elapsed time on the order of two or more years since the separation of Pa^{231} from U^{232}.

68. This reduction is found by simulation in TART.
69. The competing background is dominated by the decay of Th^{232}, present in many terrestrial sources, which ultimately produces 2.6 MeV photons through Tl^{208}; however, its signal can in principle be subtracted by observing other Th^{232} decay products. Fetter et al., "Gamma Ray Measurements."
70. For the first possibility, see Fetter et al., "Gamma Ray Measurements." For the second, see Bernard Phlips, "Nuclear Data for Gamma Ray Telescope Simulations," slides from presentation at Cross Section Evaluation Working Group meeting, Brookhaven National Laboratory, November 4, 2004.
71. Phlips, "Nuclear Data."
72. Calculation from figures above using formulae from the appendix.
73. Determined using TART simulation.
74. National Drug Intelligence Center, *National Drug Threat Assessment, 2006* (Washington, DC: U.S. Department of Justice, 2006). The uncertainty is due to the difficulty of estimating the amount of cocaine originally destined for the United States.
75. Office of National Drug Control Policy (ONDCP), *Estimation of Cocaine Availability* (Washington, DC: ONDCP, 2002), 27.
76. Ibid., 28.
77. Maritime seizure statistics fluctuate wildly, and may be unreliable. Using the statistic for 1998, the seizure rate jumps to 7 percent, while using the statistic for 1997, it becomes 12 percent, similar to the rate for 1997. In any case, they account for a much smaller fraction of cocaine smuggling.
78. ONDCP, *Estimation of Cocaine Availability*, 27.
79. Office of Policy and Planning, *Estimates of the Unauthorized Immigrant Population Residing in the United States: 1990 to 2000* (Washington, DC: U.S. Immigration and Naturalization Service, 2003).
80. Blas Nuñez-Neto, *Border Security: The Role of the U.S. Border Patrol* (Washington, DC: Congressional Research Service, 2005).
81. This calculation is not affected by possible multiple entry attempts, since the probability of being apprehended in any individual attempt is always equal to the ratio of successful entries to successful entries plus apprehensions.
82. Rohan Gunaratna, *Inside Al Qaeda* (New York: Berkley Books, 2002), 219.
83. U.S. Attorney's Office, Western District of Texas, "Former Mexican Immigration Official Sentenced to Federal Prison for Role in Alien Smuggling Organization," press release, November 30, 2001.
84. Steven A. Camarota, *The Open Door: How Militant Islamic Terrorists Entered and Remained in the United States, 1993–2001* (Washington, DC: Center for Immigration Studies, 2002).
85. Ibid., 30.
86. Ibid., 32.

87. Ibid., 34.
88. Office of the Inspector General, *Inspection of INS' Strategy for Securing the Northern Border* (Washington, DC: U.S. Department of Justice, 2000), 6.
89. "Smuggling Boat Dumps 150 People on Canadian Coast," *Reuters*, August 11, 1999.
90. Dene Moore, "Nine Ships, Five Countries Cited for Illegal Fishing in North Atlantic Last Year," *Canadian Press*, January 20, 2005.
91. Stephen Flynn, personal communication, September 2006.
92. "Mexico's Drug Runners Taking to the Skies," *Arizona Republic*, November 20, 2005.
93. "Designation of Ports of Entry for Aliens Arriving by Civil Aircraft," 8 CFR Part 234.
94. Michael A. Braun, Testimony before House Subcommittee on Crime, Terrorism, and Homeland Security and House Subcommittee on Western Hemisphere, September 21, 2006.
95. Her Majesty's Royal Customs, *Annual Report and Accounts 2003–04* (London: HMRC, 2004), 150.
96. John Martin Corkery, *Drug Seizures and Offender Statistics, UK, 2000*, www.homeoffice.gov.uk (accessed November 25, 2006), 16.
97. *Disrupting Crack Markets—A Practice Guide* (London: Home Office, 2003), 12, 33.
98. Michael Jandl, "Estimates on the Number of Illegal and Smuggled Immigrants in Europe," presentation at eighth International Metropolis Conference, August 17, 2003, slides at www.icmpd.org (accessed November 25, 2006).

5. Warning

1. One can find such assessments in, for example, Charles Ferguson and William Potter, *The Four Faces of Nuclear Terrorism* (Washington, DC: MIIS, 2004), 14–45; Graham Allison, *Nuclear Terrorism* (New York: Times Books, 2005), 17–120.
2. Defense Science Board, *Preventing and Defending Against Clandestine Nuclear Attack* (Washington, DC: Office of the Undersecretary of Defense for Acquisition, Technology, and Logistics, 2004).
3. I thank Matthew Bunn for this observation.
4. Barbara Slavin, "Nuclear Weapons Threat Lurks in Russia," *USA Today*, November 24, 1998.
5. Gary L. Jones, "DOE's Efforts to Secure Nuclear Material and Employ Weapons Scientists in Russia," testimony before the U.S. Senate Committee on Armed Services, May 15, 2001.

6. Matthew Bunn, "Mayak Fissile Materials Storage Facility," www.nit.org (accessed August 4, 2005).
7. Guarav Kampani, "Safety Concerns about the Command and Control of Pakistan's Strategic Forces, Fissile Material, and Nuclear Installations," cns.miis.edu (accessed August 26, 2005).
8. See the review of command and control for Pakistani weapons in ibid.
9. Hui Zhang, "Evaluating China's MPC&A System," proceedings of the forty-fourth Institute of Nuclear Materials Management (INMM) annual meeting (July 13–17, 2003, Phoenix, Arizona).
10. Nathan Busch, "China's Fissile Material Protection, Control, and Accounting: The Case for Renewed Collaboration," *Nonproliferation Review,* Fall–Winter 2002, 89–106.
11. Rensselaer W. Lee, *Smuggling Armageddon* (New York: St. Martin's Press, 1998), 30–31.
12. For an introduction to the HEU Agreement, see Richard A. Falkenrath, "The HEU Deal," in Graham Allison et al., *Avoiding Nuclear Anarchy* (Cambridge, MA: MIT Press, 1995), 229–293.
13. Oleg Bukharin and Helen M. Hunt, "The U.S.-Russian HEU Agreement: Internal Safeguards to Prevent Diversion of HEU," *Science and Global Security* 4 (1994): 189–212.
14. Ibid., 199.
15. Ibid., 200.
16. Marvin M. Miller, "Are IAEA Safeguards on Plutonium Bulk-Handling Facilities Effective?" Nuclear Control Institute, Washington, DC, 1990.
17. James W. Tape, "International Safeguards and Verification Challenges," Proceedings of the European Safeguards Research and Development Association (ESARDA)/Institute of Nuclear Materials Management (INMM) workshop "Safeguards Perspectives for a Future Nuclear Environment," Como, Italy, October 14–16, 2003, 6. Lawrence Scheinman, a senior aide to the IAEA director general during the LASCAR (Large-Scale Reprocessing) process, confirms that safeguardability judgments regarding Rokkasho depended heavily on the strength of C/S measures. Lawrence Scheinman, private communication, November 7, 2005.
18. Miller, "Are IAEA Safeguards Effective?" Miller indicates that one or two inventories per year is typical.
19. To calculate this, first calculate the detection threshold at which the required rate of false positives is achieved; then calculate the likelihood that the inventory measurement will exceed this threshold in the presence of an eight-kilogram (one significant quantity) theft. The standard deviation in a one-year measurement of plutonium throughput is seventy-two kilograms.

20. This combines the 25 percent likelihood of an inspection occurring within three months of a theft and the 6 percent likelihood that the inspection will detect the theft with high confidence.
21. Tape, "International Safeguards and Verification Challenges." The deliberations and reports of the LASCAR project are classified as safeguards confidential, and thus are not publicly available; moreover, the participants in various Rokkasho-related safeguards activities are prohibited from discussing them in detail.
22. Department of Energy 5633.3B, September 7, 1994, *Control and Accountability of Nuclear Materials.* All quotes below are from this document.
23. ASTM International, *Standard Guide for Application of Radiation Monitors to the Control and Physical Security of Special Nuclear Material* (West Conshohocken, PA: ASTM, 2005).
24. Vladimir Orlov, "Addressing the Challenge of Illicit Nuclear Trafficking," presentation at the second International Forum of the JAIF [Japan Atomic Industrial Forum] Study Group on Peaceful Uses of Nuclear Energy and Non-Proliferation, March 2001. First parenthetical remark in the original; second inserted.
25. International Atomic Energy Agency, *IAEA Illicit Trafficking Database (ITDB),* www.iaea.org (accessed on November 25. 2006).
26. Matthew Bunn and Anthony Weir, *Securing the Bomb 2005: The New Global Imperatives* (Cambridge, MA: Belfer Center for Science and International Affairs, Kennedy School, Harvard University, 2005), 31.
27. Ibid., 29.
28. Krystyna M. Dziewinska et al., "Development of an Enhanced Materials Protection, Control and Accountability Plan at the Mining and Chemical Combine," proceedings of the fortieth Institute of Nuclear Materials Management (INMM) annual meeting (July 25–29, 1999, Phoenix, Arizona).
29. Ibid., 4.
30. Ibid., 5.
31. Office of Technology Assessment, *Nuclear Safeguards and the International Atomic Energy Agency* (Washington, DC: OTA, June 1995), 112–114.
32. Miller, "Are IAEA Safeguards on Plutonium Bulk-Handling Facilities Effective?" Edwin Lyman has recently reviewed Miller's analysis, and concludes that it is still correct. Edwin S. Lyman, "Can Nuclear Fuel Production in Iran and Elsewhere Be Safeguarded against Diversion?," paper presented at the Nonproliferation Policy Education Center (NPEC)/King's College London conference, "After Iran: Safeguarding Peaceful Nuclear Energy," October 2–3, 2005, London. Draft cited with permission.
33. Miller, "Are IAEA Safeguards on Plutonium Bulk-Handling Facilities Effective?" The expected error in measuring plutonium throughput is proportional

to the total plutonium throughput between consecutive inspections; hence longer periods between inspections lead to larger expected errors.

34. A slightly higher critical mass (a significant quantity is normally defined as being eight kilograms) is used because the material at large reprocessing plants is not weapons grade, and thus more is required; however, this should not be taken to imply that all bombs made using reactor-grade plutonium would use ten kilograms of material. See Carson Mark, "Explosive Properties of Reactor-Grade Plutonium," *Science and Global Security* 4, no. 1 (1993).
35. To calculate the numbers, assume, as before, that the standard deviation of the measured plutonium throughput about the actual plutonium throughput is 72 kg and that the error is normally distributed. Given a fixed false positive rate, one can calculate the detection threshold that, if used to produce alarms, would generate that rate. One can then use that detection threshold to determine the size of the actual diversion that would be detected with the required confidence.
36. NRTA reduces uncertainty by reducing throughput between inspections.
37. The standard deviation of the measurement error would drop to (72 kg / 1 yr) × (1 yr / 52 weeks) = (1.4 kg / week)—well below 10 kg.
38. OTA, *Nuclear Safeguards and the International Atomic Energy Agency*, 119.
39. I thank several former and current government officials for emphasizing this problem.
40. Lawrence M. Wein et al., "Preventing the Importation of Illicit Nuclear Material in Shipping Containers," *Risk Analysis* 26, no. 5 (2006): 1–16.
41. Interview with Thomas Kornack, July 2005.
42. This analysis can be carried out mathematically. Without loss of generality, one can approximate the background radiation as normally distributed with mean zero and standard deviation one. Fix a particular background positive rate, BP, and a particular false negative rate, FN. Then $1 - BP = S(T)$ and $T = S_I(1 - BP)$, where S is the cumulative distribution function for the standard distribution, and S_I is its inverse. ($S(T)$ is the probability that a standard random variable is less than T.) In addition, $FN = S(T - M)$ and $M = T - S_I(FN)$, where M is the signal from the contraband material. When a terrorist group subdivides the material into F pieces, the probability of detection for a single inspection becomes approximately $P_1 = 1 - S(-M/F + T)$. This assumes that the radiation signal of a piece of nuclear explosive material is proportional to its mass. In practice, the signal will not be reduced proportionally—the reduction will be deeper for neutrons due to reduced multiplication in the material, greater for gamma rays due to reduced self-shielding, and either greater or lesser depending on the way the shape of the nuclear material changes. Assuming proportional reduction still provides useful and transparent insight; further analysis could explore other variations. The probability of

a single detection across the multiple inspections now becomes $P = 1 - (1 - P_1)^F$. Combining these, one finds $P = 1 - S(-[S_1(1 - BP) - S_1(FN)]/F + S_1(1 - BP))^F$. This can be evaluated for a variety of *BP* and *FN*.

43. If a group used more material in order to make its plot more robust, a more complicated calculation shows that it could still only reduce its probability of defeat by 33 percent, not a meaningful difference for such a crude calculation, suggesting that the increased probability of success at the border might not be worth the added risk involved in acquiring additional materials.
44. Samuel Glasstone and Philip J. Dolan, *The Effects of Nuclear Weapons* (Washington, DC: Government Printing Office, 1983), 356.
45. I thank Thomas C. Schelling for emphasizing this point to me.
46. Jeffrey T. Richelson, "Defusing Nuclear Terror," *Bulletin of the Atomic Scientists,* March/April 2002.
47. Ibid.
48. I thank Peter D. Zimmerman for this observation.

6. A Wider Universe of Nuclear Plots and Defenses

1. Robert S. Norris et al., "U.S. Nuclear Weapons, 2001," *Bulletin of the Atomic Scientists,* March/April 2001, 77–79.
2. Li Bin, "Nuclear Missile Delivery Capabilities in Emerging Nuclear States," *Science and Global Security* 6 (1997): 311–331.
3. For a review of PAL technology, see Peter Stein and Peter Feaver, *Assuring Control of Nuclear Weapons* (Boston: University Press of America, 1987).
4. Charles Ferguson and William Potter, *The Four Faces of Nuclear Terrorism* (Washington, DC: Monterey Institute for International Studies, 2004), 61–62.
5. Thomas B. Cochran and Christopher E. Paine, "The Amount of Plutonium and Highly-Enriched Uranium Needed for Pure Fission Nuclear Weapons," unpublished.
6. Robert S. Norris and Hans M. Kristensen, "Russian Nuclear Forces, 2006," *Bulletin of the Atomic Scientists,* March/April 2006; Robert S. Norris and Hans M. Kristensen, "U.S. Nuclear Forces, 2004," *Bulletin of the Atomic Scientists,* May/June 2004.
7. For a review of issues concerning tactical nuclear weapons, see Alistair Millar and Brian Alexander, eds., *Tactical Nuclear Weapons: Emergent Threats in an Evolving Security Environment* (Dulles, VA: Potomac Books, 2003).
8. All figures in this paragraph are from Bin, "Nuclear Missile Delivery Capabilities in Emerging Nuclear States."
9. Alexander H. Montgomery, "Ringing in Proliferation, How to Dismantle an Atomic Bomb Network," *International Security* 30, no. 2 (Fall 2005): 153–187.

10. For Little Boy, see Richard Rhodes, *The Making of the Atomic Bomb* (New York: Simon and Schuster, 1986), 701. For the South African bomb, see David Albright, *South Africa's Secret Nuclear Weapons*, ISIS Report, May 2004.
11. Steve Fetter et al., "Detecting Nuclear Warheads," *Science and Global Security* 1 (1990).
12. Howard Morland, "The H-Bomb Secret: How We Got It and Why We' Telling It," *The Progressive*, vol. 43, November 1979.
13. The thickness of shielding needed would depend not on the size of the weapon, but rather on the amount and type of nuclear material contained inside.
14. For example, Daniel Byman, *Deadly Connections: States That Sponsor Terrorism* (Cambridge: Cambridge University Press, 2005).
15. Part of this discussion is based on Michael A. Levi, "Deterring Nuclear Terrorism," *Issues in Science and Technology*, Spring 2004.
16. The most prominent example of an attempt to trace state acquisition of nuclear technology has been in the IAEA investigation of Iranian acquisitions from the A. Q. Khan network. Steve Coll, "Blueprints for Disaster," *New Yorker*, August 7, 2006.
17. For careful discussions of pre-attack forensics, see M. J. Kristo et al., *Model Action Plan for Nuclear Forensics and Nuclear Attribution*, UCRL-TR-202675 (Livermore, CA: Lawrence Livermore National Laboratory, 2004); Kenton J. Moody et al., *Nuclear Forensic Analysis* (New York: Taylor and Francis, 2005); and Gabriele Renie, "Tracing the Steps in Nuclear Material Trafficking," *Science and Technology Review*, March 2005.
18. I thank both Will Happer and Tony Fainberg for the general point that pre-attack attribution is easier than postattack attribution.
19. Michael May et al., "An International Databank of Nuclear Explosive Materials," unpublished draft. Other discussions are Jay Davis, "The Attribution of WMD Events," *Journal of Homeland Security*, April 2003; and Levi, "Deterring Nuclear Terrorism."
20. The fraction of atoms fissioned—the weapon efficiency—is roughly 1 percent. For each important isotope, the number of atoms transformed through neutron capture is at least five times smaller than the number fissioned. One can see this by comparing the capture cross sections with the fission cross sections for all relevant isotopes. The fission cross sections for U^{232}, U^{234}, U^{235}, U^{236}, and U^{238} at fission spectrum average energies are 2.0, 1.2, 1.2, 0.59, and 0.31 barns respectively, while the radiative capture cross sections, which dominate neutron capture, are 28, 218, 89, 108, and 66 millibarns respectively; the corresponding ratios are 71:1, 5.5:1, 13:1, 5.5:1, and 5.0:1 respectively. It is useful to note the analogous numbers for a weapon using plutonium, which would be altered even less during a detonation. The fission cross sections for Pu^{238}, Pu^{239},

Pu^{240}, Pu^{241}, and Pu^{242}, are 2.0, 1.8, 1.4, 1.6, and 1.1 barns respectively, while the radiative capture cross sections are 99, 53, 93, 118, and 88 millibarns respectively; these correspond to ratios of 20:1, 34:1, 15:1, 14:1, and 13:1 respectively.

21. Those isotopes with greater fission cross sections will endure greater reductions.
22. One can show this by assuming that reductions are proportional to the initial concentration of each isotope and to its fission cross section; this linear approximation should be valid for small efficiencies. Given that, one can calculate the percentage reductions in each isotope, and hence the changes in isotopic ratios. This calculation assumes a weapon efficiency of 1 percent or less.
23. Accounting for large efficiencies is more difficult. Assume 10 percent efficiency. Then simple calculations, duplicating those in the last note but letting amounts of various isotopes decrease exponentially, rather than linearly, suggests that for 50 percent or greater uranium enrichment, ratios of pairs of isotopes will not be altered by more than 20 percent, with the ratio of U^{235} to U^{238} altered by less than 10 percent. For plutonium, assuming greater than 80 percent Pu^{239}, no isotopic ratio is altered by more than 5 percent, with the ratio of Pu^{239} to Pu^{238} altered by no more than 4 percent. As a result, if the defining characteristics of various material origins differ from place to place by less than 5 percent (plus some amount to account for measurement and intelligence errors), it is not clear that attributing postdetonation debris by isotopic signature will be possible. There is no reason, however, to believe that this is a fundamental limitation, rather than a limit on the calculations given here, as noted in the main text.
24. Davis, "The Attribution of WMD Events"; National Research Council, *Making the Nation Safer: The Role of Science and Technology in Countering Terrorism* (Washington, DC: National Academies Press, 2002), 59–60; William J. Broad, "Addressing the Unthinkable, US Revives Study of Fallout," *New York Times*, March 19, 2004.
25. For one example of such an unclassified study, see Maria Wallenius, "Origin Determination of Reactor Produced Plutonium by Mass Spectrometric Techniques: Application to Nuclear Forensic Science and Safeguards" (master's thesis, University of Helsinki, 2001).
26. The separation factor of an individual enrichment unit depends on the masses of the isotopes being separated, but in different ways for different technologies; hence two technologies that achieved the same separation between U^{235} and U^{238} would achieve different separation between either of those isotopes and other uranium isotopes. Whether different cascade arrangements, or different variations on the same technology (for example, different centrifuge types), would produce useful differences would be a valuable topic for future study,

presuming that results obtained in a proprietary or classified setting have not already provided sufficient information.

27. Jessica T. Matthews et al., *A New Approach: Coercive Inspections* (Washington, DC: Carnegie Endowment for International Peace, 2002).
28. Thomas C. Schelling, "Deterring Nuclear Terrorists," *Issues in Science and Technology*, Summer 2004. Also see G. P. Gilfoyle and J. A. Parmentola, "Using Nuclear Materials to Prevent Nuclear Proliferation," *Science and Global Security* 9 (2001): 81–92.
29. For example, Anders Corr, "Deterrence of Nuclear Terror: A Negligence Doctrine," *Nonproliferation Review* 12, no. 1 (March 2005): 127–147; Robert L. Gallucci, "Averting Nuclear Catastrophe: Contemplating Extreme Responses to U.S. Vulnerability," *Annals of the AAPSS* 607 (September 2006): 51–58. The latter article makes an exception for states that have inadvertently leaked nuclear weapons or materials despite their best efforts to control them, though it is unclear who would determine which states qualified for this exception.
30. Graham Allison, "Nuclear Accountability," *Technology Review*, July 2005.
31. Michael O'Hanlon and Mike M. Mochizuki, *Crisis on the Korean Peninsula* (New York: McGraw-Hill, 2003), 61.
32. For example, Michael O'Hanlon, "What If a Nuclear-Armed State Collapses?" *Current History*, November 2006, 379–384; Jon Wolfsthal, CSIS Briefing on North Korea's Nuclear Test, Center for Strategic and International Studies, Washington, DC, October 11, 2006.
33. See, for example, Robert I. Rotberg, ed., *When States Fail: Causes and Consequences* (Princeton, NJ: Princeton University Press, 2003).
34. See Victor D. Cha and David C. Kang, *Nuclear North Korea: A Debate on Engagement Strategies* (New York: Columbia University Press, 2003), for two complementary perspectives.
35. "Efforts to induce [Pakistan] to roll back [its] programmes—as South Africa did—have gradually been weakened and are now largely abandoned." Hans Blix et al., *Weapons of Terror* (Stockholm: Weapons of Mass Destruction Commission, 2006), 60.
36. For example, Kimberly Ann Elliott, *Economic Leverage and the North Korean Nuclear Crisis* (Washington, DC: Institute for International Economics, 2003), 2.
37. For example, David Wright, "Cut North Korea Some Slack," *Bulletin of the Atomic Scientists*, March/April 1999.
38. For example, see Alex Wagner, "U.S. Offers Nuclear Security Assistance to Pakistan," *Arms Control Today*, December 2001.
39. David Albright, "The AQ Khan Network: Case Closed?" Testimony before the Subcommittee on International Terrorism and Nonproliferation, House International Relations Committee, May 25, 2006.

40. Coll, "Blueprints for Disaster."
41. Jon Wolfsthal, "U.S. Needs a Contingency Plan for Pakistan's Nuclear Arsenal," *Los Angeles Times*, October 16, 2001.
42. Debate over the 2005 U.S.–India nuclear cooperation deal, for example, reflects the tension between engaging proliferators and preventing proliferation. See Michael A. Levi and Charles D. Ferguson, *U.S.–India Nuclear Cooperation*, Council Special Report no. 16 (New York: Council on Foreign Relations, 2006).
43. The first three options are discussed in Michael A. Levi and Michael E. O'Hanlon, *The Future of Arms Control* (Washington, DC: Brookings Institution Press, 2005).
44. Richard L. Garwin, personal communication, 2004.
45. Most prominently, see Seymour M. Hersh, "Watching the Warheads: The Risks to Pakistan's Nuclear Arsenal," *New Yorker*, November 11, 2005.
46. Michael O'Hanlon, *Dealing with the Collapse of a Nuclear-Armed State: The Cases of North Korea and Pakistan*, Working paper for the Princeton Project on National Security, April 2005.
47. North Korea has roughly 2,500 kilometers of coastline along the Yellow Sea and East Sea that can be immediately accessed from Russia or Japan. Pakistan has roughly 1,000 kilometers of coastline along the Arabian Sea that can be immediately accessed from India.

7. The Way Forward

1. The most recent edition is Matthew Bunn and Anthony Weir, *Securing the Bomb 2006* (Cambridge, MA: Belfer Center for Science and International Affairs, Kennedy School, Harvard University, 2006).
2. Graham Allison, *Nuclear Terrorism* (New York: Times Books, 2004); Charles D. Ferguson, *Preventing Catastrophic Nuclear Terrorism*, Council on Foreign Relations Special Report no. 11 (New York: CFR, 2006).
3. For an overview, see National Commission on Terrorist Attacks, *The 9/11 Commission Report* (New York: Norton, 2005). See especially chapters 11–13.
4. Although this recommendation may seem obvious, such analysts often do not work together, even when collaboration would seem an obvious route. For an example, see Commission on the Intelligence of the United States Regarding Weapons of Mass Destruction, *Report to the President* (Washington, DC: U.S. Government Printing Office, 2005), 274–275.
5. Jon Fox, "Lawmakers May Cut Nuclear Detection Office Funding," *Global Security Newswire*, August 3, 2006.
6. For example, Government Accountability Office, *Combating Nuclear Smuggling* (Washington, DC: Government Printing Office, 2006).

7. For example, see Vayl Oxford, Testimony before the House Homeland Security Committee, Subcommittee on Prevention of Nuclear and Biological Attack, April 20, 2005.
8. Defense Science Board, *Defense Science Board Task Force on the Role and Status of DoD Red Teaming Activities* (Washington, DC: Department of Defense, 2003), 4.
9. Richard L. Garwin and Hans A. Bethe, "Anti-Ballistic-Missile System," *Scientific American* 218, no. 3 (1968): 21–31.

Appendix

1. Steve Fetter et al., "Detecting Nuclear Warheads," *Science and Global Security* 1 (1990): 225–302.
2. Jonathan Katz, private communication.
3. Jonathan Katz, "Detection of Neutron Sources in Cargo Containers," *Science and Global Security* 14, nos. 2–3 (September–December 2006): 145–149.
4. Lawrence M. Wein et al., "Preventing the Importation of Illicit Nuclear Materials in Shipping Containers," *Risk Analysis* 26, no. 5 (2006): 6.
5. For the specific neutron production rate, see Figure 1 in Stephen Croft and Ludovic C. A. Bourva, "The Specific Total and Coincidence Cosmic-Ray-Induced Neutron Production Rates in Materials," *Nuclear Instruments and Methods in Physics Research A*, vol. 505 (2003): 536–539. The specific neutron production rate in lead is approximately 0.15 n/s-kg.
6. This calculation neglects contributions from surrounding containers. Katz, "Detection of Neutron Sources in Cargo Containers."
7. A steel, tin, or copper cargo would be less dense, and hence have a greater volume-to-area ratio for a given mass, but that would be offset by the lower number of neutrons produced per kilogram of material.
8. Samuel Glasstone and Philip J. Dolan, *The Effects of Nuclear Weapons* (Washington, DC: U.S. Government Printing Office, 1983), 349, shows a range of neutron-shielding factors; a tenfold reduction may actually be a pessimistic defensive assumption.
9. Gilbert C. Binninger et al., *Mathematical Background and Programming Aids for the Physical Vulnerability System for Nuclear Weapons* (Washington, DC: Defense Intelligence Agency, 1974) and help files for the Defense Nuclear Agency code WE (Weapons Effects), as reported in Matthew G. McKinzie et al., *The U.S. Nuclear War Plan: A Time for Change* (Washington, DC: National Resources Defense Council, 2001).
10. Office of Technology Assessment, *The Effects of Nuclear War* (Washington, DC: OTA, 1979), 19.
11. D. J. Strom, *Health Impacts from Acute Radiation Exposure* (Richland, WA:

Pacific Northwest National Laboratory, 2003), 21. This assumes medical care typical of response to a mass casualty incident.

12. Several models for population density are discussed in Jeffrey J. Hunter, "An Analytical Technique for Urban Casualty Estimation from Multiple Nuclear Weapons," *Operations Research* 15, no. 6 (November 1967): 1096–1108. Hunter cites Sherratt's empirical work as the basis for choosing a Gaussian distribution over an exponential distribution: G. G. Sherratt, "A Model for General Urban Growth," in *Management Sciences, Models, and Techniques,* vol. 2 (New York, NY: Pergamon Press, 1960), 147–159. More recently, Bracken and Tuckwell, in reviewing the literature, note that a Gaussian distribution may be more accurate near a modern city center, while an exponential distribution may be more accurate over larger areas; since I wish to explore deviations from the most lethal terrorist attacks possible—that is, terrorist attacks against city centers—the Gaussian distribution is appropriate. See Anthony J. Bracken and Henry C. Tuckwell, "Simple Mathematical Models for Urban Growth," *Proceedings of the Royal Society of London A,* vol. 438 (1992): 171–181.
13. Lynn E. Davis et al., *Individual Preparedness and Response to Chemical, Radiological, Nuclear, and Biological Terrorist Attacks* (Santa Monica, CA: RAND, 2003), 40.
14. Although hospitals may be overwhelmed in the immediate aftermath of an attack, immediate treatment is generally unnecessary and not useful, as "irradiation has no emergency treatment." Mark H. Beers, ed., *The Merck Manual of Medical Information,* 2nd ed. (West Point, 'A: Merck and Company, 2003), 1660.
15. Figures obtained using HOTSPOT.
16. K. P. Ferlic, *Fallout: Its Characteristics and Management* (Bethesda, MD: Armed Forces Radiobiology Institute, 1983), 89. Sheltering in a basement, which provides greater protection, is not a practical option for most inhabitants of tall skyscrapers, which would dominate any very dense city center, as assumed here.
17. If sheltering could provide only a protection factor of ten, this reduction would be to 7 percent of the original area, still an order of magnitude reduction. Broken windows outside the blast zone might sharply reduce the effective shielding, though not enough to make a difference to the qualitative results here.
18. For example, one group of scholars has estimated 62,000 immediate deaths from a 12.5 kT attack at the Port of New York, but they also estimate that fallout would kill 200,000 more. The figures are low because their work uses census data, which does not reflect daytime populations. Matthew Bunn et al., *Controlling Nuclear Warheads and Materials* (Cambridge, MA: Belfer Center for Science and International Affairs, Kennedy School, Harvard University,

2003), 18. If the number of fallout deaths could be reduced by 90 percent, as above, the total casualty count would be reduced by nearly 70 percent. Ira Helfand et al., "Nuclear Terrorism," *British Medical Journal* 324 (2002): 356–359.

19. This approach can significantly underestimate the number of deaths, since people who spend part of their time inside the area while beginning their evacuation, and part of their time outside but near the area after evacuating, may receive a dose exceeding 500 rem, but would be considered "outside" the area, and thus safe, for the present calculation.

Acknowledgments

This book would not have been possible without the help and support of many people. I am most grateful to Peter Zimmerman and Lawrence Freedman for their guidance, insight, and support. Our discussions at the Department of War Studies at King's College London, where I did most of the research for this book, invariably sharpened both my thinking and my writing. At the Council on Foreign Relations, Richard Haass, James Lindsay, and Gary Samore have encouraged me to explore broadly, a privilege too rarely afforded young scholars. Jim was supportive as I overhauled my manuscript, helping me to connect my ideas about nuclear terrorism with concrete thinking about policy. Gary arrived as I was fine-tuning my manuscript, offering his own invaluable insights. Patricia Dorff kindly helped guide me through the publication process. I was also aided by two excellent research associates. Ripal Patel ably supported me during my first months at the Council. Susan Basu joined later, tracking down facts and challenging my arguments in ways that invariably improved them.

Steve Weinberg kindly introduced me to Michael Fisher, editor-in-chief at Harvard University Press, who provided expert guidance and frequent encouragement as I reshaped my book. Elizabeth Gilbert, my manuscript editor, carefully sharpened my thinking and my prose.

I was fortunate to work with a Council on Foreign Relations study group as I connected theory to policy. Gerald Epstein chaired meetings in Washington, DC, while William Schneider, Jr., chaired sessions in New York. Ashton Carter also chaired an invaluable meeting with Council national members in Boston. In addition, I benefited from responses to presentations hosted by Princeton, Stanford, the Norwegian Institute of International Affairs, and the Fondation pour la Recherche Stratégique. I also had the privilege of engaging policymakers in some of my arguments in testimony before the House Committee on International Relations and the Senate Judiciary Committee.

Dozens of people discussed my ideas with me, and there is too little space here to do each one justice. I am especially grateful to Matthew Bunn and Steve Fetter who, despite being in high demand, regularly found time to assist me with some of the more challenging parts of my research. Matthew Bunn, Lawrence Freedman, Richard Haass, Jonathan Katz, Steven Koonin, Jack Levi, Gary Samore, Thomas Schelling, William Walker, and Peter Zimmerman read entire drafts (some several times) and provided the sort of unvarnished feedback that I needed. Two anonymous reviewers did the same.

My work on this book has been generously supported by the John D. and Catherine T. MacArthur Foundation through grants both to King's College London and to the Council on Foreign Relations, by the Social Sciences and Humanities Research Council of Canada through its William E. Taylor Fellowship, and by an ORS award from the Government of the United Kingdom.

Index